WHO ARE YOU, REALLY?

A PHILOSOPHER'S INQUIRY INTO THE NATURE AND ORIGIN OF PERSONS

JOSHUA RASMUSSEN

ivp
Academic
An imprint of InterVarsity Press
Downers Grove, Illinois

InterVarsity Press
P.O. Box 1400 | Downers Grove, IL 60515-1426
ivpress.com | email@ivpress.com

InterVarsity Press® is the publishing division of InterVarsity Christian Fellowship/USA®. For more information, visit intervarsity.org.

The publisher cannot verify the accuracy or functionality of website URLs used in this book beyond the date of publication.

Cover design and image composite: David Fassett
Interior design: Jeanna Wiggins

ISBN 978-1-5140-0394-7 (print) | ISBN 978-1-5140-0395-4 (digital)

Printed in the United States of America ♾

Library of Congress Cataloging-in-Publication Data
A catalog record for this book is available from the Library of Congress.

29   28   27   26   25   24   23 | 13   12   11   10   9   8   7   6   5   4   3   2   1

"In *Who Are You, Really?*, Joshua Rasmussen probes vexing philosophical problems related to the meaning and nature of personhood. He considers issues we take completely for granted—concerns like thinking, feeling, willing, and personal identity—and lays bare many problems that the casual thinker would never have known were there. He then does a masterful job of engaging these problems using the light of critical introspection. Though he leans heavily on the power of such introspection, I think his results justify the weight he has placed on it. All in all, it is an excellent work that I heartily recommend."

Rick Langer, Talbot School of Theology, Biola University

"Joshua Rasmussen is a treasured friend and esteemed colleague. Based on the quality of his work, he is regarded as an elite philosopher among secular and Christian scholars alike. But he is much more than that. Joshua is a warm-hearted Jesus follower with a passion to help thoughtful believers, and with the skills to take difficult topics and make them accessible. *Who Are You, Really?* is the fruit of these abilities. With fresh, original, perceptive insight, this book addresses the central question that underlies most of the issues debated in contemporary culture and the academy. Having specialized in philosophy of mind and theological anthropology for decades, I can confidently say that there is nothing like this book. With fairness and rigor, Rasmussen carefully works through all the issues and arguments fundamental to his topic. Happily, he does all of this while making the book marvelously accessible. This should be a required text in all Christian colleges and seminaries, and it is must-read for all who care about this crucial subject."

J. P. Moreland, distinguished professor of philosophy at Talbot School of Theology at Biola University, and author of *The Soul: How We Know It Is Real and Why It Matters*

"*Who Are You, Really?* is beautifully written and very well organized! Overall, I think this is an excellent book. It makes a core assumption about the nature of matter very clear, and it shows brilliantly what follows."

Eric Steinhart, professor of philosophy at William Paterson University and author of *Believing in Dawkins: The New Spiritual Atheism*

"The question, What does it take to be conscious? has two senses. What does consciousness involve? Where does consciousness come from? In this stimulating book, Joshua Rasmussen addresses both. As with *How Reason Can Lead to God*, he again shows his considerable skill in delving deep into philosophy in an inviting and engaging manner. Rasmussen takes the reader on a journey into some of the central topics in philosophy to help us understand something of great importance: ourselves."

Kevin Timpe, William H. Jellema Chair in Christian Philosophy at Calvin University

"Josh Rasmussen is one of the deepest and most interesting thinkers of our time. He is one of the leaders of a new generation of philosophers building a more conciliatory and fruitful dialogue between believers and atheists. *Who Are You, Really?* is a novel and intriguing exploration of some of the biggest questions of human existence. It's essential reading for anyone interested in consciousness and what it means to be a human being."

Philip Goff, associate professor of philosophy at Durham University

"Professor Rasmussen's new book is both a pleasure to read and a welcome change of pace. You will find here a rare achievement: it is written in a style that will engage both students and philosophers, and it presents original ways to explore and defend a mind-first ontology. Rasmussen's flair for new ideas is fully on display. Challenging current physicalist conceptions of the mind, he articulates a conception of personal identity that combines ancient spiritual ideas with novel ways to understand physical reality."

Evan Fales, University of Iowa

"As we have come to expect, Josh Rasmussen has written another volume that is clear, carefully reasoned, and illuminating, and it is full of marvelous analogies and accessible illustrations. Rasmussen's account of personhood and its origin, and what constitutes personal identity is not only masterful in its logically structural layout; it is also modest, wise, engaging, and persuasive. A fine work!"

Paul Copan, Pledger Family Chair of Philosophy and Ethics at Palm Beach Atlantic University and author of *A Little Book for New Philosophers*

For seekers of wisdom

CONTENTS

PREFACE

THIS BOOK IS ABOUT YOU. If anything is true about you, it is this: you are real. But out of this truth springs a great mystery. How could there be anything like you? This question inspires my quest. My purpose in this book is to seek to uncover the deepest possible explanation of the nature and existence of a conscious, personal being like you. I hope that by joining me on this quest, you will gain resources to see a grander picture of who you really are.

My interest in writing on this topic grows out of my research into the fundamental nature of reality. Over my career, I have sought to better understand the fundamental nature of things—such as truth, time, and the foundation of existence. In response to my work, many people have asked me how I think fundamental reality might relate to personal, conscious reality. For example, are there ways to determine whether fundamental reality is itself personal? How might qualities of a personal being arise from the resources of fundamental reality? What resources does it take to make beings like us? In this work, then, I will investigate the connection between the nature of persons and fundamental reality.

The time is ripe for a new look at the nature of conscious, personal beings. Theorists have identified a minefield of problems in analyzing the emergence of conscious beings from ordinary matter. These problems are not conjured up by advocates of a particular worldview. Rather, they are center points of discussion by leading experts with diverse perspectives who are trying to understand how conscious beings could fit into our world by *any* means.

A challenge in writing a book like this is that clouds of controversy occlude paths to insight. The topic of consciousness and the nature of persons touches on significant, sensitive issues related to ultimate meaning, purpose, and existence. Heated debates arise as we hash out competing explanations of conscious beings. Oftentimes, we are locked into continual sparring as we seek to explain something so universal and familiar as our own conscious experience.

I want to highlight a path that can bridge the insights from many brilliant minds on opposing sides of the debate. Instead of starting and ending with one of the familiar packages of views (materialism, dualism, idealism, etc.), I want to show how we can build a new understanding of persons from basic concepts and observations. By reframing the discussion and digging into fundamental concepts, I believe we can integrate more insights from more perspectives, thereby positioning ourselves to see a greater picture of our existence as personal beings.

Whatever your viewpoint, I hope this book will help you analyze relevant data by your own light. I have encountered evidence that people have power to extend their current sight beyond what they may have realized. A couple years ago, I worked with a student to collect data on people's beliefs about consciousness. We created a survey with randomized premises in deductions for and against different views about the nature of consciousness. One striking, preliminary result of our study was this: a statistically significant number of participants reported beliefs that entail conclusions that the participants themselves did not previously realize. This result suggests to me that people can see more by further analysis. My hope is that this book will help you extend your own analysis of the nature of persons in view of a wider range of data.

By seeking to display a vision of persons, I also hope to inspire a greater perception of the significance of your existence. This outcome, I suggest, will be achieved through the beholding of a greater picture of personal reality at the most fundamental level. The fullness of this picture will come into view by the end of the book.

I write this book to serve *anyone* interested in the nature of personal beings. Toward this end, I have worked to write in a style that is both accessible to a wide audience and also deep enough to contribute to the analyses of experts. To increase accessibility, I define all technical terms using ordinary language. You do not need to know any philosophical jargon to follow along.

The ideas in this book spring from my own original reflections, including recent reflections (and some original discoveries) that have led me to change my mind about some previous ideas. The pathway I will mark out is one you will not find anywhere else.

Enjoy the journey.

ACKNOWLEDGMENTS

I AM GRATEFUL FOR INVALUABLE FEEDBACK and resources from many friends, colleagues, and peers. Thank you, Andrew Bailey, Michael Bacon, Zach Blaesi, Brianna Bode, Ben Crandall, Dustin Crummett, Ryan Downie, Patrick Flynn, Philip Goff, Tyron Goldschmit, Eli Haitov, Bill McClymonds, Mia Mendoza, John Michael, James Porter Moreland, Nathan Ormond, Adam Redwine, Bell Sarian, Joseph Schmid, Parker Settecase, and Eric Steinhart, for your inspiration and insights, which added great value to this project beyond what you could know. I am also grateful to my children, Micah, Lana, Chloe, Jonah, and Kaleb, for putting up with many questions about whether their toys could become conscious and, if not, how they could know. Finally, big thanks to my wife, Rachel, for helping me process every idea in this book. Any remaining infelicities have their origin in mindless grains of reality, or they are mine.

1

INTRODUCING THE INQUIRY

The subject of mind involves certain difficulties.

ARISTOTLE

THE QUESTION

Your existence is familiar, like your breath. But despite your familiarity, your existence is far from insignificant. It is not obvious how something like you could ever exist. What are you? How did you come to be? Could a sandstorm produce a being like you?

You are a peculiar kind of reality. You are a conscious being. You can think. You can feel. You can decide to read this book. But how can there be something that *thinks*, *feels*, or *decides*, anywhere, ever?

When I reflect on the familiar reality of my own existence, I sometimes have the thought that reality is too strange. It would be simpler if there were just nothing at all. But if there is going to be something, surely there would never be conscious beings, like myself. Here is a simple argument for that conclusion:

1. If conscious beings can exist, then there is some possible explanation of their existence.

2. There is not a possible explanation of the existence of conscious beings.

3. Therefore, conscious beings cannot exist.

Ah, simplicity. The mysteries of reality are now solved.

Not convinced?

Well, maybe we could explain conscious beings in terms of conscious-being-*makers*. A conscious-being-maker is something that has powers to sprinkle into our world thoughts, feelings, desires, hopes, and other contents of consciousness. But the existence of conscious-being-makers would only deepen the mystery. Why and how could reality include any conscious-being-makers? Suppose some clumps of matter can make conscious beings. Still, how does matter like *that* exist? If conscious beings are mysterious, is the existence of something that can make a conscious being any less mysterious?

Suppose we appeal to a supreme being. We say, "A supreme being made consciousness!" Then we push back the mystery all the way down into the foundation of reality. If the foundational reality is a supreme being, then this being is itself capable of consciousness (at least analogically). So, what explains its consciousness? If we say "nothing," then there is no explanation of the existence of consciousness—which presents its own mystery. (We will return to the question of what, if anything, could be an ultimate explanation of consciousness as we approach the end of our inquiry.)

So, we have a great mystery. There are conscious beings, like you and me.[1] Yet it is not obvious how any such beings can exist. How can any reality—big or small, simple or complex—unfold into real, conscious beings?

To seek insight, I will investigate the nature of a reality that can give rise to conscious beings. My investigation will organize around this question: *Who are you?* I will divide this question into two big questions. First, what are you? Second, how could you have come to be? For convenience, I shall call the sort of being you (and I) are "a personal being." My quest, then, is to pursue a greater understanding of the nature and origin of personal beings.

In this quest, I aim to put light on a path leading, step by step, to a greater vision of our existence as personal beings. By highlighting the steps, I hope travelers from a wide range of perspectives will see a greater vision of who they are by their own clearest light.

A thesis that will emerge from this inquiry is that our existence is deeply rooted. I have come to believe that the roots of personal, perspectival reality go deeper than many people imagine. In fact, it is my conviction, forged

---

[1]For sake of inquiry, I will not take even this premise for granted. One of my first tasks in this inquiry will be to see how we might see that any conscious being is real.

through my research for this book, that personal reality has its roots all the way down into the fundamental nature of reality. By tracing these roots to their foundation, I hope to bring into greater light the nature of a world in which beings like you and I can exist.[2]

THE STAKES

I do not believe I can overemphasize the significance of the question at hand. The stakes extend without measure. On some theories of personal beings, you are the sort of being that can live perpetually, without end. On other theories, you are more fragile. For example, some theories analyze personal beings in terms of specific configurations of matter—such as molecules organized into a functioning brain. On these theories, either "you" flicker out of existence as soon as any molecules are replaced, or you are able to persist through a wider range of molecular changes.[3] Either way, a time is coming when you will experience your last act of awareness. When the light of your consciousness goes out, you will never be aware of anything again, not ever. The differences between these theories are infinite in their ramifications.

It is not just your future that is at stake. It is also the meaning and value of your life. Does your life have purpose? What is a life? What is "purpose"? If the path of your life reduces to the paths of point particles, can you have any assurance that your future is bright?

These questions point to the value of our quest. We may want certain answers to be true, but only certain answers are actually true. Embarking

---

[2]The resources that contribute to my analysis range from works of ancient philosophers to contemporary developments in science and analyses relevant to this inquiry. Highlights include Aristotle's *De Anima* (350 BC), Descartes's *Discourse on Method* (1637), Locke's *An Essay Concerning Human Understanding* (1690), Berkeley's *An Essay Towards a New Theory of Vision* (1709), Leibniz's *The Monadology and Other Philosophical Writings* (1898), Russell's *Analysis of Mind* (1921) and *Analysis of Matter* (1927), Dennett's *Consciousness Explained* (1991), Chalmer's *The Conscious Mind* (1996), Hasker's *Emergent Self* (2001), Kim's *Physicalism or Something Near Enough* (2005), Roveli's *Reality Is Not What It Seems* (2014), Hoffman's *Case Against Reality* (2019), and most recently, pioneering articles on quantum brain theory and the informational theory of matter. I hope my analysis will help display some fruits of these (and related) works in a larger light.

[3]It is not trivial to say how, precisely, you continue to exist on any of these theories. T. Merricks, *Objects and Persons* (Oxford: Oxford University Press, 2001) provides a thorough analysis (and the best I've seen) of different proposals about how persons persist through time. We will zoom in on the challenge of accounting for your persistence when we examine theories of personal identity in chap. 11.

on the quest to understand the nature and origin of persons will position us to discern answers to these questions for ourselves.

Not only does one's theory of consciousness have immense practical and philosophical implications, but the inquiry into consciousness is also interesting in its own right; to unravel the mystery of consciousness is to unravel the mystery in all mysteries. After all, to understand consciousness is to understand the realm in which all understanding is possible.

Finally, consciousness connects to everything you could ever care about. Without consciousness, you experience nothing; you see nothing; you know nothing. Without consciousness, nothing matters to you; nothing is significant to you. In consciousness, you experience all your thoughts, your questions, your sensations, your emotions, your intentions, your hopes, your dreams, your fears, your imaginations, your visual images, your pains, your inferences, your memories, your feelings of curiosity, your feelings of doubt, the sense that something is true, the sense that something is wrong, your every feeling of purpose, and every other sense you ever have. Your consciousness is the storehouse of everything significant in your life.

So, why do any conscious beings exist? An answer to this question would be a great reward.

OBSTACLES TO PROGRESS

There are several obstacles that keep people from even beginning to embark on a journey like this. I will point out three obstacles here.

The first obstacle is the mist of uncertainty. The inquiry into consciousness is like entering a dark cave. People don't see what is ahead. What they do see are shadows of ideas that disappear into the darkness. Is there a way to light the darkness?

One place people turn to get answers is the sciences. Perhaps we can unlock the mysteries of consciousness by studying the inner workings of the physical structure of the brain. However, even as we are able to make significant advancements in our understanding of how brains function, there are questions left unanswered. How can first-person perspectives emerge from third-person brains at all? Why do certain brain states connect to certain conscious experiences and not others? Is it possible to build a machine that consciously thinks? How might conscious intentions translate into bodily motions? Thinking about these questions invariably lead to considerations that lie beyond the scope of a purely quantitative investigation of brain behaviors.

Where, then, might we find answers? If we look to philosophy, the worry is that we will only find endless speculation. Can we tether our theories to clear observations? How? If we can't see how to test our theories of consciousness, how can we even begin our investigation?

A second obstacle I see is widespread disagreement about the nature of consciousness. Those who dedicate their lives to exploring the nature of consciousness (whether neuroscientists, philosophers of mind, or Buddhist monks) display no consensus. The controversy can leave one feeling disempowered at the start.

Third, perhaps the biggest obstacle is prior paradigms. Prior paradigms filter our vision of the world. The problem here is not that we think answers are impossible. The problem is that we think the answers are already known. If we think we already know the answers, we might be right, but we might also be unaware of our own blind spots.

Sometimes a compelling story can limit our vision by covering over other potential explanations. In academic settings, I sometimes hear stories passed along about what experts have supposedly shown. These stories can become blue skies in the background of our thinking. The blue skies are so familiar that we take them for granted. As a result, we can easily miss new ways of looking at things, even when new information comes along.

These obstacles do not need to stand in our way. I believe it is possible to illuminate a path deep into the cave of consciousness. We just need the right tools. I will next describe the tools that I believe can help us the most on our journey.

TOOLS OF INQUIRY

To illuminate the steps in our journey into the cave of consciousness, we will use tools that anyone can use to see things for themselves. Two tools will be our primary lights: introspection (by which we can collect relevant data firsthand) and reason (by which we can analyze data). I will share how I think these lights can help us on our quest. The third tool is a broadly scientific method of inquiry. I will describe that method and how our primary tools can help illuminate scientific data relevant to our inquiry.

Tool 1: Introspection. The first tool is introspection. Introspection is the tool for collecting "first-person" data about consciousness. For example, if you smell coffee, you can detect your experience of the smell. This experience of a smell is a bit of first-person data. By collecting first-person data, we prepare ourselves to test hypotheses about the nature of consciousness itself.

Immediately, you might wonder: Can introspection actually help us detect things about consciousness? Some theorists have expressed doubts about the utility of introspection to help illuminate consciousness.[4] I even met a philosopher who said he wasn't sure whether he could rely on introspection to reveal his own existence. "How can we trust introspection?" he asked. Fair question.

Since introspection will be one of the primary tools for our journey, I will offer three notes about why I think introspection can illuminate data relevant to our quest. My first two notes are clarifications that follow Bertrand Russell's response to skeptics of introspection via the precisification of key concepts.[5] My third note is about why I think introspection is foundational to other things we know.

So first, to clarify what I mean by "introspection," I offer a minimal definition: introspection is any power to sense or be aware of something in consciousness by directing one's attention inward. For example, if you can be aware of your own thoughts, feelings, or your experience of reading these words, then these are examples of things revealed by introspection. On this minimal definition, we can leave open at the outset different theories about the nature of the things revealed via introspection (or even whether introspection reveals anything).

A second clarification: I do not claim that you cannot make mistakes about your own contents of consciousness. On the contrary, I think you can

---

[4]For a representative development of key distinctions and considerations relevant to the reliability of introspection, see K. Dunlap, "The Case Against Introspection," *Psychological Review* 19, no. 5 (1912): 404-13; R. E. Nisbett and T. D. Wilson, "Telling More Than We Can Know: Verbal Reports on Mental Processes," *Psychological Review* 84, no. 3 (1977): 231-59; and E. Schwitzgebel, "A Phenomenal, Dispositional Account of Belief," *Noûs* 36, no. 2 (2002): 249-75.
[5]B. Russell, *The Analysis of Mind* (New York: Macmillan, 1921).

make mistakes—such as if you misremember what you were thinking a moment ago. The possibility of mistakes does not remove the possibility of using introspection to detect anything within your consciousness.

In my view (based on introspection), mistakes from introspection ultimately have their origin in some shaky inference—an inference that leaps beyond what one can witness in the introspective experience itself. To illustrate, suppose you see a gray cube in front of you. One of the faces of the cube is darker than two other faces that you see. You might infer that your visual experience represents a light gray cube with one face in shadow, but this thought could be a mistake. Suppose you adjust the light source and rotate the cube such that your experience of gray changes slightly. This change in your experience could lead you to believe that the cube is actually dark gray instead of light gray. You might now say that you made a mistake in your initial belief that the cube was light gray. The mistake here would not be in your belief that you had a certain experience, but in your inference about what that experience implies.

We intuitively make inferences about the things we are acquainted with. Sometimes the inferences we make are mistaken. Regardless, I believe we can be directly consciously acquainted with contents of consciousness prior to forming a theory-laden, conceptual analysis of what we are acquainted with. If that is correct, then any mistaken belief about our experience (e.g., about whether a certain image matches something else, external or internal) derives from an analysis, based on inference, that goes beyond what we actually know by direct experience.[6]

Whatever you make of this analysis, my more fundamental thought is this: you don't need to have perfectly infallible, clear awareness to have some introspective awareness. Some things in consciousness can be clearer

---

[6]Some readers may be familiar with the "gray squares" illusion, where squares with the same shade of gray appear to have different shades of gray. Some have suggested that this illusion calls into question the reliability of judgments based on introspection, for it shows that we can be mistaken about the shades of gray in our own visual field. On my analysis, however, the illusion here (the reason for error) is not in a failure to know how the squares *appear* (via introspection) but in an inference from how they appear to what they *represent* (or how they compare to each other). For example, we may think they represent different shades, even if they do not. Here is the crucial point: without introspection, we could not say anything about how the squares *appear*, or even that we have an experience of gray squares at all. So, if we make a mistake in our judgment, it is from an inference, not from direct awareness of the experience itself.

to you than others. It may be clearer, for example, that you feel vaguely hungry, even if it is less clear what exactly you feel hungry for. So long as introspection can illuminate something (leaving open what exactly it is), we can use introspection for our inquiry.

Third, and fundamentally, I believe introspection is a foundational source of many things we know. On my definition of "introspection" (as a power to sense something within consciousness), introspection is your source of knowing contents of consciousness, including your feelings, thoughts, and your experience of these words. Without the light of introspection, you would be in the dark about whether you can even question whether introspection is reliable. That's darker than things are.

Now I want to be careful not to step ahead too quickly. In the next chapter, I will investigate the prospect of eliminating contents of consciousness altogether; maybe there are no feelings, thoughts, or questions at all. I will consider a certain motivation some philosophers have for eliminating contents of consciousness.[7]

Here I want to draw attention to a more fundamental problem with turning off the light of introspection (or not turning it on). The problem is this: without the light of introspection, all possible reasons to doubt introspection would themselves be in the dark too; you could not even recognize the very reasons in your own mind to be skeptical. Your mind would be completely dark. Call this problem "the darkness problem."

To further draw out the darkness problem, suppose someone presents an argument against the reliability of introspection. And suppose this argument actually feels quite convincing to you. Should you then believe their conclusion that introspection is unreliable? Well, there is a problem: if introspection is unreliable, then you could not rely on introspection to recognize your very experience with their argument. You could not even tell whether the argument *seemed* convincing to you, since the feeling that

---

[7]Some philosophers also worry here about the prospect of *illusions*. Could our sense of what it is like to have an experience be an illusion (cf. Keith Frankish, "Illusionism as a Theory of Consciousness," *Journal of Consciousness Studies* 23 [2016]: 11-39)? I will examine the prospect of illusions when I examine the nature of perception in chap. 4. There I will share why I think illusions themselves are only possible if we can see some things *directly within consciousness* (which fail to represent other things). This analysis allows that certain things in consciousness could still be illusory in some sense.

something seems convincing is itself illuminated by introspection. Your feelings would also be in the dark. Without the light of introspection, things are too dark to even recognize you are in the dark.

So, here is my solution to the darkness problem: turn on the light of introspection. Then you can see some thoughts, feelings, and your sense of sight itself.

I would like to complete my consideration of the utility of the tool of introspection by considering how introspection contributes to scientific inquiry. When we conduct a scientific inquiry, we make observations to test hypotheses. Introspection is embedded in even these familiar practices. For to report an observation, someone must at some time be aware of making observations. While one does not need introspection to observe a thermometer, for example, one does need introspection to *notice* that one is observing a thermometer and to later recognize one's memory of that experience. Moreover, to test a hypothesis, one must be aware of logical deductions in one's mind. These acts of awareness (of one's experience with observations and one's deductions) depend on awareness of states within one's consciousness.

To draw out this connection a bit further, suppose you read a scientific report on the reliability of introspection. This report claims that we know, on the basis of many experiments, that introspection is never reliable to any extent. Do you believe the report? Maybe you could. Perhaps you trust the authors. However, logical reflection reveals a problem: the report is self-undermining. If the report were true, then the scientists would not have any access to their own experience of making observations or to the reasons in their minds leading to their conclusions. Experiences and reasons are accessed via introspection. So, without introspection, scientists could not report their observations or analysis; no one would even know what "observation" or "analysis" means. You also could not tell whether or not you are reading a report about introspection if you have no access to your own experience of reading. Without introspection, you cannot tell whether you ever experience anything at all.

There is a fundamental problem, then, with first demonstrating the reliability of introspection by scientific experiments. A scientific demonstration of introspection would run us in a circle, since we would need to use introspection to discern whether we are making observations or thinking through an analysis relevant to our experiments.

Fortunately, there is another way. We can avoid a circular justification of science if introspection is itself a tool for knowledge. If introspection is a tool for knowledge, then you don't need to first know that you have a brain to know, via introspection, that you have thoughts and feelings. Instead, introspection allows you to know something about your thoughts and feelings in a basic way; you can know them directly. By direct acquaintance with your own consciousness, you can be acquainted with your own experience of making observations and testing hypotheses. Then science can sprout. (I will have more to say about the power of direct acquaintance when we examine the nature of perception in chapter four.)

Again, I do not claim that introspection can never mislead you, such as if you misjudge what you sense by introspection. Rather, I claim that introspection can illuminate some things—thoughts, feelings, sensations, and so on—within your own consciousness. (We will return to the question of whether any consciousness is even real in the next chapter.)

As a final note about introspection, I want to suggest that the best way to see the power of introspection is to test it out. In the course of this book, I will attempt to use introspection to probe many things. You can view this book as an experiment in the use of this tool. The experiment involves seeing what you can see by collecting first-person data via introspection and then analyzing that data.

Tool 2: Reason. Another major tool we will use is reason. By "reason," I mean the power to see truths by logical analysis. For example, when carefully thinking through the definitions of a "square" and "circle," you can see this truth: nothing can be both a square and a circle. Here are some other truths you can see by reason: triangles must have angles, rocks cannot turn into numbers, trees cannot sprout into thoughts, and so on. In general, by reasoning, you can discern universal principles about what must be or what cannot be. The experience of acquaintance with universal truths is the experience of seeing truths by the light of reason.

While reason may be familiar, its applications and powers are far more significant than many people may realize. The applications of reason are comparable to the applications of the internet. When the internet first came out, we only saw a few limited uses for it, such as website searches and email. We associated the internet with these initial applications. Then new applications came to light: social media, video channels, ecommerce, and many others. As the applications of the internet expanded, we expanded the meaning of the term *internet*. In a similar way, the applications of reason have been expanding. The early application of reason gave us what we call "canonical logic." This logic includes some simple principles of reason, such as the principle that nothing can be both A and not A (for any instance of A). We associated "reason" with those original principles (so-called analytic truths). Later, we discovered many other applications of reason, which have formed many growing branches of logic. For example, in the twentieth century, we developed the logic of possibility (modal logic), the logic of parts and wholes (mereology), the logic of time (tensed logic), and many other branches illuminated by reason. Reason has continued to reveal more and more, with no end in sight.

As with the tool of introspection, I will offer a few reasons why I think we can use the tool of reason to help us in our inquiry. I begin by addressing a worry. People have sometimes asked me how we can be sure reason can reveal anything about reality. Or, if reason can reveal some things, why think reason can help us with big philosophical questions, like questions about consciousness?

I offer three considerations in reply. First, the worry invites careful testing. I will not assume reason alone will lead our inquiry into truth. Rather than rush ahead with unbridled speculations, I will seek to tether the results of reason to the real world. This project will involve tying reason to reality with the rope of observations in a systematic, scientific way. (I will say more about this scientific approach in the next section.)

Second, I believe it is possible to see, by reason itself, some truths about reality far away. For example, by reason, you can see that everything, whether a pinecone next to your foot or an electron one billion light years away, has the feature of being identical with itself. This principle of self identity is called "the law of identity," and it appears—by the light of reason—to have no restriction. Similarly, by reason, you can see that square circles don't emerge anywhere. Another example: objects cannot become both colorless and green simultaneously. These examples may seem minute, but they illustrate that reason can illuminate at least some constraints on the natures of things near and far.

In fact, some truths about far away things are more clearly illuminated by reason than by any other instrument we have. For example, we can see, quite clearly, that turtles with colorless-green shells do not inhabit galaxies far away. We can see this truth by seeing, from here, an incongruence in the nature of a shell that is both colorless and green simultaneously. Later in this book I will show how reason can reveal surprising constraints on theories of consciousness by revealing other incongruencies.

Moreover, reason's power to reveal universal truths (about things near and far) is foundational to many things we take ourselves to know locally (about things near). For example, by reason, we know that a true statement is not also false. If we did not know that, then we could not distinguish any true scientific hypothesis from any false one, and then all science would crumble.

Third, and finally, if we take skepticism of reason too far, we risk cutting off the very branch on which we stand. Everything goes dark if we turn off the light of reason entirely. After all, it takes reason to provide reasons to doubt reason. The very inferences in an argument against the use of reason are themselves illuminated by reason. The problem is that if we cannot rely on *any* reasoning, we cannot see the validity of our very reasons to doubt reason. It seems to me, then, that any argument against reason involves the use of reason itself.

The problem of cutting reason short is directly relevant to our inquiry. If we say that reason cannot help reveal any truths about conscious persons, then this very claim also depends on reasoning. How can we trust reason to tell us not to trust reason in this case? Perhaps reason can reveal some of its limits, but I do not see all the limits of what reason might reveal. I want to be careful, then, not to limit the range of reason prematurely.

In the end, I believe the best way to see what we can see is to look. It is difficult to say at the outset what we can discover via the light of reason. To see where the light of reason might shine, I see no other course than to experiment.

Tool 3: The scientific method. We will use a broadly scientific method of analysis. By this, I mean that we will test hypotheses by making relevant observations. Our observations will include data from intro-spection (e.g., about how certain things seem or feel), from logical analysis, and any other observations from scientific studies relevant to our quest. We will then test certain hypotheses about consciousness in light of those observations. If a hypothesis fails to match the observations we collect, we will push that hypothesis off the table. This observation-based approach will help us build out a theory that is anchored to the clearest observations.

Some readers might wonder how this observation-based approach fits with my work as a philosopher. People sometimes express the worry that philosophers spin webs of ideas that are untethered or untestable. Can work in philosophy contribute anything useful to our inquiry into persons?

My answer is that philosophical work can help clarify key concepts that are fundamental to understanding the data we collect. Consider, for example, data about the relationship between states of consciousness and states of brain matter. Some relatively recent studies indicate inverse cor-relations between brain activity and the richness of conscious experience in certain contexts.[8] What should we make of these studies? Interpretations vary depending on a wide range of considerations, including those not strictly in the domain of brain science. Academic philosophers have fleshed out a body of analytical work—including the logic of parts and wholes, tensed logic (i.e., the logic of time), the analysis of personal identity, the analysis of language, the analysis of rationality, and theories of mind—that are relevant to interpreting scientific results.

Logical analysis can help us tease out unexpected implications of pre-vious observations. Philosophers have developed new theorems about con-sciousness that are not widely known among scientists who study the brain.[9] These theorems, derived by deductions from first-person, introspective

---

[8] R. Carhart-Harris et al., "Neural Correlates of the Psychedelic State as Determined by fMRI Studies with Psilocybin," *PNAS* 109, no. 6 (2012): 2138-43.

[9] See, for example, Tononi's integrated information theory, which includes formal principles expressing first-person data of consciousness ("Consciousness as Integrated Information: A Pro-visional Manifesto," *The Biological Bulletin* 215, no. 3 [2008]: 216-42). Another example is Hoff-man's scrambling theorem ("The Scrambling Theorem: A Simple Proof of the Logical Possibility of Spectrum Inversion," *Conscious Cognition* 15, no. 1 [2006]: 31-45), deduced from first-person data. There is also my own deduction of the mindful thoughts theorem (about the basis of thoughts), which I will display in chap. 3.

data, expose valuable new considerations relevant to our understanding of what the current science is uncovering.

Furthermore, logical analysis can help remove conceptual obstacles to seeing things that have the potential to be quite clear. For example, as I will argue, I think your own existence, thoughts, feelings, and aspects of your field of awareness can be secure items of knowledge. Obstacles to this sight roll in, however, and it can take the instrument of careful analysis to roll them away. We will be using logical analysis to roll away barriers to sight.

As a final note, to help you get the most out of this inquiry, I aim to provide an analysis of data that anyone can independently check. For this reason, while I lean into a broadly scientific method (of testing hypotheses with relevant observations), I will not rest any claim on mere scientific authority. Sometimes authority-driven claims about what science says covers over key premises. To put light on our steps, I will tease out the hidden premises and point to observations and analyses anyone can examine for themselves.

We are now equipped to enter the cave of consciousness. Introspection will help us illuminate aspects of ourselves from the inside. Reason we will help us illuminate the logical implications of our first-person data. The scientific method will help us organize our observations into a testable theory. With these tools in hand, we are ready to illuminate the steps ahead.

Before we continue, I offer a warning: we will go deep. The journey ahead will move into rough and strange places, including places I personally had never seen before my research for this book. We will not take for granted classical ways of thinking about consciousness but will instead work to see things in a new light. This journey is for explorers who want to uncover truths buried in the depths. I do not claim it will be easy at every step. I do predict this journey will be rewarding—and perhaps surprising.

ROAD MAP

Our journey ahead has two parts. Part one is about your nature. Part two is about your origin. The majority of part one is devoted to a close-up examination of elements of you: feelings, thoughts, perception (sight), your power to choose, your value, and your body. This examination divides across seven chapters. In each chapter, I do two things: first, I collect relevant observations (via our tools); second, I use these observations to analyze these elements and remove certain theories about them. My analysis of these elements of you prepares the way for the final chapter of part one. In this chapter, I put the scope directly on you—the subject who has and unifies the elements of you. I provide an account of this unifying subject, the being who is you.

The second part of our journey is devoted to understanding the nature of a world in which something like you can possibly exist. The guiding question is this: How can there be any personal, conscious beings (ever)? The previous part of the book prepares us to appreciate the significance and challenge of this question. Building on previous observations, I describe several "construction" problems with constructing any being like you. These problems provide severe constraints on any theory of your origin. I seek to develop, within these tight constraints, a more complete theory of the nature and origin of personal beings.

As we proceed, I invite you to own this journey. Whether you are a seasoned philosopher or curious soul, I invite you to test each part by the light of your own analysis. Take whatever serves you, and leave behind whatever doesn't. We will work to illuminate the essential steps to a big thesis by the end. Wherever you rest your beliefs, I hope this inquiry will empower you in your own exploration of who you are.

Let us now enter the cave of consciousness to see what we might see.

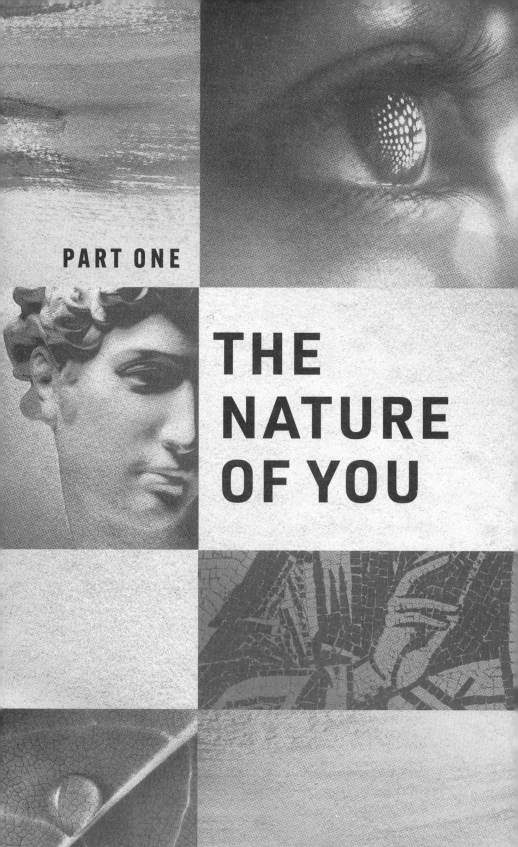

PART ONE

THE NATURE OF YOU

2

YOUR FEELINGS

Mind precedes all mental states.

THE BUDDHA

WE WILL BEGIN OUR INQUIRY into personal beings by shining light on the feeling aspect of consciousness. The feeling aspect of consciousness is what it feels like to be conscious of things, such as a desire, an intention, a thought, a hope, the smell of coffee, and so on. By illuminating the feeling aspect of consciousness, we will bring to light the first paint stroke in a larger picture of your nature.

This chapter is a building block chapter. By zooming in on feelings, we will begin to uncover a more general problem of explaining consciousness. One positive outcome of this chapter is this simple thesis: first-person feelings are real. The fuller significance of this thesis will come into greater view in the course of our journey.

WHAT CAN FEEL?

To set a stage for feelings, I begin with a puzzle. This puzzle is about how to demarcate things that have feelings from things that don't. Presumably some things can feel. For example, *you* can feel. You can feel happy, sad, afraid, angry, excited, puzzled, loved, and so on. Yet, other things do not have feelings.[1] For example, rocks, leaves, and sand presumably do not have feelings. What makes the difference? What *could* make the difference? In general, what does it take for something to be able to have feelings?

---

[1]Even the panpsychist, who says consciousness is ubiquitous in nature, will say that there are constraints on what it takes to be conscious.

To avoid leaping ahead too quickly, I will not assume at the outset which materials can or cannot make conscious beings. While it may seem obvious that certain things like rocks, leaves, or sand do not have conscious feelings, I will not even assume this at the outset. Instead, I want to take a step back and consider how we might, in principle, demarcate the difference between things that feel and things that do not.

Consider that consciousness could take different forms than we are accustomed to. For example, suppose some grains of sand collectively think, *I feel afraid*, as you toss them into the air. If some sand did think that, the sand couldn't let you know about their feeling of fear. The sand couldn't yell or shout or implant feelings into your mind. So how can we actually be sure that some sand is not experiencing feelings? Maybe sand simply enjoys consciousness in a different way than we do.

In preparing for this book, I asked some friends why they think throwing sand in the air won't make the sand feel afraid. The most common answer was this: consciousness requires a nervous system. The idea here is that since sand doesn't have a nervous system, we can infer that sand is (probably) not conscious.

However, this answer cloaks a deeper question: How does a nervous system make the difference? The question here is not whether we have *evidence* that conscious things have a nervous system. Rather, the question is more fundamental. It is about how, in principle, organizing atoms into a nervous system could, just on its own, suffice to explain the emergence of any conscious beings.

A rising tide of philosophers and scientists have been uncovering reasons to think that at least certain materials, like sand, are insufficient to explain consciousness, no matter how they function.[2] Some materials just can't explain consciousness, they argue. We will explore their reasons in the course of this book.

---

[2]Some examples include D. Chalmers, "Facing Up to the Problem of Consciousness," *Journal of Consciousness Studies* 2, no. 3 (1995): 200-219; R. Henry, "The Mental Universe," *Nature* 436, no. 29 (2005); P. Goff, *Consciousness and Fundamental Reality* (New York: Oxford University Press, 2017); B. Kastrup, *Why Materialism Is Baloney: How True Skeptics Know There Is No Death and Fathom Answers to Life, the Universe, and Everything* (Winchester, UK: Iff, 2014); B. Kastrup, *The Idea of the World: A Multi-Disciplinary Argument for the Mental Nature of Reality* (Winchester, UK: John Hunt, 2019); and D. Hoffman, *The Case Against Reality: How Evolution Hid the Truth from Our Eyes* (New York: W. W. Norton, 2019).

For now, I will highlight a seed of one reason one might think that some materials lack the means to explain consciousness. Consider that, from a logical standpoint, we cannot derive first-person, perspectival experiences from a mere third-person description of atoms. To illustrate, suppose we dumped loads of sand into a special machine that causes the sand to function like a nervous system. The grains of sand act like a functioning brain. Still, logic alone does not reveal whether the resulting storm of sand would thereby have its own first-person, conscious feelings. Therefore, third-person materials are the wrong materials, one might think, to logically derive first-person conscious reality all on their own.

Moreover, an inability to derive first-person realities from third-person descriptions could explain why sand cannot become conscious. Sand is a third-person material: descriptions of sand reduce to third-person, quantitative descriptions of positions and motions of little grains. None of these descriptions, on their own, add up a description of first-person feelings. Nor do they suffice to explain how feelings could emerge. So, to avoid multiplying inexplicable states of reality, one might conclude that conscious feelings cannot arise out of unconscious grains of sand.

But if sand cannot become conscious, what can? What difference in material could be relevant to consciousness?

This question is not easy. It is not obvious how to turn things, whether cosmic dust or chains of carbon atoms, into conscious beings. If consciousness can emerge out of certain materials, the deep question remains: which ones? These questions point to what I call "the construction challenge."

The construction challenge is the challenge of seeing how to construct conscious beings by any means. There are two pieces to this challenge. The first piece is about consciousness. This piece is the premise that some conscious beings exist—for example, we exist, and we are conscious. The second piece is about construction. There are constraints on constructing conscious beings. For example, if some grains of sand in a certain position do not comprise a conscious being, then it may seem that merely changing some positions or motions of those grains will not thereby transform them into a conscious being. The thought here stems from a more general thought about relevant differences: one might think that mere quantitative changes (in size, shape, motion, etc.) cannot, on their own, add up to the relevant categorical difference required to construct a conscious being. In other words, mere quantitative changes in some materials will not thereby transform them into a conscious being. This principle, if true, is an example of a construction constraint. The challenge, then, is to see how these two pieces—the existence of conscious beings, on the one hand, and the construction constraints, on the other—could go together. How can conscious beings be constructed out of any actual materials of reality?

I believe great insight can spring from wrestling with the construction challenge. A large part of my task in this book will be to draw out the challenge, from many angles, and to identify resources that will help us put the pieces together in a satisfying way.

THEORIES OF MIND: A TAXONOMY

To help us think about what is at stake in making conscious beings, it will help to consider some different theories of what consciousness is. Over the last seventy years, philosophers of mind have developed a set of standard options for understanding consciousness. I will survey these options here.

For ease of reference, I shall call something that can include (or contain) contents of consciousness a "mind." A mind, in this sense, is a realm of consciousness. This minimal definition is a seed for other ideas that will sprout in the course of this book. For now, I note this result: where there are feelings (in consciousness), there is a mind (a realm of consciousness).

We can divide all the theories of mind into two broad types: reductive and nonreductive theories. Reductive theories analyze aspects of mental states (of thinking, feeling, intending, etc.) in terms of material states, such as neurological states of a brain. Nonreductive theories, by contrast, say that mental states (at least some of them) do not reduce to material states. On nonreductive theories—a feeling of happiness, for example—is not the same as (say) chemical reactions in a brain.

To elucidate these views, it will help to have a closer look at the terms *mental state* and *material state*. While these terms are not easy to define, paradigm examples can orient us to the distinction. Examples of mental states include feelings, thoughts, and intentions. The term *material state*, on the other hand, picks out states of matter that are analyzable in terms of quantities and spatial aspects, such as shape, size, location, or motion. An example of a material state is an axon firing in a brain, where the axon is analyzable in terms of quantitative and spatial aspects. The analysis of a material state can also include functions or equations that specify changes or relations between quantities and spatial aspects.

One way of distinguishing "mental state" from "material state" is in terms of whether they depend on a first-person perspective. Material states are typically thought to be able to exist—at least in principle—apart from someone's first-person experience; for example, you don't need to experience your brain from your first-person perspective for your brain to exist. By contrast, a mental state of feeling love depends on someone's first-person experience. I will call states that depend on a first-person perspective "first-person states." I will call states that can (at least conceivably) exist apart from a first-person perspective "third-person" states. I make no assumptions at the outset about whether any particular states are first-person or third-person.

In light of these clarifications, we can sharpen the distinction between reductive and nonreductive theories. Standard reductive theories of mind analyze first-person, experiential states (thoughts, feelings, emotions, and so on) in terms of third-person states, such as spatial or functional states of axons in a brain. Nonreductive theories deny this. They say that a complete third-person description of third-person material states (e.g., chemical reactions) leaves out certain first-person aspects of consciousness.

Here, then, is a bird's-eye view of all the major reductive and non-reductive theories of mind. Nonreductive theories separate into the following three options: eliminativism (which eliminates consciousness), varieties of idealism (which flips the picture by treating mental states as fundamental to the analysis of everything else), and varieties of dualism (which countenances both mental and material states, while viewing each as irreducible to the other). On the other side are reductive theories. These include behaviorism, type-identity theory, token-identity theory, and reductive functionalism.

In this chapter, I will zoom in on the theories that either eliminate or reduce consciousness. My aim is to draw out what is at stake in eliminating or reducing consciousness. By seeing what is at stake, we will be in better

position to see something special about what it takes for something like you
to have feelings.

Eliminativism. Let's start with eliminativism. According to the strongest
form of eliminativism, nothing is ever conscious.[3] Initially, one might think
this idea is crazy talk: How could nothing be conscious? However, eliminativists sometimes refer to ordinary beliefs about consciousness as expressing
our "folk ontology." Folk ontology is just what ordinary folk ordinarily
believe to exist, such as rocks, people, and conversations. Eliminativists
point out that these ordinary beliefs can be mistaken. In the case of consciousness, they say that many of our ordinary beliefs about consciousness
probably are mistaken.

I want to emphasize that eliminativism is not a reductive theory of consciousness. Reductive theories reduce mental states to third-person
material states, such as brains states. Eliminativists don't do that. Instead,
eliminativists eliminate mental states altogether. They say there are no
beliefs, feelings, thoughts, and so on. So, elimination and reduction are
importantly different. (One can also be an eliminativist about *certain*
mental states without eliminating all mental states. For example, one might
eliminate feelings without eliminating thoughts.)[4]

Still, eliminativists and reductionists are allies on a significant point.
They agree on this: felt aspects of consciousness are not fundamentally as
they seem through the window of introspection. For example, consider a
feeling of happiness. You may seem to know some subjective aspects of this
feeling—for example, what it feels like to have that feeling. However, a
reductionist may analyze this feeling in terms of certain motions and
activities of molecules in a brain. Thus, while you may think you know the
feeling via introspection, you don't know what the feeling *really is* via

---

[3]Some representative defenses of eliminativism with respect to (at least certain) mental states
include Patricia Churchland, *Neurophilosophy: Toward a Unified Science of the Mind/Brain* (Cambridge, MA: MIT Press, 1986); Paul Churchland, *A Neurocomputational Perspective* (Cambridge,
MA: MIT Press, 1989); S. Stitch, *Deconstructing the Mind* (New York: Oxford University Press,
1996); E. Irvine, *Consciousness as a Scientific Concept: A Philosophy of Science Perspective* (New
York: Springer, 2013); and A. Rosenberg, "Disenchanted Naturalism," *Kritikos* 12 (2015): https://
intertheory.org/rosenberg.htm.

[4]Illusionists eliminate *phenomenal consciousness* (i.e., *what it is like* to have a certain feeling), but
they are not thereby committed to eliminating everything within consciousness, including feelings, thoughts, and visual imagery.

introspection. For when you introspect a feeling, you do not witness any molecules as molecules. By reductionist lights, then, your feelings reduce to things (brain states) you would not recognize merely via introspective experience. That's because feelings are not fundamentally characterized in terms of subjective (felt) aspects as they appear in introspective experience. Instead, feelings are fundamentally and exhaustively characterizable in terms of third-person vocabulary (shapes, motions, quantities, etc.). On this point, eliminativists (with respect to feelings) agree: eliminativists say there are no irreducibly subjective aspects of feelings. Third-person descriptions of material systems, like brains, describe all the aspects (of you) there are.

But here is the crucial difference between eliminativists and reductionists. Eliminativists generally say that feelings would actually have the subjective aspects that people ordinarily say they have. For example, a feeling of happiness would have the felt positive aspect it seems to have introspectively. In this respect, eliminativists respect certain ordinary intuitions about consciousness. For example, you might think your feeling of happiness feels to you a certain way. Eliminativists can agree with this much: your happiness would, *if it were real*, have the subjective aspect of feeling a certain way to you. However, since eliminativists think that nothing has subjective aspects (as they appear via introspection), eliminativists, unlike reductionists, infer that therefore there are no feelings.

In a sense, then, eliminativists take first-person, subjective aspects of consciousness seriously. They take the subjectivity of consciousness so seriously, in fact, that they resist explaining consciousness away in terms of nonsubjective configurations of matter. In this respect, it seems to me that the eliminativist actually does more than the reductionist to take seriously common intuitions about consciousness. Unlike the reductionist, the eliminativist takes seriously the common conviction that a feeling of love is not reducible to (say) a chemical reaction in a brain (or any other state describable in purely nonpsychological terms). Instead of dismissing this conviction as misguided (or as just part of "folk" thinking), the eliminativist says that first-person consciousness does not reduce to third-person brain states.

By taking consciousness seriously, eliminativists also take seriously the "hard problem" of consciousness. The hard problem of consciousness at the most general level is the problem of explaining consciousness in terms of purely third-person material states. Some philosophers have argued that (i) everything must be explicable in terms of more fundamental, third-person material states, but that (ii) consciousness cannot be explicable purely in terms of third-person material states. If one accepts (i) and (ii), then the only option left is to eliminate consciousness. Elimination can be an implicit acknowledgment of the hard problem of explaining consciousness. The problem is so hard, one might think, that it cannot be solved unless we eliminate consciousness altogether.

From my survey of the literature on eliminativism (and from correspondence with eliminativist sympathizers), it appears to me that a root motivation for eliminativism grows out of a certain *epistemology* (about how to know the nature of reality). Eliminativists tend to approach the question of consciousness with a certain view about how to reliably acquire information about anything. Eliminativists often emphasize the tools of empirical observation, theoretical virtues, and scientific methodology. These tools, they point out, give us information about brains and bodies. Moreover, these tools fail to reveal any clear information about first-person subjective experiences. For this reason, we are unable to use our scientific tools to verify that first-person, subjective experiences actually exist.

To be clear, the thinking here is not that it is impossible in principle to discover consciousness. Many eliminativists suppose that, in principle, there could be reasons to posit consciousness to explain other things we see, just as we posit electrons to explain other things we see. The problem, however, is that we cannot verify consciousness by any direct means. So, if we are to verify the existence of consciousness, we need to make an *inference* based on other things we observe. The thought, then, is that we have no sufficiently good reason to posit consciousness to explain other things we see. We can explain everything more simply without positing the things people associate with first-person consciousness.

So, is there good reason to think consciousness exists? As you may anticipate, I think so. In particular, I think it is possible to detect at least some contents of consciousness directly using introspection. Before I develop this thought further, I want to briefly walk through a sequence of three objections to eliminativism and possible replies. Walking through these objections and replies will help further illuminate what is at stake. By the end of this walk, I hope to display what I think is the best way to navigate this dialectical landscape.

First, perhaps the most common objection to eliminativism is that the thesis is itself self-defeating. For suppose eliminativism is true. Then there are no mental states. But if there are no mental states, then no one could *think* that eliminativism is true. To think that there are no mental states is to have a mental state (a thought). Even to question the existence of mental states is to have a mental state (a question). Is that not a contradiction?

Here is a reply. Per eliminativism, no one actually thinks that there are no thoughts. Instead, in the place of thoughts, there are nonmental brain states that function like thoughts would.[5] So the eliminativist doesn't think there are no thoughts. Rather, she thinks* there are no thoughts. Thinks* is like thinks, except there is no subjective feeling or experience involved in having a thought*. The eliminativist's "thought" here is that we can replace references to mental states, like thoughts, with reference to something else.

Here is a second objection. If we replace talk of thoughts with talk of thoughts*, then what exactly does "thoughts*" mean? William Hasker raises this question in his analysis of Paul Churchland's arguments for eliminativism. Hasker observes, "Churchland, having reached his negative conclusion about folk psychology, nevertheless continues . . . to make to make assertion after assertion assuming the truth of what eliminativism denies."[6] Hasker's point is not that eliminativism is flatly self-defeating. Rather, he is concerned with how to interpret claims made in support of eliminativism. The problem here is this: if there are no mental states, then there are no affirmations, and thus there are no affirmations of eliminativism. What, then, could someone mean if they say they "affirm" eliminativism?

In response, an eliminativist could perhaps leave the translation project as an open inquiry. Sure, the translations have not been worked out so far. But perhaps they could be worked out in terms of brain functions. While

---

[5]See Rosenberg, "Disenchanted Naturalism."
[6]W. Hasker, *The Emergent Self* (Ithaca, NY: Cornell University Press, 2001), 36.

we don't (yet) have the actual translations, perhaps an eliminativist could point to our best current theory of human behaviors, which we do understand. Those theories, they may say, are not in terms of mental states. The eliminativist could then offer a promissory note: the cost of the translation problem will be paid, and the cost is worth the theoretical benefits of eliminativism. I think this is sort of response is the best strategy on behalf of eliminativists.

I turn now to a third objection, which I think points to a root problem. The problem is that eliminativism contradicts what I think one can know *directly*. According to this objection, one does not need to posit consciousness or witness one's feelings through a microscope. Instead, one can witness one's consciousness directly—just by noticing it.

For our purposes, I do not take for granted that we have direct access to mental states. In the previous chapter, I suggested that introspection can give us information about inner conscious states. But we may wonder, why think that is true? Some eliminativists I've talked with express skepticism that introspection illuminates any reality. Why think we can use introspection to know that we are conscious?

In view of this question, I took some time in the previous chapter to offer some reasons for thinking that introspection can reveal aspects of reality within consciousness. To review, I argued that introspection is a basic tool of knowledge. This tool allows us to know something about our experiences, including the experience of questioning whether introspection is reliable. Without introspection, we fall into a deep pit of skepticism, and I see no possible way out.

Previously, I also argued that introspection is foundational to scientific inquiry itself. The gist of the argument was that we use introspection in the activities of science, such as the activity of recalling observations and analyzing scientific reports. So, without introspection, I believe all of science (including any science that could cast doubts on introspection) would crumble.

My analysis of eliminativism, then, is fundamentally this: by the light of introspection, I think it is possible to know something about your experiences directly. In particular, you can know some thoughts, feelings, and intentions. On this analysis, the subjective aspects of consciousness are not theoretical posits that explain some data; you do not need to posit your feelings to explain other things, like your behavior. Rather, conscious states are part of your data—which I think you can access directly. (I will say more about the power to access things directly in chapter four on perception.)

Suppose instead you are not conscious. Then things aren't as they seem. But without introspection, you could not even tell whether you *seem* to be conscious. Even if everything is an illusion, your very experience of an illusion is itself an item of consciousness illuminated by introspection.[7]

To be clear, I am not saying that introspection illuminates everything perfectly clearly. Rather, I say that introspection allows you to detect at least some aspects of your mental states. For example, when you pay attention to inner states, you can witness thoughts and feelings by direct acquaintance, which I believe is the clearest and most direct way to know that anything is real.[8] So, the way out of the eliminativist's territory, on my analysis, is by the light of introspection, which shines on realities right within you.

We can summarize this analysis in the form of an argument:

1. You can tell, by introspection, that some of your feelings differ from others (e.g., happiness differs from sadness).

2. If some of your feelings differ from others, then you have some feelings.

3. Therefore, you have some feelings.

At this stage in the dialectic, someone could wonder whether my analysis depends on presupposing the things whose very existence is in question—introspection, feelings, seemings, considerations, and so on. Does my analysis presuppose the very thing I am arguing for? If so, isn't that cheating?

My answer is that my case for consciousness does not fundamentally rest on the edifice of an argument from independent premises. Rather, it rests on a basic act of awareness. Just as your eyes allow you to be aware of shapes and colors within your visual field, introspection allows you to be aware of your

---

[7] I will say more about the prospect of consciousness itself being an illusion in chap. 4 when we zoom in on theories of perception.

[8] For the sake of modesty, my arguments allow for the possibility of mistakes. However, in my analysis, a belief based directly and solely on a direct experience is the most secure a belief could possibly be, for it has the fewest sources of possible error. We could call it "infallible" in the following sense: necessarily, if one directly experiences x (a thought, feeling, visual image, mathematical truth), and on that basis alone believes that x exists, then that belief is true.

experiences. If you can notice something within you by the light of direct, inner awareness, then no argument for its existence is necessary.

There is certainly a longer discussion to be had with eliminativists, and I do not claim to have the last word. Still, I hope the connection between introspection and science may serve eliminativists whose toolkit includes scientific instruments. Perhaps these considerations may encourage some eliminativist sympathizers to take up the instrument of introspection with more confidence.[9]

As usual, I invite you to test my ideas by your own light. Focus your awareness within. Do you sense anything? Do you sense any thoughts, feelings, or emotions? Do you sense that some feelings differ from others? If you are like me, by focusing inward, you can sense some thinking and feeling right within you; you can even witness your *sense* of thinking and feeling. Even if you notice yourself feeling unconvinced by my presentation, then you notice some feeling. If so, then that you've noticed enough to eliminate eliminativism.

Behaviorism. I turn next to reductive theories. Recall that these theories don't deny that consciousness exists. Rather, they deny that conscious experiences (happiness, love, hope, etc.) are fundamentally characterizable in terms of experiential aspects (e.g., what it feels like to you to be happy) as they appear in one's first-person perspective. Instead, according to reductionism, consciousness reduces to things expressible in the vocabulary of third-person physics ("shape," "size," "momentum," etc.). For example, the experience of happiness is fully describable in terms of purely third-person aspects, such as a pattern or function of particles in a brain.

To draw out the implications, I will walk through a sequence of iterations of reductionism. Some of the earliest reductive theories in contemporary analytic philosophy are behaviorist theories. These divide into logical (sometimes called "analytical") and ontological versions. I'll consider these theories in turn. First, logical behaviorism is about the meaning of our words. According to logical behaviorism, talk about a conscious state (e.g., a feeling) is analyzable in terms of talk about behaviors. For example, when

---

[9]For those worried about *illusions* with respect to first-person data, hold on to that worry. We will examine the prospect and nature of illusions in chap. 4, when we examine the nature of perception.

you say, "I am happy," what this means, according to logical behaviorism, is that you are disposed to behave a certain way. In particular, you are disposed to smile or to say "I am happy" when someone asks. The logical behaviorist supposes that all terms that express feelings (like "pain" or "happy") can be translated in terms of purely third-person vocabulary.[10]

As far as I have seen, logical behaviorism is no longer an active research program. A major challenge has been to provide suitable translations. To illustrate the challenge, suppose you feel sad but decide to behave as if you are happy. Surely that is possible. But then how do we translate "sad" into behaviors if a sad person can behave like a happy person? It seems there is no way.

To draw out the problem, consider this translation strategy. Translate "sad" as follows: "you do things like cry and frown unless you pretend to not be sad." Here "pretend to not be sad" expresses a mental state ("pretend"). So, if we are to translate mental states into behavioral states, we will need to translate "pretend to not be sad." How might we do that? We might try this: translate "pretend to not be sad" as "behaves as if you are not sad." But then the definition of "sad" becomes a trivial tautology. To see this, let us unpack the definition at hand: "sad" means "you will cry and frown unless you behave as if you are not *sad* [unless you don't cry or frown]." This definition tells us nothing about the meaning of "sad." The challenge, then, is to find a nontrivial, noncircular translation purely in terms of behaviors.

The problem of translation is a symptom of a deeper problem. The problem is that we can know what terms like "happy" and "sad" mean independently of behavioral definitions. For example, when my child tells me she feels thirsty, she does not first check her behaviors to determine whether she feels thirsty. She knows the feeling of thirst within her. Her behavior may be evidence of her thirst, but her behavior is not what she means by the word *thirsty*.

Moreover, mere facts about behavior leave out internal cognitive experiences. As Graham puts it, "Behavior without cognition is blind."[11] For while

---

[10]G. Graham, "Behaviorism," *Stanford Encyclopedia of Philosophy* (2019) provides an overview of the historical roots of this form of behaviorism (what he calls "analytical behaviorism").
[11]Graham, "Behaviorism."

internal cognition may result in outer behaviors, the cognition is not the same as behaviors.

The tool of introspection illuminates this same result. By introspection, one can recognize that a description of behaviors does not thereby describe one's feelings. For example, suppose you are feeling curious. You don't need to look at your face in a mirror to verify that you are curious. You know this feeling directly within you. While you may not know whether someone *else* feels curious apart from their behavior, that's not because the word *curious* just means some behavior. On the contrary, you can know the meaning of *curious* by your direct acquaintance with a curious feeling.

In view of these problems, philosophers of mind have abandoned the project of translating psychological terms into purely behavioral terms. To my knowledge, the purely semantic project is no longer on the floor of debated options; it has been swept away by careful analysis.

Let us turn, then, to the other version of behaviorism: ontological behaviorism. This theory is not about semantics: it does not suppose that our talk about feelings is literally translatable in terms of third-person behavioral language. Instead, this theory supposes that first-person experiential states reduce to (i.e., are the same as) behavioral states. This theory is a version of a more general theory that first-person, mental aspects reduce to certain third-person, material aspects. I will look at this general theory next.

Type identity. According to type identity, first-person mental aspects (e.g., a subjective quality of pain) are the same as (identical to) some third-person material aspects.[12] (Note, I use the term *aspect* to express any characteristic—such as, red, round, or rough. We could alternatively call these properties, features, or attributes. For our purposes, I use these terms interchangeably.)

To illustrate type-identity theory, let us consider the subjective, experiential aspect of being in pain. Call this aspect "Painy." Suppose, for sake of illustration, that Painy is identical to some neurological aspect of a C-fiber firing. There are now two options to consider. Option one: the nature of this neurological aspect is best characterized as a first-person, subjective,

[12]U. T. Place, "Is Consciousness a Brain Process?," *British Journal of Psychology* 47, no. 1 (1956): 44-50 and J. J. C. Smart, "Sensations and Brain Processes," *Philosophical Review* 68, no. 2 (1959): 141-56 provide representative defenses of type identity.

experiential aspect. In other words, the material brain state reduces to a mental state. This option is one that an idealist might accept, since it analyzes the neurological aspect as a subjective, mental feature. Type identity theory is not generally regarded as a version of idealism, however. Instead, type-identity theory reduces the first-person mental to the third-person material, not the other way. So, the type-identity theorist takes the other option: the nature of Painy is best characterized as the neurological aspect. According to this option, the first-person experiential aspect, Painy, reduces to a third-person material aspect (not the other way around).

An advantage of type-identity theory is that it avoids the behaviorist's problem of translation. For translation and reduction are not the same. To draw out this distinction, consider by comparison the term *water*. We can understand what someone means when they ask for water without knowing anything about H_2O. That's true even if water happens to be reducible to H_2O. In the same way, even if the term *pain* is not translatable in terms of neurological behaviors, it does not follow that pain is not reducible to neurological behaviors.

One important challenge to type-identity theory is the problem of multiple realizability.[13] The problem here is that the same type of consciousness (e.g., a sharp pain) can, it may seem, be realized (or programmed) into different types of material systems. For example, suppose a carbon brain can be conscious. Then it is at least conceivable (logically consistent) for a silicon brain to also be conscious. For example, we could swap the carbon atoms in your brain for functionally equivalent silicon atoms. Some philosophers of mind have suggested that by swapping functionally equivalent parts, different types of brains could have the same types of consciousness. If they are right, then there is a problem with reducing conscious types (which are multiply realizable) to particular material types (which are not themselves multiply realizable). The problem, then, is that multiply realizable aspects of consciousness are not reducible to material aspects.

I do not think the problem of multiple realizability is decisive, however. While philosophers of mind often cite the problem of multiple realizability

---

[13]See J. Bickel, "Multiple Realizability," *Stanford Encyclopedia of Philosophy* (2020), https://plato .stanford.edu/entries/multiple-realizability for an overview of reasons in support of the multiple realizability of consciousness.

as motivating a trend away from the purely type-reduction analysis of consciousness, the problem does not knock away all versions of type identity. A type-identity theorist could still account for multiple realizability by working with a broader notion of "type." For example, one may include functional types, which have a wide range of inputs and outputs (e.g., silicon or carbon). Functional types allow for multiple realizations. This version of type identity is a form of functionalism, which I will examine shortly.

In my view, a more forceful challenge comes from considerations I raised against eliminativism. I think both views face a deep challenge in accounting for things one can witness directly in one's own experiences. In particular, just as one can directly witness aspects of one's own feelings, one can also directly witness certain distinctions between certain aspects of one's feelings and certain aspects of brain states. For example, one can compare the feeling of a pain with the structure or motion of some molecules. By comparing these things, I believe one can see some differences directly. I will expand on this proposal (and assess possible replies) in the next section when I return to the question of what it takes to be conscious.

As a final note about type-identity, my impression is that most philosophers of mind today have moved away from a purely type reduction. While they tend to still identify as "physicalist" in at least some sense, their analysis of first-person conscious states (feelings, desires, hopes) leads many to argue against a purely reductive analysis of consciousness, often contrary to initial expectations.[14] I hope to display some of the deepest reasons that motivate this conviction throughout this book.

Token identity. While the type-identity theorist reduces mental aspects of a mental state, the token-identity theorist reduces the individual (token) mental state itself.[15] To draw out this idea, consider again Painy. Painy is a

---

[14]Unger's transition away from a third-person physicalist reduction typifies a trajectory of many I know working in this field (see P. K. Unger, "I Do Not Exist," in *Perception and Identity*, ed. G. F. Macdonald [London: Macmillan, 1979]; *All the Power in the World* [Oxford: Oxford University Press, 2006]). See also Goff's story (in P. Goff, *Consciousness and Fundamental Reality* [New York: Oxford University Press, 2017]), where he describes a strikingly similar transition. The eminent philosopher of mind Jaegwon Kim told me personally that after forty years of research and reflection, he didn't think a fully reductive analysis of consciousness was possible.
[15]For a representative of token identity, see D. Davidson, *Essays on Actions and Events* (Oxford: Clarendon, 1980).

subjective, experiential aspect of pain. The token-identity theorist says that some brain state (event or process) B has Painy. For example, B might be a particular axon firing. Here the state that has Painy reduces to (or is) a particular, material brain state.

Token-identity theory does not itself tell us what the character of consciousness is. As far this theory goes, first-person sense aspects of consciousness may be irreducibly subjective aspects of token events or states. For example, Painy could be an irreducibly subjective aspect of a third-person brain event. Token-identity does not rule that out. For this reason, token identity is compatible with a form of dualism (in particular, property dualism or dual aspect theory), according to which first-person experiential aspects exist along with third-person material aspects. In this respect, token identity is not by itself completely reductive.[16]

Reductive functionalism. A final type of reductionism is reductive functionalism. A functionalist theory analyzes mental states in terms of functional aspects that relate inputs to outputs. For example, being a doorstop is a functional aspect. It is analyzable in terms of the relationship between a door moving toward a wall (the input) and the door stopping before it hits the wall (output). According to reductive functionalism, mental aspects are functional aspects whose inputs and outputs are microphysical events (e.g., motions of atoms). Reductive functionalism is an instance of theories that analyze consciousness in terms of relations between underlying things.[17]

Not all functionalist theories of mind are reductionist. A functional state only reduces to a third-person brain state, for example, if all its inputs or outputs are third-person brain states. But some nonreductive functionalist

---

[16]I am assuming here that token identity can be distinguished from type identity. Making this distinction is not trivial, however. Hasker argues that token identity inherits the same problems as type identity given Jaegwon Kim's analysis of events and a fine-grained theory of properties (*The Emergent Self* [Ithaca, NY: Cornell University Press, 2001]). On Kim's analysis, a token event consists of three things: (i) a particular, (ii) a property, and (iii) a time. Then a token mental event M reduces to a token brain event if and only if the property encoded in the event reduces to third-person material properties (e.g., shapes or motions). In that case, token identity is true if and only if type identity is true. I bracket this problem for sake of argument and assume one can distinguish these theories.

[17]For a wide-ranging elaboration on the role of relations in analyzing mental aspects, see C. Fritjof and P. L. Luisi, *The Systems View of Life: A Unifying Vision* (Cambridge: Cambridge University Press, 2014).

theories allow for inputs and outputs to include irreducibly subjective aspects of consciousness.

To appreciate what is at stake, it is critical to distinguish between *being a function* and *having a function*. To illustrate, consider the shape of a key. The shape of a key has a function—for example, to help you open a particular door. But the shape of the key is not itself a function (a set of inputs and outputs). It's a shape.

Seeing this distinction between being a function and having a function helps us avoid a certain error. The error is in thinking that consciousness could be entirely functional just by playing a functional role in a brain. In some sense, all aspects of all things may play some functional role. But it does not follow that all aspects *are* functional roles. Again, to *have* a functional role is not the same as *being* a functional role. Just as a shape may play a functional role in a key, a feeling aspect of consciousness may play a functional role in a nervous system; in both cases, the item that plays the functional role is not the same as the functional role itself. The reductive functionalism in view reduces aspects of consciousness to functional roles.[18] By getting clear on the distinction between having a function and being a function, we can avoid a Pyrrhic victory on behalf of the functionalist.

One consequence of reductive functionalism is that only material systems could possibly have feelings. For suppose there were a nonmaterial angel who can have feelings. Then the general state, having some feeling, would have some possible nonmaterial inputs related to the angel. In that case, the general state of having some feeling would not qualify as a fully material functional state, since some of the possible inputs and outputs that constitute the definition of that state would fail be material states. In other words, the general state of having some feeling would lack a completely reductive functionalist analysis. If reductive functionalism is true, then all feelings are analyzable in terms of functional relations between material inputs and material outputs. It follows, then, that if reductive

---

[18]This version of functionalism is called "*role*-functionalism." We can distinguish role functionalism from *realizer* functionalism, which identifies mental aspects with whatever it is that plays—realizes—certain functional roles. Realizer functionalism does not require that we reductively analyze phenomenal aspects of consciousness in terms of functions. Thus, realizer functionalism is outside the scope of what I'm calling "reductive functionalism."

functionalism is true, there cannot be angels or any feelings prior to third-person material systems.

We have now surveyed the major theories of consciousness in the philosophy of mind. In the next section, I will propose a way to test (via direct comparison) certain reductionist hypotheses, including reductive functionalism.

HOW NOT TO MAKE SAND SAD

Let us return to the question of what might demarcate things that can feel from things that cannot. For the sake of focus, I will consider the prospect of making sand conscious. Then I will see if I can draw out some general constraints on what it may take for anything to have feelings. Due to the fundamental nature of our inquiry (and the depth of the controversies), I will drill deep into some very basic concepts. I hope that by digging deep, this section will help bring into greater light the reality and nature of feelings.

The direct comparison test. To begin, I offer a test that taps into a power you have to compare certain things directly. I call this "the direct comparison test." To see how the direct comparison test works, follow these steps. First, consider any sandy shape—for instance, a swirl of sand in the wind. Then consider any feeling. Compare them. See if you notice any differences between the feeling and the shape. I predict you will easily notice differences between them. For example, you will see that the vertices in the shape differ from the sense aspects of the feeling. If you can see these differences, then you can see by direct comparison that at least certain aspects of consciousness are not the same as certain aspects of sand.

The direct comparison test is empowered by a power to see certain differences clearly and directly. This power is so familiar that it is easy to take it for granted. Yet the power to see differences is fundamental to many things we know. For example, we know that the number three is not the same as the number four, that true is not the same as false, and that black is not the same as white. How do we know these things? We know them by direct comparison.

We are skating across an icy patch of ideas. To help us proceed carefully, I want to have a closer look at this power to compare things. How reliable is this power?

At this point, questions can arise from certain foggy cases. For example, there are cases where it is unclear whether one is seeing a real difference. To illustrate, suppose I see Venus in the morning. I call what I see "the Morning Star." Then in the evening, I look up again at the sky and see a light. I call this light "the Evening Star." I might be tempted believe the Morning Star is different from the Evening Star. After all, I saw them in different parts of the sky. Yet, they aren't different: they are the same planet viewed at different times. I may *think* the Evening Star is different from the Morning Star, but I would be wrong. In this case, comparison is misleading.

Could the comparison of sandy states with conscious states similarly be misleading? Perhaps feelings can appear in different ways, just as Venus can appear in different parts of the sky. If so, then perhaps a state of sadness could appear as a swirl of sand. Is there a way to rule that out?

My answer involves distinguishing between two types of comparisons. One type of comparison is *direct*, such as when you see directly that true is not false or that happiness is not sadness. In the case of direct comparison, the differences you see are not behind a veil of appearances. You are able to be directly aware of them.

Direct comparison works when you are directly aware of the items you are comparing. For example, see if you can be aware in your mind of the numbers expressed by "three" and "four." If you are directly acquainted with the items, then you can apply the test: when you compare these things, you can then see—by direct acquaintance—a difference.

Direct comparison is safer than *indirect* comparison. In an indirect comparison, you do not see things directly. For example, you do not see Venus directly. Instead, you can see the way Venus appears to you (e.g., as being in the evening sky or being in the morning sky). Another example: you do not see H_2O directly; you see its effects. When you don't see things directly, you aren't in position to apply the direct comparison test. You can only compare them indirectly by comparing (directly) how the items *appear*. For this reason, indirect comparisons can lead to errors.

Fortunately, direct comparison lacks the source of error that indirect comparison has. In the case of direct comparison, you see directly the items of comparison. For example, when you compare truth with falsity, this comparison is not behind a veil, like a man behind a mask.[19] Instead, you can see directly—within your own consciousness—that truth is not the same as falsity.

In the same way, you can directly test whether certain aspects of consciousness are the same as certain aspects of sand. To perform this test, focus on a sensation within your own consciousness. Then focus on a swirl of sand. Compare the sensation with the swirl. If the swirl shape is entirely *outside* of your consciousness, then you can deduce that the swirl shape is not a sensation *within* your consciousness. If, on the other hand, the swirl shape is also in your consciousness, then you can compare it directly with your sensation. You can see directly that the swirl shape is not a sensation, just as you can see directly that an itch in your leg is not a thought in your mind.

A benefit of the direct comparison test is that it can help us see certain things clearly. From my applications of the test, I've come to think one can have perfectly clear sight in certain cases. For example, by direct comparison, one can be sure that true is not false, two is not three, and a sense of sadness is not a swirl of sand. I think one can be even surer of these differences than that there is any sand, that trees have leaves, or that the earth is round. For when it comes to trees, leaves, and the shape of the earth, it is possible—though highly unlikely—that our experiences with these things are all part of an elaborate hallucination. By contrast, when it comes to feelings, I think one can verify their reality by direct awareness of them. One can then verify certain differences between feelings and purely spatial patterns of sand by direct comparison.

The awareness argument. We can put these considerations together into what I call "the awareness argument." The argument is as follows:

1. You can be (introspectively) aware of first-person sense aspects of a feeling without being (introspectively) aware of spatial aspects of sand (e.g., sand swirling in the wind).

2. Therefore, there is a difference between first-person sense aspects and spatial aspects of sand.

---

[19]The direct comparison test therefore avoids the masked man fallacy, where one mistakenly infers that a man behind a mask is not someone one knows. For an analysis of this fallacy, see C. Taliaferro, "Masked Man," in *Bad Arguments: 100 of the Most Important Fallacies in Western Philosophy*, ed. R. Arp, S. Barbone, and M. Bruce (New Jersey: John Wiley & Sons, 2018).

3. If A is B, then there is no difference between A and B.

4. Therefore, first-person sense aspects of feelings are not as spatial aspects of sand.[20]

Let us look closer at each premise. Start with (1): you can be aware of first-person aspects of a feeling without being aware of spatial aspects of sand. I want to be clear at the outset that (1) does not require that you are aware of every aspect of a feeling. Maybe some aspects of your feelings are outside your conscious awareness. And maybe some aspects outside your consciousness are spatial. The direct comparison test does not rule that out. Rather, (1) is about sense aspects *within consciousness*. The idea is that even if a feeling has some aspects (outside consciousness), a feeling is not entirely characterizable in terms of aspects outside consciousness.

To test (1), I take up the tool of introspection. I begin by focusing my attention on any state of consciousness, such as my sense of contentment. Then I check to see if my awareness of its sense aspect (how it feels) includes awareness of spatial aspects of sand. When I consider my current feelings, I find that I can be introspectively aware of some aspects of them, such as their quality (e.g., happy, sad, curious), intensity, and even how much I like the feeling. I also find that this introspective awareness does not include introspective awareness of spatial aspects, like shape, size, or any other third-person sandy structure.

Implicit in this verification is direct comparison. I am able to directly compare awareness with lack of awareness. By direct comparison, I see that awareness is not the same as lack of awareness, just as I can see that black is not white, true is not false, and happiness is not sadness. In this case, I am aware of aspects of my feelings, while I am also aware that I lack direct, introspective awareness of sandy states.

---

[20]The argument differs from F. Jackson's famous "knowledge argument" ("What Mary Didn't Know," *Journal of Philosophy* 83, no. 5 [1986]: 291-95). Jackson's argument is about whether a colorblind person could know what it is like to see in color just by knowing all physical facts about brain states. Jackson's argument requires that we can have insight into what someone *else* might be able to know under certain circumstances. The awareness argument, by contrast, is more direct. It is about what you can personally check right now by your own immediate awareness of your consciousness. This difference in directness makes a difference to analyzing the "opaque context" objection, which is the objection that "knowledge" arguments depend on a fallacious inference in "opaque" contexts— i.e., a context where someone knows the same thing in different ways without realizing it. In the main text, we will consider how the awareness argument can help us see past opaque contexts.

Note that the power of direct awareness also explains why a complete description of a sandy state leaves out a description of consciousness. Suppose you knew the position, shape, orientation, and motion of every grain of sand. Still, seeing all these aspects does not thereby give you sight of a feeling of curiosity. Maybe the sandy states are correlated with feelings somehow, but even then, seeing the sand does not give you sight of feelings. I think this observation can become clear upon reflection.

This reasoning taps into your power to be aware of your own awareness. For example, you can be aware that you are introspectively aware of a feeling. You can have this awareness while also being aware that you are not introspectively aware of sand blowing in the wind or what someone else is thinking. The root reason you can be sure you aren't aware of those things is that if you were, the awareness of them would make a conscious impact. So, you could tell. For if you are introspectively aware of something, then this very introspective awareness feels a certain way. If you aren't introspectively aware of something, then you could notice this difference in feeling. In other words, you have a power, by introspection itself, to be aware of whether you are directly, introspectively aware of things (like feelings, sand, carbon atoms, etc.).

Line (2)—that there is a difference between first-person sense aspects and spatial aspects of sand—follows from (1). For by (1), there is a difference between that which is within your introspective awareness and that which is not. The difference is this: first-person sense aspects of feelings can be within your introspective awareness even while spatial aspects of sand are not.

Line (3)—that identity implies sameness—follows from Leibniz's general principle of identity: if A is (identical to) B, then there is no difference between A and B, for they are one and the same. I take this principle to be a basic truth of reason: by reason, we see that if A is one and the same as B, then whatever is true of A is true of B. (We may also treat this principle as part of the definition of the relevant notion of "identity" in play.)

From these premises, the conclusion follows: first-person sense aspects of feelings are not the same as spatial aspects of sand. If that is correct, then we can identify at least one constraint on the construction of consciousness.

Something does not acquire first-person aspects of consciousness just by swirling into a certain sandy shape. It takes more than shapes for there to be sensations.

To avoid error, it is important here to separate the hypothesis that a sandy state *is* a conscious state from the more modest hypothesis that something could be both sandy and conscious. I have not argued here that something couldn't be both sandy and conscious. Maybe something could look like a sand crystal *and* have a sensation. The direct comparison test leaves that open, for the hypothesis that something could have multiple aspects is not a reductive thesis (i.e., a thesis that reduces a sensation to a sandy state). The point of the direct comparison test is to test certain reductive hypotheses. So far, my suggestion is that you can directly recognize some distinctions. In particular, you can see that certain aspects of consciousness differ from certain aspects of sand.

Time for an objection. Some philosophers have replied to similar arguments with what is called "the phenomenal concept strategy." According to this strategy, we can account for the sense of a distinction between mental aspects and material aspects in terms of different concepts. Consider, for example, water. The concept of water is distinct from the concept of H_2O, even if water itself is H_2O; hence, water is merely conceptually distinct from H_2O. In the same way, perhaps certain spatial aspects of sand are only conceptually distinct from phenomenal (feeling) aspects of consciousness. In that case, shape and sensation would be different ways of conceiving the same aspect. This proposal is an instance of what is called "conceptual dualism."[21]

To increase the resolution of our analysis, a couple distinctions will help. First, there is an important difference between contents outside of consciousness and contents within consciousness. The difference here reflects a difference in what one can detect directly via introspection. For example, one can directly detect what one is feeling; that is how one can know if one feels a pain without looking inside one's

---

[21] D. Papineau, *Thinking About Consciousness* (Oxford: Oxford University Press, 2002) argues for conceptual dualism with respect to phenomenal (felt) consciousness and third-person physical aspects of brains; he proposes that these are only conceptually distinct.

head to see what molecules in one's brain are doing. In the case of water, by contrast, one does not have direct, introspective awareness of water. Instead, one is only introspectively aware of certain effects of water (e.g., the experience of wetness). This difference is relevant because without direct awareness of the molecular structure of water, one cannot directly compare the effects of water (within consciousness) with the causes (outside consciousness). So the direct comparison test does not apply.

Second, there is a difference between direct awareness and indirect awareness of the items in question. Take, for example, $2 + 2 = 4$. Compare it with $4 + 4 = 8$. Are they different? Here you are not in a dark, opaque context. You can witness these abstract equations directly within your own mind. By comparing these (directly), you can thereby see that these equations are not the same. In the same way, you can compare sensations with shapes by witnessing them directly within you own consciousness.

My thought here does not rely on first showing that you have a reliable *intuition* that certain things are distinct. I am not appealing to what Papineau calls "the intuition of distinction,"[22] which is an intuition that conscious states differ from material states. Rather, my thought is that we have a power to see certain distinctions *directly*—by direct acquaintance with certain differences.

Direct acquaintance might feel like an intuition, but it doesn't depend on first recognizing that you have an intuition. It is more direct. To draw out what I mean, consider these differences: the number two differs from the number one, red differs from white, true differs from false, a circle of sand differs from feeling of shyness. If you can have direct awareness of these things, you can see these differences directly.

In the end, the phenomenal concept strategy itself depends on our ability to see certain distinctions by direct comparison. If we didn't have a power to see differences directly, we couldn't even make *conceptual* distinctions. But we can: introspection allows us to see that the concept of a swirl of sand, say, differs from the concept of sadness (per conceptual dualism).

---

[22]Papineau, *Thinking About Consciousness*, 161.

This same power to see distinctions between concepts empowers us to see, with equal clarity, that a swirl shape itself is not a sense of sadness. We can see these distinctions by directly comparing the items within direct, conscious awareness.[23]

If this much is correct, then sand cannot be sad just in any way. For example, even if some shape somehow makes some sand sad, the shape is not itself the sadness. To see how sand could be sad, then, involves more than seeing that it is has a certain shape.

Removing a barrier to sight. Sometimes an analysis can create a barrier to recognizing what is in one's awareness. I want to identify a certain common barrier to recognizing the reality of one's own feelings and then show how I think we can remove it.

This barrier begins with an analysis of feelings in terms of brain activity. Consider, for example, that we can describe a certain happy feeling as an effect of dopamine in a brain. This description gives us a deeper understanding of the causes of feelings, and in that sense provides an analysis of feelings. In view of this analysis, we might then be tempted to replace (remove or reduce) the feelings. The analysis acts as a barrier to recognizing the reality of the first-person feelings themselves.

We can remove this barrier by distinguishing one's data from an *explanation* of one's data. To illustrate the distinction, imagine a philosophy professor explains his existence in terms of the causal activities of his parents. The professor's existence is an example of some data. From this data, the students may agree with his hypothesis that some parents gave birth to this professor; that hypothesis would indeed help explain the data. Once the explanation is in place, however, it would be a mistake to turn around and eliminate the data itself. If the professor goes on to tell the class that there is no reason to posit, in addition to the causal activities of his parents, his own existence, then the professor has effectively conflated the data with an explanation of that data.

In the same way, it would be a mistake to conflate first-person data, such as a feeling of curiosity, with candidate explanations of that data. Again, we

---

[23]In chap. 4, we will have a closer look at how we could be consciously aware of items, like feelings or shapes, within consciousness. That analysis will further increase the resolution of my analysis here.

can distinguish between data and an explanation of that data. An explanation of a feeling in terms of brain activity may illuminate the data, but it does not thereby replace it.

For this reason, the direct comparison test leaves open the relationship between feelings and candidate explanations, such as in terms of their causes or composition. To make this point clear, suppose axons in your brain were to cause you to experience a certain sensation. It would not follow that your experience just *is* axons. Consider, again, that a first-person conscious experience can be within your introspective awareness, even while third-person axons are not; hence, there is a difference. In this way, you can see directly (by direct comparison) that things within your field of awareness differ from the causes or contents outside your field of awareness, just as you can see that a professor differs from his parents. (We will revisit the question of how causes and other contents of reality may relate to your consciousness when we examine the mind-body problem in chapter seven.)

By seeing this distinction between a feeling and its potential explanations, we clear away an obstacle to recognizing the reality of the feelings right within us.

GENERAL CONSTRAINTS

My observations about sand suggest some general constraints on any theory of the nature of feelings. I would like to highlight three constraints. First, the theory should not reduce feelings within awareness to things wholly outside your awareness, whether sandy states or brain states. Your feelings can be within your conscious awareness (by the light of introspection). Things within your awareness are not the same as things wholly outside your awareness. Therefore, feelings within awareness are not the same as things wholly outside your awareness.

Second, a theory of feelings should pass the direct comparison test. You can directly compare a sense aspect of a feeling with a triangle (for example), for you can be directly aware of both items within your consciousness. When you compare items directly, you can see if they are different. When you see a difference, this difference is not a theoretical posit behind a veil. It is among the things you are directly aware of; it is part of your data.

Third, a theory of feelings should pass the irrelevant difference test. The irrelevant difference test is a way to distinguish feelings from things that fail to be relevantly different from nonfeelings. To illustrate, suppose one sees, by direct comparison, that a feeling of happiness is not a small crystal shape. Might happiness be instead a large crystal shape? We are not in the dark. We can see, by direct awareness of the aspects in question, that a mere difference in size is not itself a difference in a sensation.

The irrelevance of shape and size to the identity of a feeling may seem clear enough, but this clarity provides a steppingstone to see other things that may otherwise be out of sight. Instead of checking every single shape, say, to compare that shape with some sensation, we can see an irrelevant difference between shapes and any sensation. By checking irrelevant differences, we can expand our perspective from seeing that sadness is not a square, for example, to seeing a wider landscape of things consciousness cannot be. (Note that I am focusing here just on the *identity* of conscious states, not their *basis*. We will return the question of what could be a relevant basis of consciousness later in our inquiry.)

Here are some other differences that, to me, do not appear to be relevant to the identity of a sensation: size, velocity, acceleration, spin, structure, number of atoms, type of atom, or any combination or function of these. Differences with respect to any of these do not display a difference with respect to being identical to sadness, or any other form of consciousness. Here again I believe we can see this irrelevance directly, just as we can see that differences in shapes are not a difference with respect to being sad. Seeing the irrelevance of these differences provides a significant constrain on one's theory of the nature of felt consciousness.

To extend our analysis, we can also compare certain general types. For example, we can see that the general type of being a truck is categorically different from the general type of being a sandwich. From this we can infer that we will never see a truck that is a real sandwich (setting aside atypical definitions of "truck" and "sandwich"). In other words, differences in truck are not relevant to being a difference with respect to being a sandwich. In the same way, we can compare being some shape with being some sensation. By comparing these general types, we can see a categorical difference between particular shapes and particular sensations.

These constraints lay the groundwork for understanding what, in general, could be relevant to consciousness. So far, I've argued that certain differences (e.g., color, shape, size) can be seen to be irrelevant to the identity of certain forms of consciousness. Whatever consciousness is, and however it comes to be, the general constraints can help guide us in developing a theory of what consciousness is, or at least what it is not.

In summary, the tools in hand (introspection and reason) can help us identify these constraints on consciousness:

1. The identity constraint: by direct comparison, one can see that a sense aspect of a feeling is not the same as certain other aspects (shapes, colors, sizes).

2. The relevant difference constraint: by reason, one can see that certain differences, just by themselves, are irrelevant to make a difference with respect to being or making a subjective, sense aspect of feelings (e.g., a difference in number of vertices, shade of color).

These constraints can illuminate guiderails for any theory of consciousness.

As a disclaimer, my goal in writing this book is not to settle all the disputes but rather to point to tools anyone can use to investigate things for themselves. Here I offer the tests of direct comparison and irrelevant differences. I do not claim that these tests apply in every context or settle every question. But I do think they can help reveal some clear constraints on theories of consciousness. I leave it to readers to see what constraints make the most sense to them.

Here are how things look to me. When I use these tools, it becomes evident to me that feelings depend on certain constraints. In particular, things do not have feelings solely by having certain shapes, colors, configurations, motions, or functions of atoms, whether in sand or in brains. Feelings involve something more, or something else.

SUMMARY

We began our investigation into personal beings by examining the nature of feelings. By the light of introspection, I believe it is possible to discern at least three truths about feelings. First, feelings exist. Second, feelings have a subjective, first-person aspect. Third, this first-person aspect is irreducible to standard third-person, material aspects (e.g., shape, motion, extension).

These results add up to a bit of information about who you are: you are a being who can have real, first-person feelings. This information contributes to the challenge of explaining your existence. If your first-person feelings are indeed real, then a description of the purely third-person features of sand, molecules, or neurons leaves out the first-person feeling aspect of your consciousness. So, whatever you are, a complete explanation of you will include more than an explanation of third-person aspects of matter. There is more to you than that.

■   ■   ■

You navigate into the cave of consciousness. Light from your lantern flickers against the smooth cave walls. As you inspect the cavern, you notice some imperfections in the wall on your right. You hold up your lantern. To your surprise, the rather unnatural-looking marks appear to convey meaning. Carved into the rock are shapes that form the following words:

YOU ARE NOT YOUR FEELINGS.

3

YOUR THOUGHTS

I very rarely think in words at all.

ALBERT EINSTEIN

In this chapter, I will share the latest iteration of my thinking about thoughts. First, I will collect some observations about some aspects of thoughts. Second, I will show why I think these aspects of thoughts are not reducible to certain third-person, chemical aspects of brain states. Third, I will share some original discoveries I made about logical links in the contents of thoughts (including a deduction of the mindful thoughts theorem); I will show how these discoveries, if correct, reveal general constraints on the nature and basis of a thought. Finally, I will offer an account of what it takes to make a thought. My analysis of thoughts will provide another paint stroke in my picture of you—as something that can think.

ASPECTS OF A THOUGHT

In this section, I will use the light of introspection to highlight four aspects of thoughts: aboutness, structure, logical links, and truth-value. Bringing these aspects into the light will help us see some special things within any being that can think. This sight will also prepare us to see another edge of the great challenge of explaining our existence.

Aboutness. Let's start with the aboutness of a thought: thoughts are about things. For example, my thought that the sky is blue is about the sky and the color blue. My thought that $2 + 2 = 4$ is about some numbers. My thought that I am curious to better understand consciousness is about me, my curiosity, and consciousness. I see that these thoughts are about these things by examining these thoughts within my own mind.

Are all thoughts about things? I think so. When I inspect any thought I have, I notice that it is about something. I have never had a thought that was not about anything. This observation leads me to think that aboutness marks all thoughts.

Let us look more closely at how thoughts can be about things. Some philosophers have wondered how a thought could be about fictional things, like hobbits or other fictional characters. Fictional things don't exist, at least not in concrete reality. Some argue, then, that since fictional characters don't exist, you can't literally think about them (since there is no "them"). How, then, might a thought be about something fictional? An answer to this question would give us deeper insight into the nature of aboutness.

Philosophers are split on their views about how to analyze thoughts about fictions. One option is that, strictly speaking, you cannot think about fictional characters, like Spiderman or the Flash, since they do not exist. On this analysis, aboutness is a relation between existing things.[1] Thus, the thought that Spiderman is different from the Flash is not strictly about Spiderman or the Flash, since those characters don't exist. (Later, I will suggest how this view may work best on an externalist notion of "aboutness.")

Another view is that fictional characters exist in some sense (e.g., in a fictional realm or story). On this view, thoughts about fictional characters are about something, such as characteristics or possible objects.[2]

Other philosophers (myself among them) endorse a hybrid between the above views. On my view, thoughts can be about fictional characters, in some sense, even if those characters do not literally exist. I develop a version of this view in "About Aboutness."[3] To unpack my view briefly, I propose that a thought encodes essential aspects within an abstract structure (what I call a "proposition"), and that these aspects determine what the thought is about. To see how this might work, consider the thought that the Flash is fast. I propose that this thought encodes aspects like being fast, being a

---

[1]Cf. R. Stalnaker, "Merely Possible Propositions," in *Modality: Metaphysics, Logic, and Epistemology*, eds. Bob Haley and Aviv Hoffmann (Oxford: Oxford University Press, 2010).
[2]Cf. P. van Inwagen, "Creatures of Fiction," *American Philosophical Quarterly* 14 (1977): 299-308.
[3]See J. Rasmussen, "About Aboutness," *Metaphysica* 15, no. 1 (2014): 117-86.

superhero, being described by certain stories, and so on. Then to say that this thought is about the Flash is to say that the thought encodes aspects that uniquely characterize the Flash—that is, only the Flash could have all those aspects if the Flash were real. On this account, aboutness is not itself a fundamental relation between existing things. Instead, aboutness is analyzable in terms of more fundamental relations between aspects (or concepts). This analysis shows, therefore, how thoughts could be about fictional characters.

Whichever view one takes about fictions, we can further clarify a core concept of aboutness (a concept that spans different theories) by distinguishing two notions of "aboutness": internal aboutness and external aboutness. The internal notion of aboutness is what philosophers call "narrow content." You can examine this aboutness (narrow content) directly by inspecting any thought in your mind. For example, consider the thought that hobbits will not come into your house tonight. You can see that this thought is in some sense about *hobbits*, while it is in no sense about *unicorns*. You can see this internal aboutness without seeing whether any hobbits actually exist external to the thought itself. Internal aboutness is a core concept that we know directly and is foundational to our understanding of references to things external to our mind.

The external notion of aboutness, by contrast, goes beyond what you can examine just by introspection. To illustrate, consider the thought that water is leaking from the ceiling. Suppose water is identical with the molecular structure, H_2O. Then there is an externalist sense in which your thoughts about water are about H_2O. But you cannot determine this just by introspection. You need other information to see whether thoughts about water are about certain molecules external to your mind.

This distinction between internal and external aboutness can help us make sense of thoughts about nonexistent things. A thought about the Flash, for example, may not be externally about anything. For there is no one with the characteristics of the Flash in external reality. So a thought about the Flash is not externally about the Flash. Still, there is an *internal* sense in which thoughts (internally) about the Flash are about the Flash (by encoding the attributes the Flash would have), whether or not the Flash exists.

Since I am interested in what we can see by the light of introspection, I shall focus on the internal aboutness of a thought. This aboutness is an intrinsic aspect of thoughts, which I believe we can detect directly by introspection. As we continue, then, unless otherwise stated, I will use the term *about* to mean internal aboutness (narrow content) in my analyses of thoughts.

Finally, for our purposes, we do not need to choose between theories of aboutness to see that thoughts are about things in some sense. Whatever theory one takes, there is this general point of consensus: aboutness is a common mark of a thought. By seeing this mark, we see a special aspect of a special item in a person's mind.

Structure. Another aspect of thoughts is structure. To illustrate the structure in thoughts, consider the thought that snow is white. Inspect this thought in your mind. What do you see? When I inspect this thought, here is what I notice. I notice three conceptual components: (i) a concept of snow, (ii) a concept of is, and (iii) a concept of white. That isn't all I see. I also see a certain *organization* of these components—what I shall call "the structure."

Seeing the structure of a thought allows one to distinguish different thoughts that have the same conceptual components. For example, my thought that snow is white differs from my thought that white is snow, even while they both contain the exact same conceptual elements ("snow," "is," and "white"). The difference between these thoughts, then, is not in their conceptual components. The difference is in the *order* of components—their structure.

Can we say more about what this structure is? Bertrand Russell offered a theory of structure called "logical atomism."[4] According to logical atomism, all structures are all analyzable in terms of logical combinations of basic, atomic structures. The atomic structures are themselves unanalyzable. On this model, some structures have an analysis, while other (atomic) structures are bedrock pieces of reality; they have no further analysis.

In my research on the structures in reality, I came to agree with Russell in thinking that some structures are basic and not analyzable in terms of unordered (unstructured) items.[5] I have developed my own version of

[4]B. Russell, *The Problems of Philosophy* (New York: H. Holt, 1912).
[5]Rasmussen, "About Aboutness."

Russell's theory in my work on propositional structures. According to my account, we do not come to understand what a basic structure is by first coming to understand a deeper analysis. Rather, we come to understand what a basic structure is by *direct awareness* of a structure. For example, you can know the structure of the thought that snow is white by direct acquaintance (direct awareness) of that structure in your own mind. By having awareness of basic structures in your mind, you can then combine structures via logical relations to form more complex conceptual structures in more complex thoughts. So complex structures are analyzable in terms of basic structures.

We see the structure of a thought by the light of introspection. We can see, for example, that a thought that snow is white has a certain structure involving certain components. We can also see that this structure is different from other structures we can see in our minds.

Could you see the structure of a thought by instead seeing a certain structure of molecules in someone's brain? No. Seeing molecules in someone's brain will never give you firsthand sight of the conceptual structure of a thought. Unlike brain activity, the conceptual structure is not posited to explain other things you know about. On the contrary, you know the structure of your thoughts by seeing your thoughts directly under your own clear and private light. (I will examine this idea more closely in the next section when I consider the relationship between thoughts and brain states.)

True versus false thoughts. Next, by introspection, you can also see the truth or falsity of some thoughts. While it is not my purpose here to embark on a thorough investigation of theories of truth or falsehood, I will summarize the core elements of my theory of truth to help illustrate a core concept.[6]

My theory of truth has four parts. First, truth is an aspect of the content of a thought. The content of a thought is determined by (or entailed by the existence of) the thought's structure together with the conceptual elements of that structure. For example, my thought that snow is white has the content that snow is white. I call the content of a thought "a proposition." (For the sake of neutrality, I leave open the main theories of propositions. In particular, I leave open whether contents of thoughts are abstract, concrete, Platonic, or something else.)

---

[6]For a fuller articulation of my theory of truth, see J. Rasmussen, *Defending the Correspondence Theory of Truth* (Cambridge: Cambridge University Press, 2014).

Second, on my analysis, different thoughts can share the same proposition (the same content): for example, your thought that snow is white has the same propositional content as my thought that snow is white. By sharing the same content, we are able to communicate with each other.

Third, a correct thought encodes a true proposition (content). An incorrect thought encodes a proposition that is not true.

Fourth and finally, truth relates to reality. By this I mean that truth is a relational aspect (e.g., of matching or corresponding with). Truth relates the content of a thought to the reality the thought describes. To illustrate, consider the thought that you are feeling hungry. This thought is about your hunger. You can see if this thought is correct by checking whether its propositional content matches how you actually feel. If you do indeed feel hungry enough, then I believe you are able to see (by direct awareness) that the propositional content, *that you feel hungry*, corresponds with (accurately describes) your feeling. Thus, it counts as true.

To draw out a bit further how truth relates to reality, I offer a structural theory of the link between a true proposition and the reality it describes. To illustrate, suppose proposition p is true. Then p has a structure of aspects that characterize things in a certain way. For example, let p = <snow is white>. In this case, p has a structure of the aspects, being snow and being white. This proposition counts as "true" if something actually has these aspects in the way the proposition specifies.[7]

Details aside, you can use introspection to identify truths in your mind. For example, suppose you feel hungry. You can see that it is true that you feel hungry by seeing these three things within you: (i) your hunger, (ii) your thought of being hungry, and (iii) the match between the content of that thought and your hunger. If you see this match, then you see the truth of the thought's content. In this way, you can see truths by direct acquaintance with examples in your mind. The awareness of truth within your mind is foundational to everything you think and say is true about the world outside your mind.

So, those are the main parts of my theory of truth. Whether you agree with every part of this theory or not, my primary goal here is to show how

---

[7]I develop this version of a "correspondence" theory (and address hard cases and classic objections) in Rasmussen, *Defending the Correspondence Theory of Truth*, 120-46.

to see some truth. By the light of introspection, you can see some truth inside some thoughts.

Logical links. Something else I believe you can see by introspection is logic. To see logic, it will not suffice to read a logic textbook. When you read a logic textbook, you see patterns of ink on a page. This ink represents another reality, a logical reality, which you see only within your mind. The logical reality consists of logical links between thoughts (or more exactly: between propositional contents of thoughts).

There are different types of logical links. Some of the logical links one can observe (by introspection) are these: and, or, if, only if. One can use these links to combine simpler thoughts into more complex thoughts. For example, I can form the thought that snow is white *or* the sky is blue. I can form the thought that snow is white *and* the sky is blue. I can form the thought that snow is white *only if* the sky is blue. And so on. I call these links, "logical links." Logical links form the structure of logically complex thoughts.[8]

We have collected some observations about the nature of thoughts. By paying attention to your own thoughts (via introspection), you can discern various aspects of thoughts. We considered these four aspects of thoughts: (i) they can be about things, (ii) they have a structure, (iii) they can be accurate (true) or inaccurate (false), and (iv) they can link together to form more complex thoughts.[9] While these aren't the only aspects of thoughts, these provide a foundation for my analysis of thoughts.

Our observations are preparing the way for a deep analysis of our existence. We have observed familiar items, like aboutness, structure, and truth. We may easily take these items for granted. But it is not trivial that these items exist. What are logical links, for example? Why do they exist? How can any reality give rise to any logical links at all? These questions point back to the big question that inspires my inquiry: how can there be any personal reality at all? By illuminating familiar things within our consciousness, we

---

[8]I offer a theory of logical links in Rasmussen, *Defending the Correspondence Theory of Truth*, 85-119. My theory there is in terms of a "property arrangement" theory of propositions, where a logically complex proposition is an arrangement of properties linked by basic logical relations.
[9]These are not the only aspects one can see by introspection. I think one can also see that thoughts have a sense aspect—or phenomenal character. See D. Pitt, "The Phenomenology of Cognition, or, What Is It Like to Think That P?," *Philosophy and Phenomenological Research* 69, no. 1 (2004): 1-36.

are preparing the way to illuminate a more fundamental understanding of who we really are and how we could have come to be.

WHAT YOU CANNOT SEE INSIDE A BRAIN

Our observations so far give us useful bits of information about thoughts. We observed four aspects of thoughts: aboutness, structure, truth-value, and logical links. We can now compare these aspects of thoughts with third-person material aspects (shape, size, velocity, mass, etc.) that figure into third-person descriptions of brain states. By comparing first-person aspects of thoughts with third-person aspects of brain states, we can illuminate something about how thoughts relate to brain states.

Here I want to share why I think there is more to a thought than what you can see just by looking inside a brain. I have two points I wish to make. First, any purely third-person characterization of brain chemistry in the vocabulary of physics leaves out certain first-person aspects of thoughts. Second, you have more direct access to certain aspects of thoughts than you do to certain aspects of brain matter.

Start with brain chemistry. To compare aspects of thoughts with third-person aspects of chemical reactions, we can use the direct comparison test. Recall the test. In the previous chapter, we compared certain (first-person, qualitative) aspects of feelings with certain (third-person, nonqualitative) aspects of brain states. In the same way, I believe we can compare certain aspects of thoughts with material aspects of brain states. By direct comparison, we can see that certain aspects of thoughts are not included in any standard list of third-person material aspects.

To consider a clear case of comparison, compare being true with being triangular. Are these different? When I compare truth with triangularity, it is evident to me that truth differs from triangularity. When I see the truth of 2 + 2 = 4, for example, I do not thereby see a triangle. Moreover, when I see a triangle, I do not thereby see the truth of something. Instead, I see directly that being true differs from being triangular.

My analysis of truth and triangularity illustrates a general analysis. By focusing on this clear case, we gain light to shine into other places and extend our vision. For example, we can see that differences in shape make no difference to the analysis. If triangularity is not of the same as truth, then neither is any other shape.

To be clear, the comparison test leaves open different theories of how aspects of thoughts might relate to aspects of brain matter. As far as the comparison test goes, it could be that thoughts have both material and mental aspects, such as if an axon has both shape and conceptual structure. Or, perhaps thoughts and brain states are windows into a more basic, underlying reality. The direct comparison test leaves these options open.

My point here is just that there is more to a thought than what we find in third-person matter. In particular, a complete third-person description of chemical reactions (in the vocabulary of standard physics) leaves out first-person aspects of thoughts.

This analysis is further supported by my next observation: we have a direct access to our thoughts that we do not have to material brain states. Consider a thought in your mind. Focus on it. See what it is about. By seeing what your thought is about, you can distinguish this thought from other thoughts that are about other things. By distinguishing your thoughts from each other, you can verify that your thoughts are not in the dark (outside your conscious awareness). If they were in the dark, you could not distinguish one thought from another. If thoughts were outside your conscious awareness, then different thoughts would be like different socks in a closed drawer; they would be in the dark. But your thoughts aren't in the dark. They are like socks on your feet. They aren't hidden away. Therefore, you are consciously aware of them.

Now consider, by contrast, bits of your brain. You do not have direct, conscious awareness of third-person bits of your brain. Bits of your brain are like socks in a closed drawer: they are in the dark. While you may have good reason to believe you have a brain (based on reports of other brains), you are not currently witnessing third-person aspects of your brain in your own consciousness. Instead, you infer that you have a brain with the third-person aspects that people tell you about (of axons, etc.).

These observations expose a salient difference between the first-person aspects of your thoughts and the third-person aspects of bits of your brain. The difference is in your means of accessing them: first-person aspects of thoughts (aboutness, structure, truth-value, and logical links) are contents of your immediate, direct conscious awareness, whereas third-person aspects of brain states are not. Seeing this difference supplies an additional reason to think that there is more to a thought than is characterized by third-person, chemical aspects of brain matter.

I realize there are deep controversies and complexities surrounding any analysis of thoughts in relation to brain states. For this reason, it can be difficult to feel confident in any proposed analysis. For my part, I find it helpful to separate what is clear to me from what is less clear. It seems to me that the reality of some aspects of thoughts can be as clear as anything. In particular, it seems to me that it is possible to be *directly aware* of certain aspects (e.g., structure, aboutness, truth-value) within my mind. Direct awareness creates clarity. By contrast, chemical aspects of brain matter are not within my direct awareness. For this reason, it seems to me that I have clearer (more direct) access to first-person contents within my own mind than to third-person chemical contents within my brain.

On this note, I agree with Sean Carroll when he says, "To start with the least-well-understood aspects of reality and draw sweeping conclusions about the best understood aspects is arguably the tail wagging the dog."[10] Although Carroll applies this point to our understanding of physics (which he takes to be well-understood), I apply it to my understanding of certain aspects of consciousness. Certain aspects of consciousness can be well-understood by the light of one's own direct acquaintance (while mysteries remain).

In summary, I believe it is possible to see some aspects of thoughts directly within your own consciousness. Thoughts are not merely theoretical posits. Rather, you can witness thoughts in your own mind. By seeing thoughts in your mind, you can verify the reality of first-person aspects of your thoughts (aboutness, conceptual structure, truth-value, and logical

---

[10]S. Carroll, "Consciousness and the Laws of Physics," *Journal of Consciousness Studies*, preprint (2021): http://philsci-archive.pitt.edu/19311/. Carroll was interested in showing that, by the light of physics, introspection does not reliably reveal that aspects of consciousness can exist uncorrelated with what physically happens in brains. My purpose here is not to contest this point. In fact, one of my interests in this book is to see how physics can help us understand the role of consciousness in brains. We will return to the question of how consciousness might fit with physics in chap. 13, when we consider how consciousness could emerge.

links). When you see these aspects, you don't see third-person aspects of brains. If that is correct, then thoughts, like feelings, have aspects that a purely third-person description of brain states leaves out. In other words, there is more to a thought than a (third-person) brain state.

A NOTE ABOUT MATERIALISM

Let us stand back and consider the bigger picture. So far, I have been chipping away at a certain mindlessness frame. The mindlessness frame either eliminates your existence or analyzes you entirely in terms of mindless bits, such as mind-independent particles. I have argued that, by the direct comparison test, one can see that at least certain first-person aspects of your thoughts (aboutness, structure, truth-value, and logical links) do not reduce to purely mindless (third-person) aspects of matter.

That said, I would like to offer a friendly note for readers who may call themselves "materialists." By materialism, I mean the thesis that reality is fundamentally material (or physical). The purpose of this book is not to target materialism, broadly conceived. On the contrary, my interest is to better understand what "matter" could be, such that conscious beings (who can think and feel) might arise out of matter (if they do).

In fact, my impression is that the strongest objections people raise against materialism more squarely target a version of *mindless* materialism, not materialism in its broadest form. For this reason, I share Montero's recommendation: "Rather than worrying about whether the mind is physical, we should be concerned with whether the mind is ultimately non-mental."[11] By distinguishing materialism from mindless materialism, I hope to separate objections to mindless materialism that do not target materialism per se.

Later, we will consider how recent neuroscience and physics may shed light on the relationship between minds and material systems. In particular, I will articulate an analysis of matter that fits well with many observations (and which also fits with a parsimonious, realist interpretation of recent physics).

At this step, however, I want to convey a more basic thought: you can use your own inner light to see aspects of your own thoughts directly. When

---

[11]B. Montero, "The Body of the Mind-Body Problem," *Annals of the Japan Association for Philosophy of Science* 9, no. 4 (1999): 216.

you do, you can see some things that you could never directly see just by looking inside brains.

THE COUNTING ARGUMENT

In this section, I will extend my analysis of thoughts by sharing a breakthrough in my research on the logical nature of thoughts. This analysis will provide additional insight into the aspects of thoughts you don't see in brains.

The seed. In the fall of 2005, I got an idea that challenges certain theories about the nature and origin of thoughts. The seed idea came to me in the form of a picture. I saw in my mind a conceptual landscape made of thoughts overlaying a material landscape. This picture inspired a thought: there may be more ways to construct conceptual landscapes using logical links than there are ways to construct material landscapes using spatial links. If so, then we have a counting argument for an interesting conclusion: the conceptual nature of a thought is not reducible to third-person, material states.

Little did I know at the time just how much would sprout from the initial seed. After ten years of developing the idea, I published my first counting argument in an article, "Building Thoughts from Dust."[12] Soon after that, I saw additional ways to develop the argument, leading to additional publications.[13] More recently, I've also come to see new implications that I've not presented anywhere else. I am excited to share with you the latest developments here for your consideration.

Counting shapes. I will give three iterations of the counting argument. To display the core logic of the argument, I will first give a version of the argument that is about *shapes*. The conclusion of this argument will be that shapes, whether shapes of sand or shapes of neurons, are insufficient by themselves to construct (determine or make) all the types of thoughts that can be logically constructed. I will then apply this same reasoning to brain states. The result will be that third-person brain states are

---

[12]J. Rasmussen, "Building Thoughts from Dust: A Cantorian Puzzle," *Synthese* 192 (2015): 393-404.
[13]J. Rasmussen, "Against Nonreductive Physicalism," in *The Blackwell Companion to Substance Dualism*, eds. Jonathan J. Loose, Angus J. L. Menuge, and J. P. Moreland, 328-39 (Malden, MA: Wiley-Blackwell, 2018); A. Bailey and J. Rasmussen, "A New Puppet Puzzle," *Philosophical Explorations* 23, no. 3 (2020): 202-13.

insufficient to construct, all on their own, all the types of thoughts that can be logically constructed. In the next section, I'll give a third version of the argument that builds on these results to expose a problem with any purely mindless account of the basis of thoughts. These results, if correct, provide constraints on any theory of the nature and origin of thoughts. These arguments also contribute to the larger challenge of explaining the existence of thinking beings in the first place. (We will seek a solution to this challenge in the second part of this book, which investigates the origin of persons.)

Let's start with "The Shapes Argument":

1. For any shape S, the thought that S exists is a thought about a shape.

2. For any thoughts about shapes, linking them together with logical links forms a more complex type of thought (e.g., thinking that S1 exists *or* that S2 exists).

3. If (1) and (2) are true, then there are more logically constructible types of thought than constructible shapes.

4. Therefore, shapes alone are insufficient to construct all the logically constructible types of thoughts.

Let us look closer at each step. The first step is (1): for any shape S, the thought that S exists is a thought about a shape. I am thinking of this premise as expressing the meaning of "a thought about a shape." We understand the meaning of the phrase "that shape S exists" in part because of our awareness of the structure of a thought. By seeing the structure of thoughts in our minds, we can see that any thought of the form S exists (where S is a shape) has a certain structure. We may then classify any thought with this structure as a thought about a shape.

Note that (1) does not say that anyone is *actually* thinking about a particular shape. The premise says just this: if there *were* any thought of the form, *shape S exists*, then that thought would count as a thought about a shape (by definition).

Consider next (2): for any thoughts about shapes, linking them together with logical links forms a more complex type of thought. To illustrate, the thought that a square exists can link up with the thought that a triangle exists to form the thought that a square exists or a triangle exists.

We can understand (2) because of our awareness of logical links between thoughts. For example, we can see that a thought that a square exists or a triangle exists differs from the thought that a square exists or a circle exists. We can see this difference directly by awareness of the differences within the two thoughts.

Again, I am not assuming that anyone actually has (or even can have) all these types of thoughts. This premise merely identifies differences in conceivable *types* of thoughts that are constructable by logical links.

The next step is (3): if (1) and (2) are true, then there are more (logically constructible) types of thought than (constructible) shapes. We can support this step by a theorem in mathematics called "Cantor's theorem." According to Cantor's theorem, collections outnumber individuals. For example, suppose you have three individual items, A, B, and C. You can then construct seven collections from these items: {A}, {B}, {C}, {A, B}, {A, C}, {B, C}, and {A, B, C}. These seven collections outnumber the three individuals. This principle applies to any collection (or plurality) of items, including infinite collections.[14] From here it follows that there are more collections of shapes than individual shapes. So, since there is a constructible thought corresponding to any collection of shapes, it follows that there are more constructible thoughts than shapes (of any size and complexity).

To elaborate, the argument so far is this. Logical links allow the construction of at least as many thoughts as collections of shapes, since any individual shapes can be collected into a complex thought about each of them. Again, that is because thoughts about any particular shapes can logically link together to form a logically complex thought about any collection of shapes. These logically complex thoughts differ from each other, for they represent different collections. We just saw that collections outnumber individuals (by Cantor's theorem). It follows, therefore, that there are more constructible thoughts than constructible shapes.

---

[14]To be technically precise, the theorem states that for any plurality, the xs, there is no mapping from individuals to the xs, such that (i) each member of the xs is mapped to at most one subplurality of the xs, and (ii) for every subplurality of the xs, there is a member of the xs that is mapped to it. I give a version of Cantor's diagonal argument for this theorem in J. Rasmussen, "Building Thoughts from Dust," 194. The proof relies on an axiom schema akin to the Axiom of Separation—basically, that for any formula ψ, if there are some things that satisfy ψ, then there are the things that satisfy ψ.

While this result is abstract, it is relevant to the nature of thoughts. In particular, we can deduce that shapes alone are insufficient to construct all the logically constructible types of thoughts. For there are too many ways to construct thoughts. Another way to think of this result is that logical links have more construction power than spatial links. If that is right, then logical links in types of thoughts cannot be reducible to (identical with) spatial links.

So far, I am illustrating a general type of reasoning (from counting). One value of this type of reasoning is that it allows us to inspect the nature of thoughts by another light. Previously, we used the direct comparison test to compare aspects of a thought with material aspects (like shape). We can put that test aside here. For instead of comparing a mental state with a material state, here we only need to compare mental states with *each other*. By comparing mental states with each other, we can see that logical links can construct distinct types of mental states. We can then use mathematical reasoning to deduce something about the nature of logical links, in particular that logical links have greater construction power than spatial links. We don't need to compare logical links with spatial links directly to see their distinction; instead, we deduce their distinction by applying mathematical reasoning to distinctions we can witness between mental states. If this mathematical reasoning is sound, then it provides a second witness of the same result we can see by direct comparison.

In the course of writing this chapter, I discovered another potential fruit, which especially excites me. Unlike the direct comparison test, the counting argument implies something about potential *hidden* aspects of thoughts. A hidden aspect is an aspect you cannot directly access just by introspection. Some people have theorized that there are aspects in brains that uniquely determine certain thoughts. For example, if thoughts are determined by third-person brain states, then perhaps a certain chemical reaction determines that one think that $2 + 2 = 4$. This chemical reaction, which is outside your introspective awareness, would then be a hidden aspect that determines a certain type of thought. The conclusion of the Shapes Argument provides a constraint, however, on the aspects that determine thoughts. In particular, there are not enough shapes to uniquely determine each type of thought. For this reason, at least some type of thought has no (hidden) shape that determines that thought uniquely. (As you may anticipate, the type of reasoning here does not merely apply to shapes. We can extend this reasoning to extract additional results, as I will show soon.)

This result matches the general hypothesis that you can know a thought internally via introspection. For example, you can know the thought that snow is white by internal awareness of its conceptual contents and structure. On this hypothesis, the essence of a thought is transparent to you. It is not hidden. Whether one endorses this transparency hypothesis or not, it is useful to see how a counting argument can (in principle) help one investigate the essence of a thought in relation to aspects outside one's introspective awareness.

Counting brain states. We can achieve a more general result by replacing "shape" with any aspect (property, process, state, or item) that is analyzable in terms of third-person brain aspects. Thus, we have the following Brain States Argument:

1. For any brain state B, the thought that B exists is a thought about a brain state.
2. For any thoughts about a brain state, linking them together with logical links forms a more complex thought (e.g., thinking that S1 exists or that S2 exists).
3. If (1) and (2) are true, then there are more logically constructible thoughts than constructible brain states.
4. Therefore, brain states alone are insufficient to construct all the logically constructible thoughts.

The supports for these premises derive from precisely the same considerations as before. What is crucial is our ability to witness the logical structure of thoughts within our own minds. By witnessing this logical structure, we can see directly how new combinations of thoughts can be constructed from simpler thoughts. We can then compare the building power of logical links with the building power of brain states.

This argument has far-reaching implications. If the argument is sound, then thoughts not only have the first-person aspects we have identified (aboutness, structure, truth-value, and logical links), but we can deduce a further result: brain states are not, just in virtue of third-person spatial or functional properties, sufficient to construct all the logically constructible thoughts.

The argument also has a certain intriguing ramification for how thoughts relate to brain states. The Brain States Argument, if sound, entails certain limits to what brain states (by themselves) can construct. In particular, if a brain state causes a thought, the brain state itself was not logically sufficient for making the thought.

We may wonder, then, how brain states and thoughts can go together. Thoughts evidently connect to brain states somehow. But how? We will return to this question in chapter seven, where I will offer a theory of mind-body unification. For now, I note that my analysis removes a certain significant theory of how to make a thought. If the argument is sound, then there is more to making a thought than making a brain state.

I will now consider a few potential objections to the Brain States Argument. These will help clarify key steps in the argument.

Objection 1. The argument refers to thoughts that might not be able to physically occur. Such thoughts are hypothetical realities. We cannot deduce anything about actual thoughts by reflecting on hypothetical thoughts.

Reply. We do not need to make any assumptions about the physical world in order to examine the nature of thoughts. Instead, we can examine the nature of thoughts directly, by introspection. We can then use reason to see how new types of thoughts could logically be generated by combining more basic thoughts. Nothing in this reasoning assumes that these types of thoughts can all be instantiated in some physical structure. The key premise is that thoughts about different brain states would be different from each other. That is enough to generate more types of thoughts than types of brain states.

It may help to see a parallel argument that illustrates this same reasoning. Consider a counting argument about decimal numbers and whole numbers. Cantor famously showed that there are more decimals (reals) than whole numbers by his diagonal argument, which is a form of counting argument. Crucially, no step in Cantor's deduction depends on the assumption that every decimal number can be physically instantiated. Instead, the deduction is derived from reasoning we can access directly. The deduction in the Brain States Argument proceeds the same way.

Objection 2. How could there be more constructible thoughts than constructible brain states if both are infinite?

Reply. Some infinities are larger than others. As I noted above, Cantor
showed that the set of decimal numbers is larger than the set of whole
numbers. He did this by showing that for any natural number, we can
match it with a unique decimal, but not vice versa. According the Brain
States Argument, we can use the same reasoning to show that the infinity
of constructible thoughts is larger than the infinity of constructible brain
states. We do this by showing that for any set of brain states, we can match
it with a unique type of thought definable in terms of the logical relations
between simpler thoughts about individual spatial states. By contrast, the
argument does not show that we can use spatial relations to construct a
material structure that matches each definable type of thought.

Objection 3. The argument proves too much. For example, we can reverse
the argument to show that there are more constructible shapes than constructible thoughts. Here is how. Take any group of thoughts. We can then
define a shape in terms of the shape of neurons that could give rise to that
group of thoughts. The result is that there are more constructible shapes (of
neurons) than constructible thoughts, which contradicts the conclusion of
the counting argument.

Reply. There are two problems with this reverse argument. First, the
reverse argument includes the premise that there is a type of brain state that
could give rise to any group of thoughts. This premise is not something we
can simply check by introspection (in the way that we could check that a
thought about different shapes would differ from each other).

Second, even if there were a type of brain state that could give rise to any
group of thoughts, it still wouldn't follow that there are more types of brain
states than types of thoughts. To get this conclusion, we would need to add the
additional premise that there is a *unique* brain state for each group of thoughts.
But this additional premise contradicts our observations about the logical
linkability of thoughts. It is the logical linkability of thoughts that allows us
to identify a complex thought for any group of brain states. Logical linkabilty
is what gives us more building power with thoughts than with brain states.

Objection 4 (advanced). There are limits to combining thoughts. In particular, if we say that all thoughts are combinable, then we run into

intolerable paradoxes of self-reference. The combination of all thoughts would include itself. But now take the combination of all thoughts that don't include themselves. If you reflect on the definition of this combination, you can see that it would include itself if and only if it does not include itself. To avoid this contradiction, we must deny that there is any such combination. Therefore, it is a mistake to think logical relations can combine just any arbitrary thoughts together.

Reply. First, there is a way to avoid the paradox of combining thoughts. The paradox arises from combinations that lead to self-reference. But the premises in the counting argument do not themselves lead to self-reference. We can verify this via first-person awareness of the relevant thoughts. To see this, take any thoughts about shapes. For example, consider the thought that a square exists and the thought that a circle exists. Then combine these to form the complex thought that a square exists or a circle exists. You can see its component parts (about a square and a circle, respectively), and you can compare those parts directly with the thought as a whole. In this way, you can see that neither part is itself the whole. In general, you can see that merely linking up thoughts about individual spatial, brain states does not yield a thought that contains itself (as a whole) as one of its parts. So, we avoid paradox by limiting combinations that do not involve self-reference.

Second, we can account for why self-reference leads to paradoxical cases. It is because nothing can be a mere part of itself. If thoughts included themselves, then something could be a part of itself, which is impossible. Nothing in the counting arguments results in self-inclusion. So nothing in the counting argument results in the paradoxical cases. (The argument I give next will range over thoughts that are explicitly about *nonmental* things and so explicitly not self-including.)

A NEW COUNTING ARGUMENT

The story continues. In June 2018, while staring out a car window, I had a new thought about thoughts. I was thinking about the counting argument again. Until this moment, I had only seen how we could use the counting argument as a device for investigating the *nature* of thoughts (e.g., that shapes don't figure into the identity of a thought). However, as I looked out the window, I saw a new way to configure the counting argument. This new configuration gave me an idea about how I might investigate the *basis* of a thought.

I began to see how I could convert the original picture of logically complex thoughts into a set of principles. I shared my idea with another philosopher of mind, Andrew Bailey. We decided to join forces to write up an article on this new counting argument. We worked with a small team of philosophers and logicians to construct and check a rigorous symbolic formulation of the proof.[15] In early 2020, *Thought* published our article, "How to Build a Thought." In that article, we deduced a theorem about the basis of thoughts from a set of axioms using thirty-one steps (each step encoded in symbolic logic).

In the course of writing this chapter, I discovered yet another way to develop the argument we published. This development shares the structure of the previous two arguments and derives an additional result. I will present the key ideas next.[16]

The Mindless Noise Argument. This third counting argument is about constructing thoughts out of mindless states alone. The conclusion of the argument is that it takes more to make a thought than a mindless noise of atoms. If the argument is sound, then while thoughts may occur in the context of a mind, they cannot occur in the context of pure mindlessness (unless a mind first occurs).

I will express the first two steps as axioms, since we may treat them as implicit definitions of certain types of thoughts. You can think of the previous counting arguments as preparing us to formulate a more precise, technical counting argument in terms of axioms and theorems.

Axiom 1 (base thoughts): for any purely nonmental state M (e.g., sand blowing in the wind), the thought that M exists is a type of thought. Call thoughts of this type "base thoughts."

Axiom 2 (logical links): linking any base thoughts by a logical link forms a type of thought (e.g., thinking that B1 exists or that B2 exists). Call these "build thoughts."

---

[15]I am especially grateful for help from Robert Koons and Chris Menzel.
[16]To maintain an intuitive presentation here, I will forego a symbolic, technical formulation. To see a more technical display of the core reasoning, see A. Bailey and J. Rasmussen, "How to Build a Thought," *Thought* 9, no. 2 (2020): 75-83.

Let us have a closer look these axioms. Axiom 1 provides a definition of "base thought." A base thought is a thought of the form *that M exists*, where M is something nonmental. For example, if sand blowing in the wind is nonmental, then a thought that sand blowing in the wind exists counts as a base thought.

This axiom does not require anything to actually be nonmental. Instead, the axiom defines a certain type of thought. The axiom implies that if anything were nonmental, then a thought reporting its existence would count as a base thought.

While the axiom is definitional, it is not thereby trivial. Our ability to grasp the meaning of this definition tells us something about reality. It tells us that reality includes meaning. We grasp meaning by grasping the structure of thoughts (e.g., that M exists). It is significant that we can grasp the structure of thoughts. We don't grasp the structure of a thought by looking at brains. Instead, we grasp the structure of a thought by inner awareness of the structure of thoughts in our own minds. Without this awareness, Axiom 1 would be meaningless to our minds. Fortunately, Axiom 1 is not meaningless. The fact that we can grasp Axiom 1 (or any definition, for that matter) already reveals a significant insight we have into the structure of thoughts.

On a technical note, Axiom 1 explicitly avoids the threat of self-reference. We saw in the discussion of the previous counting argument that self-reference can lead to paradoxes. Axiom 1 avoids self-reference by defining base thoughts in terms of *nonmental* states. By putting the scope on non-mental states, there is no threat that base thoughts may be about themselves, since base thoughts are themselves *mental*.

Consider, next, Axiom 2 (logical links). I am thinking of this axiom as also definitional. We grasp this definition by having insight into the logical structure of thoughts. In particular, we can see that thoughts can link together by the logical link *or*—for example, the thought that the bush exists *or* the sky exists. By grasping this logical structure, we can understand what it means to link together base thoughts to form logically complex thoughts. This understanding allows us to understand my definition of "build thoughts," which are base thoughts linked together by *or*. Again, our ability to understand this axiom is not insignificant; we can grasp its meaning by grasping the structure of thoughts (their logical structure) using our inner awareness.

Note that this axiom does not assume that all build thoughts are physically or metaphysically possible. When I say they are "constructible," I mean that they are constructible logically—that is, there is no logical contradiction in the logical linking of any base thoughts to form more complex thoughts.

Let us now consider some results of these axioms. The axioms have implications concerning the purely mindless-first view of the world. On the mindless-first view, mindlessness is a prerequisite for mind. One version of this view is a certain materialist view on which mentality can only emerge from suitably complex material states that determine the mentality. The axioms press against a certain, common characterization of this mindless-first frame, as I will now show.

First, we can deduce that there are more (logically constructible) types of thoughts than (constructible) types of mindless states. The deduction follows from the same reasoning we saw in the previous two counting arguments. From Axioms 1 and 2, we can define a logically complex type of thought for any collection of mindless states. Take any thoughts about individual mindless states. These base thoughts can logically link together to form logically complex thoughts. In this way, logical links allow the construction of at least as many types of thoughts as collections of mindless states. It follows (by Cantor's theorem) that there are more (constructible) types of thoughts than (constructible) mindless states.[17] Hence, we have the counting theorem: there are more (constructible) types of thoughts than (constructible) mindless states.

The counting theorem is relevant to the prospect of deriving a thought from a mindless state. Here is why. Suppose each type of thought is derivable from a state that uniquely determines that particular type. For

---

[17]In "How to Build a Thought," we include an axiom of distinction (for technical completion), which makes explicit that thoughts about different things are different thoughts. This axiom allows us to distinguish logically complex thoughts that encode logical relations between different base thoughts. For example, thinking that snow exists differs from thinking that sand exists (assuming sand is not snow). The axiom follows from Leibniz's law of identity: if A is identical to B, then whatever is true of A is true of B. For if thought A is identical to thought B, then it must be true that they are about the same things. I believe one can also check this axiom directly by awareness of the contents of thoughts (where the notion of "aboutness" here is intrinsic to the thought itself—i.e., narrow content). In general, one can see that thinking that A exists is not the same as thinking that B exists, in the case where A ≠ B.

example, suppose some state α determines the thought that sand exists. Call states that determine thoughts "grounds of thoughts." Now according to the counting theorem, there are more (constructible) types of thoughts than (constructible) types of mindless states. From here, it follows that there are more (constructible) types of thoughts than (constructible) mindless grounds of thoughts. In other words, at least some type of thought cannot be derived from (or determined by) any constructible mindless state.

We have just deduced a significant theorem about the basis of thoughts. Call it "the mindful thoughts theorem": there is a type of thought, such that no type of mindless state can determine that type of thought individually.

This result again highlights the significance of logical links in thoughts. Logical links exist. We witness them in our own thoughts. But what determines their existence? According to the mindful thoughts theorem, there is this constraint: logical links in (at least) certain thoughts cannot have a purely mindless basis that determines them. In other words, mindlessness cannot be a basis for determining every type of logically linkable type of thought. If logical links in thoughts have any basis that determines their existence, that basis includes a mental context—such as a conscious being with the capacity to think.

Uniformity. We can derive an additional result about your specific thoughts if we add a uniformity principle. So far, we have seen that there are general constraints on building thoughts. In particular, if the mindful thoughts theorem is correct, then mindless states are not sufficient to individually build every type of thought. From here it follows that at least some types of thoughts are not individually buildable from mindless matter. By the uniformity of thoughts, we can deduce that *all* types of thoughts are in the same boat.

To unpack this thought further, recall that build thoughts are defined in terms of the same form of thought (that M1 exists or M2 exists or . . .). The only differences between build thoughts is in their contents (what they are about), not in their general form as build thoughts. The general form indicates a categorical uniformity: a mere difference in content of a thought does not itself display a categorical difference with respect to the type of basis of that thought. For example, consider the thought that squares exist. Suppose that thought cannot have its basis in any purely mindless state. Then consider the slightly more complex thought, that squares or triangles exist. This thought has a slightly more complex content. But a change in complexity of the content does not explain a change in category of the basis. To minimize inexplicable breaks, then, I expect that thoughts of the same form are in the same boat. In other words, if content C cannot have a mindless basis, then content C* cannot have a mindless basis, either.

We may express this "uniformity" principle as follows:

Axiom 3 (uniformity): build thoughts do not differ in whether they can have a mindless ground.

Axiom 3 is about the categorical uniformity of build thoughts. Build thoughts encode logical links. Thus, build thoughts differ from each other only by what they logically link together. The idea again is that differences in content do not account for a difference with respect to the category of things (mental vs. mindless) that might determine a build thought.

To draw this idea out a bit further, suppose state α determines the build thought that sand exists or fire exists. Suppose, for sake of argument, that α is a purely mindless state (e.g., a pattern of neurons firing). Next, consider a more complex build thought: that sand exists or fire exists or shoes exist. By uniformity, this build thought could (without logical inconsistency) also be based on a mindless state, perhaps one that is slightly more complex. Going in the other direction, if a thought about sand and fire *cannot* have a mindless basis, then neither can a thought about sand, fire, and shoes. Either way, build thoughts are in the same boat with respect to what category of thing can make them.

I believe the uniformity axiom is verifiable by reason: by reason one can see that differences in contents of thoughts cannot make (or entail) a difference with respect to whether those thoughts can be based on the same category of thing, whether mindless or mental.

So here is where we are. According to the mindful thoughts theorem, not every constructible build thought can be individually determined by purely mindless states. By uniformity, all build thoughts are in the same boat. Therefore, a mindless state cannot individually determine any build thought.

This result is especially significant if you can actually have individual build thoughts. For example, consider just (T1): that sand exists or fire exists. You can have this thought without thereby having other build thoughts in your mind. You can verify this directly. Simply consider right now whether thinking

T1 forces other build thoughts into your mind. If you can think T1 without thinking other build thoughts, then you can deduce the following consequence: whatever is a basis of T1 can be a basis of T1 uniquely.

This final step takes the argument from theoretical abstraction into concrete application. Build thoughts actually exist: you can see the reality of a build thought by direct awareness of a build thought in your own mind. See, for example, the thought that sand exists or fire exists. This thought is real. The axioms and theorems draw out the significance of this element of reality. From the mindful thoughts theorem together with the uniformity axiom, it follows that build thoughts cannot have a purely mindless ground that determines them. Therefore, this build thought in your mind has formed, somehow, without a mindless ground. This result, if correct, has real world implications about the basis of your thoughts.

Here is another way to think of these results. On one level, it may seem surprising to think that we can deduce information about the nature and basis of thoughts by such general, abstract reasoning. On the other hand, once we examine thoughts under the light of introspection, we position ourselves to see significant truths about thoughts. For by inner awareness, we can see the structure of thoughts. This sight of the structure of thoughts positions us to see the construction power of the logical links in the structure of thoughts. By insight into these logical links, we can see things about the nature of thought that we could never see in the nature of brain matter.

Now to be clear, it does not follow that material brain states have nothing do with thoughts. There are evident links between mind and matter. Part of my project will be to examine the nature of those links (in chapter seven). The result so far is just that mindless matter is not sufficient, by itself, to make all your thoughts.

Whether or not you agree with everything I am proposing here, I hope you at least appreciate the power of introspection to illuminate the inner structure of thoughts. Introspection can help us see some things we cannot see just by looking inside brains. By introspection, we can see, for example, logical links. And, by logical reasoning, we can compare the building power of logical links with the building power of other things. By moving away from hypotheses that contradict what we can see by this light, we move closer to the truth. We are clearing the way.

HOW TO MAKE A THOUGHT

So, what can make a thought?

Some ingredients clearly won't do. For example, you can't make thoughts out of blue napkins. It does not matter how long a blue napkin sits on a table. A blue napkin will never begin to think on its own. The properties are wrong. Making something blue, for example, does not by itself make something think. Having fibers does not help a napkin think. Thus, no matter how long the napkin sits, it will not, just by being blue or having fibers, begin to have thoughts.

What, then, is required to make a thought?

Answering this question seems especially difficult if the ingredients are fundamentally mindless. Mindless matter has certain explanatory limits. Here are two. First, if the counting argument is sound, then mindless states are not by themselves sufficient to determine thoughts. While this result leaves open the prospect of a nondeterministic link between mental and nonmental states, it removes the prospect of a deterministic explanation.

Moreover, without a mind, mindless materials have the wrong aspects to explain the aspects of thoughts. The blue of a napkin, for example, not only does not deterministically explain a thought, but the blue also does not *indeterministically* explain a thought. Making something blue will not, and cannot, make something able to think all on its own. More is required.

Philosopher of science Alex Rosenberg expresses this problem in terms of physics. He asks, "How can one clump of stuff anywhere in the universe be about some other clump of stuff anywhere else in the universe?"[18] His answer is that nothing in the universe can be *about* anything. He explains why he thinks this:

> Physics has ruled out the existence of clumps of matter of the required sort [i.e., the type that can be about things]. There are just fermions and bosons and combinations of them. None of that stuff is just, all by itself, about any other stuff. There is nothing in the whole universe—including of course all the neurons in your brain—that just by its nature or composition do the job of being about some other clump of matter.[19]

---

[18]A. Rosenberg, *The Atheist's Guide to Reality: Enjoying Life Without Illusion* (New York: W. W. Norton, 2011), 173-74.
[19]Rosenberg, *Atheist's Guide to Reality*, 179.

Rosenberg is pointing here to the problem of wrong materials. Clumps of matter are the wrong materials, he thinks, to make thoughts. His response is to suppose that thoughts do not even exist, for nothing in physics can account for them.

I appreciate Rosenberg's boldness to follow his argument where it leads him. He thinks physics cannot account for thoughts. So, he concludes there are no thoughts.

My response will be different. To my mind, Rosenberg's observations reveal, not that thoughts do not exist, but that there is a great challenge in accounting for the existence of thoughts purely in terms of the standard vocabulary of physics. As I have said, I think thoughts do exist—by the light of direct, introspective awareness. So, I am stuck with the problem of accounting for the existence of thoughts.

But there is a solution—or at least the beginning of a solution. The material that makes thoughts is not purely mindless. It's not napkins. Not sand. Not glass. Not any mindless clumps of matter. Instead, thoughts emerge in the context of a *mind*. Where there is a mind, there can be thoughts. A mind is a stream of consciousness in which waves of thoughts can emerge.

A mind is the right material. Recall that by "mind," I mean minimally this: a mind is something that can have contents of consciousness, such as thoughts, feelings, perceptions, and anything else that can occur in consciousness. On this definition, something that can have a thought within consciousness will count as a "mind." I witness thoughts in my own consciousness. So, I witness thoughts emerge in my own mind.

The minimal concept of a mind is a seed for a fuller concept that I will develop in the course of our inquiry. Once we have a clearer view of the nature of minds, we will investigate the origin of any thought-making materials (minds). So far, my aim has only been to identify a certain, key constraint on the nature and origin of thoughts. The constraint is this: where there are thoughts, there is a mind. Seeing this constraint will serve us later when we investigate your possible origin (in part two).

So, my appeal to a mind does not completely solve our mystery but pushes it deeper into reality. If sand can't make thoughts, sand presumably can't make minds, either. To appeal to minds, then, to explain thoughts relocates the question: what explains minds? This deeper question remains.

Still, it is valuable to see a constraint on the origin of thoughts. If thoughts have their origin in a mind, then mindless materials do not, all on their own, make thoughts. Mind is required.

I will close this chapter by offering a simple proposal about how thoughts may emerge in a mind. While this proposal is not an essential paint stroke in my larger picture, it helps illustrate the resourcefulness of a mental material. My proposal is this: thoughts are organizations (structures) of concepts, which come into being in a mind via conceptual acts. On this account, to make a thought requires putting concepts into order. For example, when you have the concept of cat and the concept of cape, you can organize these concepts into the thought that a cat wears a cape. This act of conceptualization is how you can form thoughts in your mind. In this way, you can make thoughts in your mind via an act of organizing concepts.

This proposal fits my general proposal that thoughts require a mind. Without a mind, there is no context for concepts to occur (as contents of consciousness). So, without a mind, there cannot be conceptual organization. And without conceptual organization, there cannot be the conceptual organizations that are thoughts. So, again, without a mind, there are no thoughts.

We can summarize a key outcome of this chapter as an argument for the dependence of thoughts on a mind:

1. There are thoughts.

2. There cannot be thoughts without a mind.

3. Therefore, where there are thoughts, there is a mind.

If all of this is right, then I arrive at a key conclusion: thoughts occur in the context of someone's mind.

SUMMARY

By inner awareness of your thoughts, you can see that your thoughts have at least these four aspects: aboutness, structure, truth-value, and logical linkability. These aspects are part of the visible essence of a thought. The visible essence of a thought is visible to your immediate awareness (direct acquaintance).

The visible essence of a thought does not consist of material aspects of brain matter. For the visible essence of a thought is within your immediate awareness, while the material aspects of brain matter are not. So, your thoughts have at least some aspects within your consciousness that are not the same as material aspects of brain matter wholly outside your immediate awareness.

A series of counting arguments helped us further investigate the nature of thoughts. The first counting argument illuminates a new constraint on the essence of a thought. If that argument is sound, then certain visible aspects of thoughts (structure and logical linkability) allow us to count more types of thoughts than third-person material types. The result is that third-person material types are not part of the essence of a thought, not even an invisible essence.

The second counting argument illuminates a new constraint on how thoughts could emerge. In particular, by combining the first counting argument with an analysis of the logical independence between distinct thoughts, we were able to deduce the mindful thoughts theorem. If that theorem is true, then mindless bits of reality are insufficient, on their own, to construct all the logically constructible types of thoughts. In other words, mindless matter is not a sole sufficient basis for the existence of thoughts.

Finally, we saw the beginning of an account of how thoughts can emerge. The account is this: thoughts can emerge in a mind, via the organization of concepts. The result of this analysis is that while mindless bits of matter cannot (by themselves) make thoughts, someone with a *mind* can.

■　■　■

Still pondering the strange shapes in the wall, you notice a dark tunnel in the far corner of the cavern. Out of curiosity, you decide to follow the tunnel further into the cave. You feel cold sand under your feet as you walk. After about twenty steps, you notice a rough patch on the wall of the tunnel up ahead. In anticipation, you hold up your lantern. You see a message, just as before. It reads clearly:

YOU ARE NOT YOUR THOUGHTS.

4

YOUR SIGHT

Reality is merely an illusion, albeit a very persistent one.

ALBERT EINSTEIN

*It is, I think, agreed by all that distance, of itself
and immediately, cannot be seen.*

GEORGE BERKELEY

THIS CHAPTER IS ABOUT SEEING. By seeing into the nature of seeing, I hope to expose deeper insight into the kind of reality you are—a seeing being.

THE PROBLEM OF PERCEPTION

Somehow, sight is real. If you are reading these words, you can verify the reality of your own sight. When you see, you don't merely act like you can see (as an unconscious GPS system does). On the contrary, you actually consciously see things. (If you are listening to this book or are unable to see, then I invite you to translate the contents of this chapter in terms of what you can consciously *hear*. Conscious hearing and conscious seeing are both forms of conscious awareness. The problems we will examine in relation to sight are fundamentally problems with conscious awareness in all its forms, including conscious hearing.)

It is not trivial that anything can see. Dust can't see. You can. What makes the difference? Can blind bits of matter all by themselves turn into something that is not blind? How? This question invites us to consider how sight is possible.

In this section, I will seek deeper insight into the nature of sight (and how sight is even possible) by examining a classic puzzle of perception. This puzzle is about how someone can be aware of *external* things via one's internal experiences. Examining this puzzle will position us to see more clearly what it takes for there to be sight.

To give a sense of how perception can be puzzling, consider your perception of the sun in the sky. The sun is entirely outside of you (presumably). Yet your experience of seeing the sun is entirely within you. How, then, does an internal experience of the sun allow you to perceive the actual, external sun? This question points to the puzzle of perception: the puzzle of perception is about how a perceptual experience *in* you can give you any information *outside* of you.

Philosophers of perception unpack this puzzle by drawing attention to cases where the things you think you see aren't actually there. For example, suppose the sun exploded five minutes ago. You don't know it exploded right away, for it takes about eight minutes for sunlight to reach the earth. So, if you look at the sky, you won't see any explosion yet. In fact, if you look into the sky, you'll still experience the sun holding its place in the sky. But wait: there actually is no sun; it already exploded. So, what are you seeing in the sky, if not the sun?

This question invites us to consider the relationship between things we are directly aware of in consciousness (e.g., an experience of the sun) and things external to our consciousness (e.g., the sun itself). When you experience the sun, you have a picture of the sun in your mind. You can be consciously aware of this picture directly, whether or not there is any sun. But then, how does your awareness of this picture help you see the sun outside your mind? And, while I am asking questions, here's another: Is there even a sun outside your mind? How could you ever know?

The questions I'm raising are central to our inquiry into the nature of personal beings. As a personal being, you can see. The question is, how? How, in principle, can one portion of reality consciously see any other portion of reality? An answer to this question would be a master key to unlock insight into the foundations of all knowledge. By seeing how you can see, you can see a special power that personal beings have to know anything.

In the following sections, I will pursue a greater understanding of how perception works. First, I will examine the main theories of perception on offer. I will then organize threads from these theories into my own integrated account, which will be in terms of basic, conscious awareness (direct acquaintance). Finally, I will consider what kind of material (or reality) can possibly have this power of conscious awareness.

THEORIES OF PERCEPTION

To help us consider possible solutions to the puzzle of perception, I will describe four theories of perception. These theories represent the main options developed by perception theorists. Each theory provides an account of how our perceptual experiences may relate to external things, like the sun. I will seek to highlight something helpful about each theory while also identifying limitations. The positive points in each theory will prepare the way for my own "window theory" of perception.

Direct realism. According to direct realism, you can *directly* see things "out there." For example, when you look at the sun, you see the sun. On this account, your perception of the external world involves a direct awareness of things in the external world. To see the sun, you don't first see something else (such as a mental image of a sun in your mind). Instead, you see the sun itself.

To help us appreciate what is at stake, let us consider a classic challenge to the direct realist position. The challenge is to distinguish between things "out there" and things merely in your own consciousness. For example, suppose you are dreaming of a sun. In the dream, you have a visual image of a sun. In that case, you do not see a real, external sun. Instead, if you "see" anything, you see mental imagery in your own mind. However, the imagery of a sun in a dream experience is, at least in principle, experientially indistinguishable from the imagery you experience when perceiving a real sun. How, then, does a perception of a real sun differ from a perception of inner mental contents? Call the challenge of answering this question, "the distinguishability problem."

To meet the challenge, we need an account of the difference between veridical experiences (while awake) and nonveridical experiences (such as in dreams). One type of account is an either-or account called "disjunctivism."[1] On this account, there are two cases with respect to an experience of a sun: either (i) you are seeing a real sun, or (ii) you are only having an experience of seeing a sun. In the case of real sight, the sun is an object of your perceptual awareness. In the case of hallucination, the sun is not an object of your perceptual awareness. Even if you can't consciously tell the difference between these cases, there is a difference in terms of what you are actually directly aware of.

John Searle offers a different account of the similarities between veridical and nonveridical experience.[2] According to Searle, the *contents* of your experience are the same in both veridical and nonveridical perceptual experience; the contents are constituents of the perceptual experience itself. Meanwhile, the *objects*, which the contents are *of*, are not the same in both veridical and nonveridical experiences. To illustrate, suppose you have a visual image of a sun. Then you perceive a real sun if and only if your image is of a real sun. Searle offers a causal account of "of": a sun-image is *of* a real sun in virtue of its causal relationship to a real sun. On this account, even while visual experiences in a perfect hallucination can be subjectively indistinguishable from veridical experiences, the veridical experience is different because it involves a perception of real objects. Thus, there is a difference between an inner experience of a sun and a perception of a real sun.

Still, on either account, there remains a more fundamental question about the nature of the contents of inner, conscious experience. What are these contents? Think again about an experience of a sun. When you have a visual image of a sun, this image contains various qualities (e.g., brightness, colors, shapes). Call these "visual contents." Your awareness of visual contents does not by itself tell you whether the contents themselves are wholly internal to your consciousness, or whether instead they may be part of an external world. So how does an experience of a sun give you direct, conscious sight of an external object?

We are walking on complex conceptual terrain. To help secure our footing, I want to zoom in on some key distinctions. When thinking about

---

[1] The most helpful and nuanced defense of this account I've seen is from M. Martin, "The Limits of Self-Awareness," *Philosophical Studies* 120 (2004): 37-89.
[2] J. Searle, *Seeing Things as They Are: A Theory of Perception* (Oxford: Oxford University Press, 2015).

perceptual experience, it is important to distinguish three things involved in perception. First, there is the content of the perceptual experience. Second, there are the causes of the experience. Third, there is the perceptual experience itself. By seeing these distinctions, we can describe the problem of perception more precisely. The problem is this: conscious awareness of the *contents* of a perceptual experience does not by itself give us conscious awareness of external *causes* of the experience.

Indeed, the lack of direct conscious awareness of external causes is precisely what ignites the debates over the nature of the external world. It is why we can entertain the possibility that the causes of our experiences might be radically unlike anything we could imagine. For all we are consciously aware of, it is conceivable that there might be no external world at all.

The point here is not that direct realism cannot be true. A direct realist could suppose that visual perception consists of awareness of things in an external, mind-independent world. Still, my thought is that, even if we see external things directly, we do not see their *externality* directly: that is, we do not see whether what we see directly is (only) internal or external to consciousness.

There remains a deeper question, then, about what it is that we see in conscious experience, whether we are dreaming or awake. Searle supposes (as part of our pretheoretical knowledge) that everything we perceive is mind-independent. This starting point leads him to infer that the *contents* of perceptual experience (which he thinks are mind-dependent) cannot be *objects* of perceptual experience. For example, if one has an illusory experience of seeing double, Searle says, "We do not for a moment see two of anything."[3] The "double," he says, is a *content* of a visual experience, not an *object* of sight. But then how does a content of a perception put us in conscious contact with an external object?

This question points to a deeper root of the problem of perception. The problem is not fundamentally about how we can visually perceive a world, but about how we can be *consciously aware* of a world. To elaborate on this problem, consider again your perception of the sun. Suppose you can be directly consciously aware of the sun. Then this awareness has an immediate

---

[3]Searle, *Seeing Things as They Are*, 84.

conscious impact: that is to say, you can be conscious of *whether* you are aware of the sun, just as you can be conscious of whether you are aware of a happy feeling. The problem, however, is that the sun could be removed without any conscious impact. For suppose the sun explodes. In that case, your awareness is not immediately impacted at all; it takes time for light from the explosion to reach your eyes. So it looks like you are not consciously aware of the sun after all.

We may summarize the challenge as follows:

1. The awareness premise: if you are directly aware of something, then you can tell whether you are aware of it or not (by the conscious impact of awareness).

2. The internality premise: you can only tell whether you are aware of things that are internal to your consciousness (e.g., visual images).

3. Therefore, whatever you are directly aware of is internal to your consciousness.

This result contradicts the premise that you can be directly aware of the sun, if the sun indeed exists entirely external to your consciousness.

The argument is not fatal for direct realism. Technically, a direct realist could even accept the conclusion. For it could be that some contents of awareness are both internal to your consciousness and in an external world. For example, perhaps certain aspects within a mental image, like shape and color, can exist both in your mind (as part of a mental image) and "out there" (as part of an external object). Then the external things you see would also be internal things; the aspects of the sun you are directly aware of (shape and color) would not be wholly external to you. This option is still on the table. (In fact, my own theory of perception will incorporate a version of this option.)

In summary, direct realism is helpful but limited. It is helpful because it recognizes that we have a window of direct awareness (direct, conscious acquaintance). By direct awareness, we can see things. The limit, however, is in its account of what we see. The window of awareness is open. But how do we know what we are seeing through the window? Is anything we see "external"—capable of existing apart from our own conscious awareness of it? Or is the window merely open to mental paint in our own minds?

Phenomenalism. Phenomenalism flips the focus from the external world to the internal world of conscious experience. According to phenomenalism, perception is analyzable entirely in terms of one's internal states of consciousness ("sense data"). When you perceive a sun, for example, you see a picture of a sun inside your mind. This picture is real. But this picture does not exist out there, apart from your consciousness. Nothing you consciously see exists out there.

A standard challenge for phenomenalism is to account for the external world. According to phenomenalists, the pictures in your mind do not even *resemble* an external world. The reason is this. Suppose your sight of mental pictures were a way of seeing the world. Then mental pictures would resemble the world somehow. But mental pictures of the world do not resemble external, nonmental causes. Hence, according to phenomenalism, you are not even indirectly aware of external things. The contents of your awareness, direct or indirect, are entirely within you.

In my estimation, the two best contemporary defenses of phenomenalism I have seen are from the philosopher of perception Richard Fumerton and the physicist Donald Hoffman.[4] Together they provide two grand pillars of support: (i) empirical evidence and (ii) logical analysis.

Hoffman erects the empirical pillar. He points to a series of developments in science (quantum mechanics, cosmology, evolutionary biology, and vision science) to make a case for the conclusion that we don't see things as they are.[5] A summary of part of his case is this:

1. The objects that appear in visual perception are spatial.

2. External objects are not (fundamentally) spatial.

3. Therefore, external objects are not (fundamentally) what appear in visual perception.

In support of (2), Hoffman displays evidence from many corners of recent science (including from his own original discoveries). This

---

[4]R. Fumerton, *Metaphysical and Epistemological Problems of Perception* (Lincoln: University of Nebraska Press, 1985); D. Hoffman, *The Case Against Reality: How Evolution Hid the Truth from Our Eyes* (New York: W. W. Norton, 2019).

[5]D. Hoffman, "The Scrambling Theorem: A Simple Proof of the Logical Possibility of Spectrum Inversion," *Conscious Cognition* 15, no. 1 (2006): 31-45 also makes a logical case for the variability of color experiences.

evidence paints a new scientific picture of the fabric of external reality: the "stuff" of our world is fundamentally nonspatial.

Hoffman adds to his case by supplying empirical reasons to doubt that the contents of visual perception would likely "match" external things. These reasons come from experiments in evolutionary biology and vision science. For example, Hoffman cites the "The Fitness-Beats-Truth Theorem," which he and others deduce from general principles of complex adaptive systems.[6] From this theorem, Hoffman infers that the probability is virtually zero that any of our perceptions estimate true aspects of objective (mind-independent) reality. Hoffman goes on to deduce that our ordinary way of thinking of physical objects as existing in a mind-independent spacetime is almost certainly inapt to describe reality as it is. Hoffman brings together many different lines of evidence from many corners of science to point to a single conclusion: you don't see external reality as it is.

In addition to Hoffman's empirical case, Fumerton makes a more fundamental, logical case. Fumerton's argument arises from the basic problem of perception. This problem, as we have seen, is about how to see anything external to our own consciousness (in principle). Recall the distinguishability problem. When we look through the window of awareness, we "see" (are consciously aware of) visual data (e.g., shapes and colors). This visual data is the same data we see when we dream (or hallucinate). So, what distinguishes what we see in a dream from what we see when we are awake? Unless we say the "external world" is like a large, shared dream (which we have not ruled out!), the visual data we see is not part of external objects themselves; thus, the visual data is not part of external, material objects. At minimum, the visual data we see directly (whether dreaming or awake) is internal to our own consciousness.

Here now is my analysis of phenomenalism. First, the greatest advantage of phenomenalism, in my view, is that it takes seriously the internal aspect of direct, conscious awareness. Awareness is internal to conscious experience. For this reason, awareness makes a conscious impact on you: you can be aware of whether you are aware of something. For example, you can be aware of whether you are right now aware of some thoughts, feelings, or a visual image of these words. If you only ever had *external* awareness (of

---

[6]C. Prakash et al., "Fitness Beats Truth in the Evolution of Perception," *Acta Biotheoretica* (2020): https://doi.org/10.1007/s10441-020-09400-0.

things outside of your consciousness), then you would not be able to say what you are thinking, feeling, or sensing. But you can say what you are thinking, feeling, or sensing. Therefore, your awareness is not entirely external.

So, I think the phenomenalist is right about this much: you can be aware—really aware—of elements of (or within) your own consciousness. In other words, you have access to the contents of your consciousness.

Nevertheless, phenomenalism has certain limits. I would like to point to two limits of this theory. First, it is limited in its ability to account for external reality (beyond one's own direct consciousness). This limit is the mirror image of the limit of direct realism: while direct realism faces the challenge of accounting for the internal aspect of awareness, the phenomenalists faces the reverse challenge of accounting for external reality. For suppose we have no access to the external world (directly or indirectly). Then how can we say anything about the external world? How can we even say about external world that it is inaccessible?

Hoffman addresses this question by restricting the phenomenalist analysis to empirical senses (sight, taste, touch, smell, hearing). In this way, Hoffman avoids having to say that *all* senses fail to reveal objective reality. Indeed, he remains optimistic that reason and logic reveal objective truths, such as that $2 + 2 = 4$. If reason reveals objective truths, then we can use reason to deduce something about external reality. More to the point, by allowing that reason can reveal objective truth, Hoffman avoids the problem of cutting himself off from the objectivity of his own conclusions about perception. He uses reason, together with introspection, to arrive at what he takes to be an objective truth about reality (as it is): that is, he takes it to be objectively true that we cannot visually see external reality as it is.

At this step, we might wonder, why think reason and logic can indeed reveal things about external reality? Why couldn't the same empirical considerations that Hoffman appeals to also cast doubt on the reliability of reason? For example, if fitness beats truth with respect to vision, why doesn't fitness beat truth with respect to reasoning too? While Hoffman suggests that there are relevant empirical differences, there is a more fundamental problem with trying to establish the reliability of reason by mere empirical science alone. The problem is that any argument from empirical science will presuppose principles of reason in the argument itself.

Fortunately, however, I think there is a way to verify realities beyond one's own consciousness by using the lights of reason and introspection working together. Here you will see why I think philosophy (as tool of analysis) can serve science (as an empirical study)—and that actually, these fields can unlock more mysteries by working together than they can by working apart.

So, here is how I think you can see truths of reason that transcend your sight of them. To begin, I invite you to consider this principle: if two things are added to two more things, there are four things. In other words, 2 + 2 = 4. I believe you can see the truth of this principle by being directly aware of (or direct acquaintance with) logical truths within your own mind (i.e., within consciousness). I arrive at this conviction by my own introspective awareness of myself having direct awareness of the mathematical truth. When I look within, I find that I am aware of the universal truth that any two things added to any other two things will result in four things. I see this truth in my mind by grasping the numbers and their relations to each other. If I can see this truth, then I assume you can too.

Next, here is how I think you can see that mathematical truths in your consciousness are not merely in your own consciousness. My reason is this: you can be aware (by reason) that the truth of 2 + 2 = 4 is *necessary*. In other words, you can see that 2 + 2 cannot fail to equal 4; necessarily, if two things are added to two more, then you have four things. By seeing this necessity, you can see then, by reason, that this truth of reason holds independently of your own current, contingent (nonnecessary) awareness of it; for example, even before you were born, it was true that 2 + 2 = 4. So, while you are aware of this truth in your mind, the truth itself does not depend on your mind. If that is correct, then by direct awareness of necessary truths within you, you can see that some truths are also external to (not dependent on) you. In this way, you can see at least some truths within your mind that do not depend on your sight of them.

These considerations lead me to think that the window of awareness is not entirely closed: we can see at least some reality, including some reality that does not depend on our sight of it. Again, when I am aware that 2 + 2 = 4, I see a necessary truth; that's real.

In my analysis, then, phenomenalism cannot be unrestricted in its application. If phenomenalism applied to all senses (including to reason and introspection), then everything would be dark. We would see nothing, not even that 2 + 2 = 4. We would not even see that we see nothing. Fortunately, things aren't that dark.

There is an additional problem with unrestricted phenomenalism. If phenomenalism applied to all our senses, then we would even be cut off from our own mental states.[7] We witness our mental states by an inner sense of them (introspection). But if all senses are turned off, then no sense is a window into any reality, not even the reality of how things appear! In that case, the sense of our own thoughts, feelings, and mental images would fail to reveal any actual thoughts, feelings, or mental images. We could not even know that our senses are real. By the light of introspection, things aren't that dark.

Finally, I believe a completely unrestricted phenomenalism is self-defeating. For suppose phenomenalism applies to every sense. Then it applies to any sense of phenomenalism itself (including the sense of understanding what phenomenalism is). In that case, we could not tell that phenomenalism itself is even real, let alone true.

To be clear, I see no obvious logical problem with restricting phenomenalism to certain senses, such as vision or hearing. For example, maybe we don't sense an apple *as it is*, even if we can still sense an apple *as it appears*.

I close my analysis of phenomenalism by pointing to some remaining questions. If vision doesn't reveal things as they are, what information does vision reveal, if any? Does a visual experience of a sun provide any information about an actual sun (as it is)? If so, what kind of information is that? Or if not, how can we say anything about the sun? Behind all these questions, I'm also wondering about this: could some aspects we witness within the contents of consciousness also be real aspects of a world external to consciousness? These questions remain on the table.

Thus, while I think phenomenalism gets something important right (that we enjoy inner awareness), I believe there is more to the story of how we see external realities.

Intentional theory. Some theories reject the premise that perception consists in a simple, basic relation of direct awareness. Instead, on these

---

[7] D. Armstrong, *A Materialist Theory of the Mind* (London: Routledge, 1993), 324.

theories, perception consists of a certain type of experience that is *of* or *about* elements of reality. For example, when you perceive a chair, you have a certain experience that is of a chair. These are intentional theories, because they analyze perception in terms of intentional states (e.g., an experience of a chair) that point to things (e.g., a chair) beyond themselves.

A paradigm example of an intentional theory is the adverbial theory. According to adverbial theory, perception involves a way of experiencing an object. To illustrate, suppose you experience a white sun. Then what makes your experience of a white sun is a certain way of experiencing the sun: you experience the sun *white-sun-ly*. To experience white-sun-ly is not to stand in an awareness relation. Rather, when you experience white-sun-ly, you simply have a certain type of experience—the white-sun-ly experience.

Adverbialists attempt to solve the problem of perception by cutting out a direct awareness of visual, sense data. So, for example, when you perceive the sun, you are not literally aware of a little sun in your head. Nor are you first aware of a mental picture of a sun from which you deduce that there is a sun outside your head. Instead, you perceive the sun (an external object) in a certain way.

The adverbial theory is helpful in this respect: this theory recognizes a distinction between a *manner* of experience and an *object* of experience. For example, if I have an experience of a white sun, this experience is not itself a white sun. Instead, it is white-sun-ly. The object of the experience differs from the manner of the experience.

Still, a deeper mystery remains unresolved: how does the object of experience relate to the manner of experience? Take, for example, a white-sun-ly experience. This experience is not itself white or a sun. Yet the adverbial description of the experience includes the term *white* and *sun*. These terms express the properties, being white and being a sun. How do these properties relate to the experience itself? Calling the experience "white-ly" and "sun-ly" labels this mystery but does not solve it.

Frank Jackson famously draws out this deeper mystery by drawing attention to the structure of experience.[8] To illustrate his concern, suppose

---

[8] F. Jackson, *Perception: A Representative Theory* (Cambridge: Cambridge University Press, 1977).

you sense a brown square next to a green triangle. The structure of this experience is not fully expressed by the adverbial phase, "sensing brownly, squarely, greenly, and triangularly," since that phrase leaves out which shape goes with which color. The adverbial phrase leaves out the structure of the experience.

In response, an adverbial theorist may build structure into a longer adverbial phrase: "sensing in the manner of there being a brown-square next to a green-triangle." Then we can distinguish structured experiences using different adverbial phrases. So, the adverbial theory is not dead.

Still, there remains a more fundamental question about the nature of the intentional experience. Take, for example, an experience of red. Sure, an experience of red is not red. But how is "of red" related to red? Calling the experience "of red" labels the mystery. What is *of-red*?

To draw out the question, consider an experience of seeing something *as something else*. When you see something as something else, you are aware of something as it is. For example, suppose you see a ball as a blurry image. The ball is not itself blurry. Yet something is blurry: you can see by introspective awareness your blurry image of the ball. The blurry image is the content of the experience. You are aware of this content directly in your consciousness. The question, then, is this: How is this content of your experience of a ball related to the ball?

I would like to emphasize here the invaluable role of the introspection tool in bringing to light the question at hand. Without introspection, we would not be able to appreciate the mystery of perception. Introspection allows us to inspect—directly—the contents of perceptual experience. When we have a visual experience of the sun, for example, we can identify certain aspects: brightness, colors, and shapes. Sure, the experience is not itself bright, colorful, or shaped. But it contains (in some sense) contents of brightness, colors, and shapes. By seeing these contents in a perceptual experience, we position ourselves to understand the central question of perception: how are the contents—whether they are intentional or not—within a perceptual experience related to external objects?

We do not answer this question merely by describing the manner of perception. While some theories (e.g., the adverbial theory and intentionalism) helpfully distinguish the manner of a perception from the objects of perception, I am still left wondering how the contents encoded in perception relate to the objects of perception, more fundamentally. In particular, how are the things I'm directly acquainted with in my perceptual experience (e.g., phenomenal colors and shapes) related to the objects external to my consciousness? This question remains on the table.

Representationalism. According to representational theory of perception, your perceptual experiences represent external things. For example, when you perceive the sun, your experience of the sun represents the sun. Thus, perhaps we can explain how you can see an external world in terms of internal representations.

Of course, representationalism invites the question, how does an experience *represent* something? One hypothesis is the sense data theory. According to this theory, a perceptual experience consists of direct awareness of "sense data." Sense data includes phenomenal qualities, such as color, shape, and glow, as they appear in your mind. These phenomenal qualities are the primary objects of your perception. By seeing these qualities in your mind, you are able to indirectly see what they represent. For example, by seeing a picture of a sun in your mind (sense data), you indirectly see the sun, which the picture represents.

On the sense data theory, the window to the outside world is closed. The sense data theorist joins the phenomenalist in this respect: what you perceive are only pictures on the walls of your own mind. A sense data theorist could suppose that you are able to indirectly perceive things outside by directly perceiving things inside your consciousness. The challenge, then, is to explain how that could work. How can perception of conscious elements in your mind give you perception of nonconscious elements outside your mind? This question brings us back to the very puzzle of perception we are trying to solve.

Another hypothesis (which does not exclude sense data theory) is the causal theory. This theory analyzes representation in terms of causation. To illustrate, suppose light from the sun causes you to have an experience of the sun. Then in virtue of this causal relationship to the sun, your experience of the sun represents the sun itself.

The causal theory of perception helps account for the difference between hallucinations and veridical (real) perception. The difference is in the *cause.*

A hallucination of a sun is not caused by a real sun. By contrast, a veridical perception of a sun is caused by a real sun. So the causal theory of perception offers a solution to the distinguishability problem.

Causal theorists work to explain how things cause the contents of a visual experience. This project connects with the science of perception. Vision scientist Stephen Palmer describes on a functional level how photoreceptors "see" the world.[9] According to Palmer, each receptor receives a bit of information, which contributes to a causal explanation of visual perception.

Despite the advances in vision science, one might still wonder how the contents of one's perception reveal the external world. We saw from Hoffman's empirical case that there are reasons to doubt that the contents of our perception resemble an external, objective world. If he's right, then it is unclear how our consciousness "represents" external things.

There is also the problem of the wrong object. To illustrate, suppose I cause a visual image of redness to form in my mind by intending to form an image. Is my intention, which caused the image, therefore red? Of course not. (To cross every t, I can add this: I can see that my intention is not red by the light of introspection.) Therefore, an image does not automatically represent its causes. More is required, then, to account for representation. (That is not to say that causal theorists don't have more to say.)

As I see it, the most fundamental challenge for representational theories remains the challenge of explaining how our inner experiences relate to an external world. Appeal to causation leaves unsolved the deeper mystery of how, or whether, we can have conscious awareness of anything external to our own minds. Maybe causation is part of the solution. Still, if the cause is screened off from my conscious awareness, then I'm back to wondering how I can see anything about the cause. How do I perceive a cause, whether it is a red apple or a white sun, if I have no conscious awareness of any of its aspects? That question remains.

Nevertheless, I think representational theories take a good step forward. Representationalism says *something* about the relation between perceptual experience and the external world: the contents of perceptual experience

---

[9] S. Palmer, *Vision Science: Photons to Phenomenology* (Cambridge, MA: MIT Press, 1999).

represent things, at least sometimes. This step can then lead to additional steps as we fill out the nature of representation.

The central question of perception is still on the table: How can the contents of a perceptual experience (which we are directly, consciously acquainted with) help us "see" external objects?

HOW TO SEE THE WORLD

I will now provide a fuller account of perception that draws from the four theories we have considered. I will begin by describing the basic challenge that all theories work to solve. Then I will begin to piece together the elements of what I call "the window theory" of perception.

Root of the problem. All theories of perception face the problem of how to get out of the mind. When you have a dream of mountains, for example, the sense of shape and structure of those mountains is not outside your mind. But when you are awake, you might have the very same sense of shape and structure as in your dream. This sense is not out of your mind. The sense is within you. All your senses are within you. How, then, can senses within you reveal information outside of you?

Theories of perception attempt to address this question in one of two ways: either they say that perceptual experience is like a window through which you can see things outside you, or they say perceptual experience is like a painting inside your mind caused by external forces.

Both options lead to challenges. On the window account (e.g., direct realism and versions of adverbial theory), we face the challenge of making sense of hallucinations and dreams. The experience of hallucinations and dreams is not a window into an external world; it's an experience within you—on the wall of your own mind. Yet, when you are awake, you have the same sort experiences (of colors, shapes, and sounds). The same experience cannot be both a window to the external world and a painting within your own mind. So how do we account for the difference?

The other option is that all perceptual experiences reflect "paintings" of conscious experience within you. This option includes versions of representational theory and phenomenalism. The problem with this account, however, is that it exacerbates the challenge of getting outside of your mind. If all you ever perceive are things within you, then you never perceive anything outside of you. You don't perceive chairs, people, or sunsets. But if you don't perceive any of those things, then how can you get any information about them? How can you get outside of your mind to know anything about anything beyond your own experiences?

Basic awareness. To solve the problem of perception, we need to unlock the window of awareness—so that we can consciously see at least some things directly. The basic challenge is to see how perception can be a window into both inner reality (of your experiences) and outer reality. To meet this challenge, I will make some observations about awareness itself.

My first observation is that awareness is real. By "awareness," I mean direct, conscious acquaintance. I know that awareness is real by my awareness of my own awareness.

I do not claim that awareness of awareness is simple or easy. No argument or research will give you awareness of your awareness. To be aware of your awareness, you must use your own power.

In his critique of introspection, Dunlap reports, "I am never aware of an awareness."[10] That report may be honest. Still, his report does not entail that he *cannot* be aware of his awareness.

I believe it is possible to be aware of your awareness by a certain mental effort. Here is a procedure. First, consider a picture in your mind. Focus on that picture. Be aware of that picture. Next, draw your attention to your *awareness* of that picture. If you can do that, then you can notice that you are aware of a mental picture. To notice that you are aware of something is to be aware that you are aware of something.

When you are aware of your awareness, you can see something about your own awareness. This sight gives you information about the nature of awareness itself.

The awareness here is *direct*. That is to say, direct awareness is not filtered through your awareness of something else. For example, when you are aware of a visual image, you see the visual image without first seeing something else; you don't see an image of an image to see the image itself. By being aware of the image, you experience a direct link between you and the object of your awareness (the image). Direct awareness is a transparent

[10]K. Dunlap, "The Case Against Introspection," *Psychological Review* 19, no. 5 (1912): 404-13.

window: rather than seeing an opaque windowpane, you see *through* the window to see the objects of your awareness.[11]

Through the window of awareness, then, you can see many kinds of things, which are the contents of your consciousness. The contents of consciousness are the objects of direct awareness. For example, when you have a visual experience, you can be directly aware of shapes and colors within your experience (as phenomenal contents). When you have an auditory experience, you can be aware of sounds and pitches. When you have a tactile experience, you can be aware of textures. When you have an experience of tasting, you can be aware of different flavors. When you have an experience of smelling something, you can be aware of different smells. And so on.

Conscious awareness allows you to see many things. By awareness of awareness, you can see your many senses, which are themselves windows of awareness. For example, you can see the window of introspection, through which you witness our thoughts, feelings, and intentions. You can also see the window of reason, by which you become aware of logical relations, deductions, and inferences. Furthermore, through the window of your sense of good and bad, you become aware of positive and negative aspects of things. And, through the window of your own imagination, you can be aware of certain possibilities. This list of windows is not exhaustive.

To increase clarity, it will be useful to adopt a term to pick out the qualities you are aware of (directly) in sense experience. Philosophers sometimes call these "phenomenal" qualities. For example, when you dream of a red shoe, you are aware of phenomenal red. Phenomenal red is not a wavelength of light or some external cause of your experience of the red. Phenomenal red is that quality you can be directly aware of when you experience red-ly.

To further illustrate the concept of phenomenal qualities, imagine that you are in a virtual reality simulation. This simulation takes over all your senses and gives you the experience of being on a planet just like earth. In

---

[11]Recent developments in knowledge theory appeal to the transparency aspect of awareness in "transparency accounts" of knowledge (see B. Gertler, "Self-Knowledge," *Stanford Encyclopedia of Philosophy* [2015], https://plato.stanford.edu/entries/self-knowledge), including knowledge of external things.

this simulation, everything you see and experience is indistinguishable from what you see and experience in your current life. You see people, buildings, trees, and grass. The difference is that none of these things you see are seen by anyone else. You see all these things purely within your own consciousness. The qualities you see (of people, buildings, trees, and grass) are phenomenal. They are phenomenal in the sense that you can be (directly) aware of them in your experiences.

It is not part of the concept of a phenomenal quality that these qualities are only internal to your consciousness. It is possible in principle that the phenomenal red, for example, exists in the petals of a red flower external to your mind. What makes a quality phenomenal is just that you can be directly, consciously aware of it. Thus, a phenomenal quality includes any quality (color, shape, sound) that you are directly aware of in an experience.

This analysis can help us understand what we see in an illusion. An illusion occurs when someone has an experience of something that isn't really there. For example, you might have an experience of a tree while no tree is in front of you. Your experience is an illusion. Still, you see *something*. By "see," I mean you are consciously aware. In this scenario, you are consciously aware of some phenomenal content in your experience of the tree. This content includes phenomenal qualities, like phenomenal brown and figures of bark. Your awareness of these contents allows you to identify what your experience is *of*—a tree. On this analysis, the only way you could have an illusion is if you are acquainted with contents of an illusory experience. In other words, the failure to see something external depends on the sight of something internal.[12]

---

[12]This analysis illuminates my analysis of illusionism, the theory that a certain quality of consciousness is itself an illusion and so not real. The quality illusionists eliminate is phenomenal consciousness, which is the quality of being what it is like to experience something (such as what it is like to experience smelling coffee). On my analysis, not everything in consciousness can be an illusion, for an illusion itself depends on the existence of contents of the illusory experience. Still, it could be that certain things in consciousness are illusory. To serve theorists who think phenomenal consciousness is an illusion, I offer this possible analysis: an experience of phenomenal consciousness has basic contents that are not themselves phenomenal consciousness. Then, just as you are not aware of an external tree directly inside contents of consciousness, the illusionist could suppose that you are not aware of phenomenal consciousness directly. In this way, an experience of phenomenal consciousness could be merely an illusion. This analysis accords well with François Kammerer's defense of illusionism in "The Illusion of Conscious Experience," *Synthese* 198 (2021): 845-66. (In my view, I think one can be aware of phenomenal consciousness directly as a content of immediate conscious experience. So, I don't think phenomenal

My final observation is that some qualities are real objects of awareness. By definition, a phenomenal quality is any quality one can see by direct awareness. By the conscious impact of awareness, you can be aware that you are aware of qualities. In this way, you can verify the existence of some qualities directly within consciousness.

External world. I will now provide an account of how I think you could perceive an external world. For the sake of modesty, I will not take for granted that there is an external world. Rather, I will show how I think one could perceive some elements of an external world if there is an external world. Then for completion, I'll say why I think there is probably an external world (of some form).

To start, I offer a minimal definition of "external word." I am thinking of an external world as any reality that is not entirely dependent on one's own consciousness. For example, if trees can exist outside your consciousness, then trees are external to you. Also, if I can have thoughts that do not depend on your consciousness, then my thoughts are part of your external world. This second example highlights that something that is external to you may not be external to everyone.

The next step is to see how the contents of one's awareness may be part of one's external world. I now present what I call "the external window theory." According to this account, some of the qualities you see by direct awareness are part of an external world. Mark Johnston develops a version of this account, and I follow some of his thought here.[13]

To illustrate how this account works, consider your visual field. The shapes and colors within your visual field combine to form what Johnston calls "scenes." For example, at this moment, my visual field consists of a phenomenal structure of a white rows and columns of a bookshelf. Within this structure, I am aware of phenomenal shapes and colors.

This visual scene is at least partly internal to me. After all, when I shift my eyes to the left, the visual field changes. The shapes and colors of my bookshelf are no longer in the field. This change suggests that the details of

consciousness is an illusion. Nevertheless, the main lines of my analysis of persons don't turn on this premise.)

[13]M. Johnston, "The Obscure Object of Hallucination," *Philosophical Studies* 120 (2004): 113-83. See also J. Rasmussen, *Defending the Correspondence Theory of Truth* (Cambridge: Cambridge University Press, 2014), 203-9.

my visual field depend on the direction of my eyes. The external elements of my room, by contrast, don't depend on the direction of my eyes. So, the external elements of my room are not the same as my visual field.

However, while my visual field is distinct from external elements of the room, it does not follow that the contents of my visual field are *entirely* internal to me. In principle, the scene could contain shapes, colors, and structures that are also elements of an external scene. For example, the bookshelf could be white (the same white I see in my visual field). It could also have shelves with a parallel line structure that is similar to the line structure I see in my visual field.

This account unlocks a solution to the distinguishability problem. That problem, recall, was the problem of seeing how to distinguish internal contents of experience from external objects of perception. According to the external window theory, the qualities you see when you are dreaming are the same in nature as the qualities you see when you are awake. In both cases, you see—by direct awareness—*scenes*. The difference between an inner scene (in a dream) and an outer scene (in the external world) is that an inner scene depends on you, whereas an outer scene does not. In this way, the external window account shows how internal awareness (of things within) can relate to external awareness (of things external).

This account also shows how we can combine the direct realist and phenomenalist accounts. The external window theory accepts the direct realist's proposal that we can be directly aware of external elements. It also accepts the phenomenalist's proposal that we only ever see phenomenal qualities (within consciousness). The external window theory combines these accounts by showing how phenomenal qualities can—at least in principle—also be part of an external world that doesn't depend on our awareness of them.

To close this section, I will share why I think there is an external world (of some form). First, I have reason to think at least some reality is external to my conscious awareness. As I have pointed out earlier, I take myself to be aware of necessary logical truths, such as 2 + 2 = 4. Necessary truths don't depend on my own consciousness, since they are necessary, while my particular consciousness is not. So, while I see necessary truths within my consciousness, I infer that these truths also exist apart from my consciousness.

Second, I also have reason to think my visual perception is related to causes external to my own mind. My reason is this: external causes provide a more probable explanation of my experiences than the alternative. Suppose instead nothing is external to my mind. Then nothing external to my experiences explains them or causes them. But by reason, I sense—via direct awareness—a probability relation between my total experiences (within my consciousness) and some external causes of them (outside my consciousness). Therefore, while I can't say I'm 100 percent sure there are external causes, it seems to me likely that there are.

In the interest of modesty, I leave wide open what in particular might be external to my mind. Certainly, not every quality within my visual field must be "out there." For example, my visual scene depicts angled shelf lines from my point of view. Perhaps I can use reason to surmise that, probably, lines in the structure of an external shelf are parallel (if they exist external to my consciousness), not angled. This hypothesis can explain the angled lines I see from my point of view. I don't have firm convictions about these details, however, as they go beyond my direct sight.

The big point is that awareness is a window into contents of actual reality, whether internal or external. By awareness, you can see many things: logical relations, thoughts, feelings, sensations, the contents of a visual field, and so on. These things are real. You may not always see external things as they are (since you may only see a representation), but you do at least see some things directly through the window of your direct awareness, whether internal or external.

WHAT CAN SEE?

Your power to see has profound implications concerning what you are. You can see. But how? By shinning the light of reason on our observations so far, I will highlight three implications of your power to see.

First, most fundamentally, you are the kind of reality, whatever it is, that can see. Not every kind of reality can see. Sand can't see. Wood can't see. Glass can't see. Numbers can't see. You can. So, you aren't sand, wood, glass, or numbers. By reason, we can deduce that, since you see, you are not something that cannot see. You are something else. (I will say something positive about what can see at the end of this section.)

Second, the contents of your sight are not exclusively mind-independent matter. To illustrate, suppose you see a faint, blurry image while you are dreaming. What is this image? Whatever it is, the image is not literally floating in your brain somewhere. If the building blocks of your brain are fundamentally mindless bits of reality, like swirling particles, then those bits are not faint or blurry, nor is an arrangement or composition of them faint or blurry. The contents of visual perception (images) occur in first-person experiences, not in exclusively third-person matter. Faint or blurry images, then, are contents of mental experience, not mindless matter.

To be clear, material bits may form a screen that looks faint and blurry to someone. For example, you might experience a blurry image. But that isn't because bits of your brain are themselves blurry or faint. The blurriness is in your experience of the screen, not in the screen itself.

My second observation, then, is that there is more to perception than is characterized by a purely third-person characterization of matter. This observation reinforces the results of the previous two chapters: just as feelings and thoughts are not fully characterized in terms of third-person material aspects, so too your perceptual experiences also have aspects (e.g., blurry contents) that aren't in a purely third-person description of brain matter.

Third, the power to see depends on a mind. On my minimal definition of "mind," a mind has contents of consciousness. Perception is itself a content of consciousness, which involves the organization of perceptual contents (within consciousness) into a first-person perspective. So, on my minimal definition, perception depends on a mind.

To illustrate how a mind can enable perception, suppose you perceive a red ball. According to the window theory of perception, perception is a window into reality: you perceive reality by having an experience of (acquaintance with) contents of consciousness (thoughts, feelings, visual images, etc.). So, if you perceive a red ball, then this perception consists of acquaintance with aspects of the ball within the contents of your consciousness.

A mind is also foundational to the perspectival aspect of perception. When you see, you see *from your perspective*. Unlike third-person, perspectiveless states of mindless matter, a mind organizes the things you see into a first-person perspective.

I want to be clear here that I am not talking about merely *functioning* as if you see. When I say that sight requires a mind, I don't mean that a mind is required to simulate a robot that acts aware. I mean that a mind is required to have real, first-person conscious awareness of things from a perspective.

This result—that seeing involves a first-person perspective—highlights the fundamental problem of explaining consciousness in general. Perception is a type of consciousness, which involves conscious awareness. By my analysis, conscious awareness requires, at minimum, the power of a mind—to organize an experience into a perspective. If that is right, then a sandstorm will not—and cannot—produce conscious awareness unless the sand somehow first produces a mind to organize consciousness into a perspective. Mind is the material from which conscious awareness can emerge. So, the challenge of explaining conscious awareness is part of the more fundamental challenge of explaining the emergence of any minds.

To review, I believe you can see three significant things about your power to see. First, you are the kind of thing that has this power to see; not just anything can see. Second, your sight is not fully describable in terms of third-person, mindless aspects of matter. Third, seeing requires a mind—that is, something that can organize your experiences into a perspective. (If you are wondering what it takes to make a mind, hold on: we will be digging deeper into the nature and basis of minds as we continue our journey.)

PAINTING THE WORLD WITH MIND

We have examined the problem with explaining how we can perceive the world. I offered an *epistemic* solution (about how to know reality): we know reality by looking through the window of conscious awareness to see directly real aspects of things, whether internal to us or external. But there remains a *metaphysical* problem (about the nature of reality): in particular, what accounts for the unification between what we see internally and what we presumably see externally?

Hoffman's work on the science of perception invites me to consider an intriguing diagnosis. The problem, according to Hoffman, is with supposing that the reality one perceives consists of a fundamentally mindless, perspective-less ontology. This supposition (rooted in the mindlessness frame) is precisely what leads Hoffman to suggest that we do not see things as they are. In the end, he flips things and proposes this: if reality is *not* fundamentally mindless, then we can see things as they are—for then we can then see contents of consciousness as they are within us. According to this diagnosis, mentality not only enables us to see through the window of perception (by organizing our awareness into a first-person perspective), but there is also a sense in which mentality enters the scenes we see through the window (as contents of consciousness).

The idea that mentality enters reality has its fullest expression in the view called "idealism." While idealism has various connotations, the core idea is this: all reality is fundamentally mental. Or, to use a metaphor, mental reality paints all reality from top to bottom.

My purpose here is not to make a case for or against idealism. Rather, I want to highlight the explanatory power of mental resources. Mind provides special resources to explain how any reality ever comes to consciously see another reality.

To see the resourcefulness of mental reality, suppose mentality paints reality. By this, I mean that contents of consciousness are real contents of real things. Then we can explain two aspects of perception: (i) the reality of conscious awareness, and (ii) the contents of conscious awareness.

Regarding (i), mental reality is the right kind of reality to give rise to conscious awareness. For conscious awareness emerges in the context of a mind, which can organize perceptual experiences into a first-person perspective.

Regarding (ii), mental reality can explain the match between contents of consciousness and the reality we perceive. For if mental reality enters into the scenes we see, then the objects we see through the window of perception can have aspects that are identical to aspects we see in the contents of perceptual experience (e.g., shapes, colors, structure). In other words, we can explain the match: there is a common kind of reality in our own experiences that matches "outer" mental reality, which can exist independent from our perception of it. This match between inner conscious experience and outer reality makes sense if inner conscious experience and outer reality consist of the same type of reality—mental.

Indeed, the paradigm cases of things we see in consciousness are mind-dependent. For example, we can consciously see what Johnston calls scenes, which include shapes, colors, sounds, and so on.[14] In dreams, these scenes are mind-dependent. When awake, the scenes include the same kind of contents: shapes, colors, sounds, and so on. Why? The most parsimonious answer is that all scenes, internal and external, depend on a mental realm, whether your own or a mental realm outside.

We can package these considerations into an argument for the mental nature of reality:

1. Any contents you see "out there" are the same in kind as contents you see in consciousness, even while you dream (imagery, color, extension, a feeling of solidity, etc.).

2. Contents of consciousness are mental in kind (i.e., contents of a field of awareness).

3. Therefore, the contents "out there" are mental in kind (in a wider field of awareness).

I am not suggesting that these considerations lead inescapably to an idealist vision of the world. But these considerations do highlight the role of mind in perception. Mental reality can do things that mindless reality cannot. Whether mental reality paints all reality or some smaller portion, mental reality is an essential key to unlock your power to see.

SUMMARY

Your power to see reveals special things about you and the nature of reality. In this chapter, I sought to bring to light a clearer vision of your nature by seeking a solution to the classic problem of perception.

The classic problem of perception is about how to get outside our heads to see the world. How do the contents of conscious experience (e.g., visual images) relate to things in an external reality? Is it possible to see anything external to our own consciousness?

---

[14]Johnston, "Obscure Object of Hallucination," 113-83.

To see how you can see, I surveyed the main theories of perception, which divide into two types. One type analyzes perceptual experience as a window into elements of reality, while the other type analyzes perceptual experience as painting of a conscious scene on the wall of your mind. I identified problems with both types of theories.

To review the problems, consider first the window theory of perception. According to this theory, a perceptual experience involves real sight of real things. This theory faces the distinguishability problem: how can the contents of a dream experience be distinguished from the contents of a perceptual experience while you are awake? Suppose your experience of the sun while awake is a window to a real sun. Then is your experience of the sun while dreaming also a window into a real sun? If not, how can the contents of the one experience be distinguished from the contents of the other? An answer is not obvious.

Turn, then, to the painting theory: what you see is not external reality, but the painting of consciousness within your own mind. While window theories face the problem of letting in too much sight, painting theories face the problem of shutting down sight altogether. The painting theory cuts us off from external reality. All we see are interior paintings in our mind. Thus, while you may see reality in a certain way (per the adverbial theory), you never actually see anything as it is. In the extreme case, you don't even see your own contents of consciousness as they are. But if you never see things as they are, how can you say anything about anything (whether about the contents of your dreams or about the outer world)? An answer is not obvious.

Enter representationalism: maybe internal conscious experiences somehow represent outer realities. Then perhaps you see external reality by seeing internal representations.

The representational solution, however, covers the problem with a word: *representation*. What is representation? Suppose we only ever see mental paint in our minds but never what the mental paint represents. Then we could never compare the mental painting with its representation to know whether it is an accurate representation. So, how can we know anything we see in our minds accurately represents anything external to our minds? An answer is not obvious.

I propose that we can solve the problem of perception by turning on the light of introspection. By introspection, we can directly see our own sight in perceptual experiences. By seeing this sight, we can see how we see.

Introspection illuminates a theory that combines elements of the window and painting theories of perception. Perception is a window: whether you are awake or dreaming, a perceptual experience is a window into scenes. But perception also includes mental paintings: when you are dreaming, the scenes you see are mental paintings within you. In the case of a dream, the paintings in your mind depend on your mind uniquely, not external realities. When you are awake, you also see scenes (mental paintings), except these scenes can include qualities that are also part of an external scene, which isn't entirely dependent on your mind. An external scene, then, doesn't depend on your mind uniquely, but is sharable with other minds. Thus, through the window of conscious awareness, you can see the world, internal and external.

This analysis invites us to consider how conscious awareness arises in the first place. Not just any material has the capacity for awareness. Rocks don't. You do. What's makes the difference? At minimum, I propose this requirement: the material that can make awareness must have the power of a conscious mind. This proposal points to a key aspect of reality: reality has mentality. We will further examine the nature of a mind and how deep mentality might seep into reality as we continue in the steps ahead.

■   ■   ■

The tunnel opens into a large room. It appears to be a dead end. Slightly disappointed, you wander around the edges to see if there is anything else that catches your interest. You notice that, in contrast to the smooth walls of stone in the rest of the cave, the back wall is composed of dense, fine dirt. Near the bottom of the wall, you see what appear to be letters inscribed into the dirt: M-I-N-D-L-E-S-S. Although the inscription is intriguing, without anywhere else to explore, you consider turning back. Just as you form the intention to leave, you hear a small pebble *clack-clack-clacking* against the cave wall. You then see streams of fine dirt cascading down the wall, and you step back. Suddenly, a thick layer of dirt and rock crumbles and falls to the ground. After the dust settles, you notice something strange about the pebbles that have rolled just in front of your feet. With your lantern, you inspect the pebbles on the ground before you. You look just as the final pebble rests in its place in a grand arrangement of pebbles that display a message. The message reads,

YOU ARE NOT WHAT YOU SEE.

5

YOUR WILL

There are no purposes in nature; physics has ruled them out.

ALEX ROSENBERG

IN THIS CHAPTER, I will explore another quality in consciousness: your power to willfully make choices. To appreciate this power, I will begin by presenting a classic "free will" puzzle. This puzzle exposes a problem with constructing anything that is not a mere puppet—with particles pulling the strings. I will then collect observations to help us solve this puzzle. These observations will light the way to a treasure box. Inside this box is a special material that makes choices possible. By seeing this material, we will be equipped to address the guiding question of this chapter: What sort of "material" could make a choice? An answer to this question will bring to light something special about who you are.

THE PROBLEM OF FREE WILL

I begin with a classic "free will" puzzle. This puzzle has two pieces. The first piece encodes the premise that people can make choices. The second piece encodes the premise that everything people do is determined by the motions of particles beyond their control. The challenge is to see how these pieces can go together if at all. Thinking about this puzzle will help me identify certain constraints on what it takes for something to have a power to choose.

To set up the puzzle, suppose you see a wooden puppet on a table. You have an assignment: give this puppet the power to choose. How might you do that?

Immediately, there is a problem: no matter what you do, the puppet's behaviors will be determined by the behaviors of other things. For example, suppose you attach strings to move the puppet. Then the puppet's actions are determined by the actions of someone pulling its strings. Or suppose instead you install a computer system that controls the puppet's head. Then the puppet will be controlled from within: the circuits inside the machine pull the strings. Either way, whether the puppet is moved by strings on the outside or electric currents inside, the puppet doesn't *itself* control any of its parts. It's the other way: the parts control the puppet. The challenge, then, is to see how it would be possible, in principle, to give a puppet real power to choose its behavior.

This challenge of giving a puppet the power to choose points to a general question. How does anything have a power to choose? If particles are the puppet masters, then we are the puppets. The particles pull the strings on all our behavior. How, then, can we be free? Are we not mere puppets of the particles?

We can express this "puppet" challenge in the form of an argument against the existence of free will:

1. If you have free will, then (by definition) you are not a puppet of things outside your control (e.g., particles).

2. You are a puppet of things outside your control (the particles).

3. Therefore, you do not have free will.

Premise (2) is the puppet premise: you are a mere puppet of things beyond your control. Some philosophers have supported the puppet premise in terms of a deterministic picture of reality. According to determinism, every event is completely determined by prior events, like a sequence of dominoes that can only topple one way. In that case, you cannot choose between alternative paths because there is no alternative path; reality has only one possible path. If there is only one possible path, then nothing can control which way reality goes. The problem here is that part of the concept of control includes the ability to control which way things go. So, if reality is completely determined, then it can be hard to see how anything (or anyone) could have control over anything. In other words, if there is only one path, then you are a puppet forced down that path.

But the problem is deeper: even if reality is not forced down a single path, there is still a reason to think you would be a puppet. For suppose that reality permits alternative paths (per indeterminism). Then, instead of a single path, there are forks in the path of the unfolding reality. The problem now is in understanding how you could possibly control which path you happen take. Any path you take is a product of undetermined events, such as a brain event involving an axon firing in a certain way. But an undetermined event is *random*, one might think, precisely because nothing determines it. To control a random event is like controlling whether lightning randomly strikes a street sign, or whether an electrical current in a brain randomly stops. You don't control random, undetermined events. Therefore, if indeterminism is true, then you still do not have control over your actions; you are a puppet of random events.

We can put these ideas together to form the following "no control" argument for the puppet premise:

1. You can't control events that are already determined.
2. You can't control events that are not determined (because they are random).
3. Therefore, you can't control any events (determined or undetermined).
4. Therefore, you are a puppet (i.e., you can't control any events).

The puppet argument brings to light a general challenge. The challenge is to see how to turn any materials into something that has the power to choose. If it is difficult to see how to transform a wooden puppet on a table into a real being who can make real choices, it is no less difficult to see how to transform any other materials into a being who can make real choices. The fundamental problem is this: if prior materials pull the strings on our behavior, then we don't have any real control over our behavior; we are mere puppets.

To draw out the problem a bit further, consider the behavior of a brain. A brain's behavior is determined by the behavior of more fundamental things, like particles. So, suppose particles pull the strings on the brain's behavior. Then the brain is a puppet of particles. It makes no difference whether particles operate deterministically or nondeterministically. Either way, the brain does not "decide" the micro-motions of particles. Instead, the particles move according to physical laws, which brains cannot change. So, particles are the masters of all brain activity. How, then, can a brain (or anyone with a brain) have any real control over any behaviors?

The problem here is general. Anything that has control over its behavior would, according to our concept of control, not be a mere puppet. But everything is a puppet of things outside its control (e.g., prior particles or laws). Therefore, nothing has control.

This argument challenges a common view of ourselves. If the argument is sound, then we don't have control over our behavior—and therefore don't have any power to choose. But is that true? A common view is that we have at least *some* power to choose. Is this view an illusion? Or can we escape the teeth of the no-control argument?

Reflecting carefully on these questions can unlock insight into the nature of the "material" required for choices to exist. The purpose of this chapter is to bring this insight into the light.

So, in this chapter, I will seek to offer a solution to the puppet problem. First, to get more data on the table, I will collect some observations about a common, ordinary concept of choice. Second, I will show how recent science and introspection together testify to a real power you have to willfully make choices (in line with this ordinary concept of choice). Third, I will have a closer look at the "no control" argument. I will show why I think this argument contains an insight, which reveals, not that you don't have any control, but that it takes a certain, special kind of being to have control. These results, if right, will shed additional light on the kind of being you are.

ELEMENTS OF FREEDOM

To give us more resources for thinking about the puzzle of free will, I will first seek to clarify a certain concept of free choice. In the section, I will highlight three aspects of this concept: (i) agency, (ii) intention, and (iii) options. The goal of this section is not to figure out whether we can actually make choices, but instead to get clearer on what making a choice would seem to require.

Agency. As usual, I will collect some relevant data using the light of introspection. I begin by shining this light on my own experience of trying to willfully do something. To generate this experience, right now I'm focusing on the experience of trying to willfully squint my eyes. Done. I just released the squint. Feel free to do the same. Focus on what it feels like to willfully squint. See if you notice any aspects of this experience.

When I focus on my feeling of willfully doing something, one thing I notice is that *I* seem to be involved. I felt *myself* squint my eyes. The sense that I am involved in a choice gives me a sense of agency: my act involves an *agent* who makes the act. Philosophers call this element of choice "the source condition." According to the source condition, when you willfully make a choice, you are a source (the agent) of your choice. Without you, the choice is not up to you. If the choice is not up to you, then it is not *your* choice. In other words, if you make a free choice, then, at minimum, you are involved.

The source condition was evident in an experience I had with my son, Micah. He was eight at the time. One day, while I was sitting on a couch, he tied my leg to a long string. Curious to see what he was about to do, I watched as he proceeded to pull the other end of the string to move my leg. As he was moving my leg, I asked him if I was *choosing* to move my leg. He said no. I asked him how he knew I wasn't choosing to move my leg.

He answered immediately, "Dad, I'm moving your leg, not you."

Micah's answer expresses the source condition. I was not moving my leg by choice. Therefore, the motion of my leg was not a product of my free choice. The source condition was missing. To freely move my leg, I would need to be the agent of my leg's motion.

To be clear, the source condition does not require that you are the *only* source of an action. An action could have many contributing sources. For example, Micah and I could move my leg together. And there could be many influences on an action. When Micah was moving my leg, I still had some power to resist. When I did resist, he wasn't the only source of my leg's motion. I was also involved.

So, the first aspect of a free choice I want to draw attention to is agency. There cannot be a free choice in the universe without an agent—someone who can make a choice.

Intention (goals). Another aspect of a choice is the intention behind it. For example, if I decide to squint my eyes, I form an intention, which directs the motion of my eyes. The concept of free choice I have in mind includes this intentional aspect: when I freely choose to do something, there is something I'm aiming at, such as to squint my eyes or to stop squinting.

To see why intention is different from mere agency, consider actions that are unintentional. For example, if someone taps your kneecap, you might feel yourself kick your leg upward. In that case, you may still be an agent of your action: you kicked your leg. But the action was not by your own intention. An agent that does something unintentionally does not have the same level of willful control—of free choice—as an agent that does things intentionally. Intentionality, then, is another aspect that contributes to the freedom of a choice.

Options. The third aspect I want to draw attention to is the sense of choosing between options. Sometimes I have the experience of selecting an option among other available alternatives. For example, I have had moments in conversations where I felt a choice between seeking to defend myself or instead seeking to enter the other person's perspective. Both options felt available to me. I then experienced choosing one of the options over the other. This example illustrates the experience of choosing between options.

Now to be clear, I am not yet arguing that you actually have options or any power to make any choices. Maybe the experience of making choices is an illusion. My task so far is merely to highlight the experience of having options as a way to highlight a certain *concept* of free choice. The concept exists, but it is a further question whether this concept applies to reality. I will address that question in the next section. Here I simply wish to highlight that there is a concept of freedom that implies options.

Social science provides additional evidence that the concept of options is included in a common concept of freedom. In one study, scientists found a link between believing in options and believing in free will.[1] Here is a synopsis. Participants read either a text that encouraged a belief that human behavior is predetermined by environmental and genetic factors (thereby

[1]K. Vohs and J. Schooler, "The Value of Believing in Free Will: Encouraging a Belief in Determinism Increases Cheating," *Psychological Science* (2008); cf. R. F. Baumeister et al., "Prosocial Benefits of Feeling Free: Disbelief in Free Will Increases Aggression and Reduces Helpfulness," *Personality and Social Psychology Bulletin* 35, no. 2 (2009): 260-68.

precluding alternative options), or they read a neutral text. The investigators found that the participants who read the deterministic message were more likely to report a lower belief in free will. This lack of confidence in the reality of free will also affected their actions, as they were more likely to cheat on a subsequent task. By contrast, those who read the neutral text, which did not call into question the reality of alternative options, were more likely to resist cheating and have a stronger belief in free will. This result is precisely what we would predict if options are part of a common concept of freedom.

As you may expect, there are different options for how to analyze "options." On a minimal, thin concept of options, options are a range of possibilities consistent with what one knows. For example, you have the option to raise your hands so long as you don't know about any factors that would prevent that. This thin concept allows for a *compatibilist* conception of free will, according to which freedom is compatible with determinism (that everything is determined). For even if reality determines that there is only one path, you might have no idea what that one path is. So, as far as everything you know, you have options available.

Here is a different account: on a thicker concept of "options," options require real possibilities, not just apparent possibilities. This thicker concept of options seems to be in play in the social science study mentioned above. For the participants' beliefs in free will were affected by whether they read passages challenging the reality of alternative possibilities.

My purpose here is not to enter the weeds of these debates between compatibilists and noncompatibilists about free will. For the sake of neutrality, I will instead speak in terms of different grades or degrees of freedom. Some grade of freedom requires options in at least the thin (compatibilist) sense, while a higher grade of freedom requires options in the thick (incompatibilistic) sense. The main results of this chapter—in particular, that it takes a special kind of being to be free—will apply to both grades of freedom.

We have seen enough about a common concept of choice to continue our journey. The next thing I want to consider is how one might verify the reality of choices.

HOW TO SEE YOUR POWER TO CHOOSE

So, do you have any real power to make choices? A lot is at stake. As I mentioned, studies indicate that your belief about whether you have a choice (or any free will) affects your behavior. For example, if you think you have a choice, you are more likely to help others. And, if you don't think you have a choice, you are less likely to resist pressure to cheat or treat others against their wishes.[2] So, if you can see your power to choose, that sight itself gives you power. But can you see your power to choose?

In this section, I want to show you how I think you can see at least some aspects of your power to choose. I will describe two methods of sight: (i) from direct experience and (ii) from a sense of personal responsibility. I will show how introspection can illuminate both aspects. Then I will examine a potential barrier to this sight from neuroscience.

Direct experience. I believe that introspection not only illuminates the concept of a choice but also its application to real experiences. By shining introspection on your experience of making choices, you can witness some aspects of the choice itself.

My proposal here builds on my analysis of perception (from the previous chapter). In that analysis, I made a case for the window theory of conscious awareness. According to the window theory, awareness is a window into contents of reality. You enjoy this awareness via various senses. For example, a visual sense is a window into shapes and colors. When I say that the sense is a window, I mean that the sense involves a direct acquaintance with contents of reality. Here I leave open whether these contents paint an external scene ("out there"), an internal scene within you, or both. Whatever the case, your senses put you in contact with something.

The window theory opens a realist analysis of your own sense of making choices. Suppose your senses are windows into reality. Then your sense of yourself making choices is itself a window into reality of yourself making a choice.

You might object: could the sense of making a choice be a mere illusion?

To answer this question, it will help to draw a distinction between the sense of something and the something that is sensed. To illustrate, when I

---

[2]Baumeister et al., "Value of Believing."

sense a feeling, I do not merely sense myself sensing a feeling; I sense the feeling itself. By sensing a feeling, I can discern aspects of the feeling (e.g., its intensity, positivity, quality). I witness these aspects directly. In the same way, I believe that by sensing an inner act of choosing, I can directly discern aspects involved in this act (e.g., my agency, intention, options). These aspects are not hidden behind the veil of my senses; they are direct objects of my senses—visible through a basic act of conscious awareness.

Now, you might still worry that the thing the sense is *of* isn't actually there. After all, maybe you can have a sense of something even if that thing doesn't exist. Isn't that what an illusion is?

I offer two responses for your consideration. First, even if an illusion is possible, it does not follow that an illusion is probable. On some level, it may be possible that everything is an illusion, including your sense that 2 + 2 = 4. But this possibility does not imply probability. On the contrary, the very fact that you sense something is at least some evidence for it, especially if you have no reason (via another sense) to doubt your sense. (Of course, the puzzle of free will can itself be a reason to distrust one's introspective sense of making choices. We will reexamine that puzzle soon.)

Second, I also have a bolder response. I think you have a power to remove even the *possibility* of error in certain cases. These are the cases of awareness of things directly in consciousness. For example, you can witness yourself intending to squint your eyes. You witness this intention directly, just as you can witness your own thoughts directly. When you witness something directly, there is no possibility of illusion.

Consider what it takes for there to be an illusion. An illusion by definition is an experience that fails to match (or represent) a reality outside one's immediate consciousness. But suppose the item in question (e.g., one's willful act of choosing) is within one's consciousness. Then that item cannot itself be an illusion. It is real: it really exists within one's consciousness. When you have direct, inner awareness of a dream image, for example, that image is real; it really exists within your consciousness. While the image may not match anything *outside* your consciousness, the image itself really exists.

In the same way, willful, intentional acts exist within consciousness. When you willfully direct your attention on a thought, for example, that act of attention is not wholly outside of you behind a veil. On the contrary, your willful act is something you can detect directly within your consciousness. In this respect, your choices are like your thoughts and feelings: you can see their reality right within you.

So, in response to the threat of illusion, I say that illusions are only possible when the item in one's consciousness fails to represent something outside one's consciousness. At least some aspects of your willful acts are not wholly outside your consciousness, however. Instead, you can witness yourself making choices directly within your own consciousness.

To test what I am proposing, I invite you to do a little experiment if you can. Direct your attention to your eyes. Now decide whether to squint your eyes. Make that decision now. Did you do it? Whether you decided to squint or not, you can now examine the aspects of your own experience. See whether your experience includes any of the aspects I identified earlier: agency, intention, and options (whether on the thin or thick notion). By the inner light of introspection, I believe you can witness these aspects directly. You can sense your own agency (yourself making the choice), your intention (to squint or to refrain), and your options (squinting or not). The sense of each aspect is an angle of awareness into your power to choose.

We can summarize this analysis as follows:

1. You can sense (by introspection) yourself making choices.

2. Senses are windows into reality.

3. Therefore, your sense of yourself making a choice is a window into the reality of yourself making a choice.

How to be responsible. A second light that shines on your power to choose comes via another sense—the sense of personal responsibility.

To avoid presumption, I will share how this sense seems to work within me from my perspective. First, on certain occasions, I notice that I have at least the *sense* that I am responsible for some things I do. For example, I sense that am responsible to seek to be honest in the things I share with you. Next, by reason, I also have the sense that I'm not responsible for things I have no control or choice over. When I combine these senses, I find myself with the following reason to think that some choices are real:

1. I sense I am responsible for at least some behavior.
2. I sense that no one is responsible for behavior they have no choice over.
3. My senses indicate aspects of reality (via the window theory of senses).
4. Therefore, my senses indicate that I have some choice over some behavior.

I invite you to consider your own senses from your perspective.

Once again, the analysis of perception supports the first two steps in the argument. Both steps depend on a sense of something—that I am responsible and that responsibility depends on choice. When the thing I am sensing is within consciousness, then—according to the window account of senses—the sense consists in a direct acquaintance with something within my consciousness. So, what I sense is real. By sensing my own responsibility and its dependence on my choices, I deduce the reality of my power to choose.

Neuroscience. Sometimes people suggest that neuroscience reveals that we don't have any real powers to choose. I have come to believe recent evidence indicates precisely the opposite. In this section, I'll briefly say why.

To begin, I realize some studies have been cited as calling into question our power to make choices. For example, a famous study by Libet raised some doubts about our power to choose.[3] This study indicates that unconscious brain activity precedes the feeling of making choices. One interpretation of Libet's study is that brain activity determines the subsequent brain states and so precludes (or deflates) free will.[4] On this interpretation, your sense of making choices does not correspond to real choices; the feeling of freedom is an illusion.

Subsequent studies, however, paint a different, more complex picture. Some studies suggest that contrary to a purely deterministic model of the brain, an indeterministic model may better fit the empirical data. Jedlicka makes a case from the emerging research in quantum biology for the

---

[3]B. Libet et al., "Time of Conscious Intention to Act in Relation to Onset of Cerebral Activities (Readiness-Potential): The Unconscious Initiation of a Freely Voluntary Act," *Brain* 106, no. 3 (1983): 623-42.
[4]See F. Crick, *The Astonishing Hypothesis: The Science Search for the Soul* (New York: Scribner's, 1994) and S. Harris, *Free Will* (New York: Free Press, 2012).

conclusion that brain activity may be significantly sensitive to quantum events, which are thought to be nondeterministic.[5]

Moreover, from my reading of a range of studies in this field, it appears to me that there is an increasing flood of evidence for the thesis that you can affect your brain by your conscious intentions.[6] For example, studies on mindfulness indicate that you have great power to affect your brain by how you think. According to these studies, when you choose to pay attention to your thoughts and feelings, you gain power to manage your thoughts and feelings. Many studies indicate that mind management affects your health in positive ways.[7] The results of these studies are surprising if our intentional acts actually have no effect on our brains. (If you are wondering how consciousness *could* affect brain states without violating microphysical laws, hold on to that question. I will examine how mind and body might be able to interact in the next chapter.)

Other, recent work in neuroscience amplify these results. For example, Lavazza cites evidence to suggest ways we can measure free will.[8] Lavazza points out that the apparent build-up of the brain activity preceding the sense of choice may reflect the ebb and flow of the background neuronal noise. According to Lavazza, this noise is consistent with an intuitive concept of free will. Lavazza proposes that we can even measure free will in terms of a capacity index related to neurological activity. This activity, says Lavazza, doesn't threaten free will but rather *indicates* it.

Even more recently, some models of brains explicitly build in the causal impact of consciousness. For example, McFadden provides a quantum

---

[5]P. Jedlicka, "Revisiting the Quantum Brain Hypothesis: Toward Quantum (Neuro)biology?" *Frontiers in Molecular Neuroscience* 7 (2017): https://doi.org/10.3389/fnmol.2017.00366.

[6]See J. Schwartz and S. Begley, *The Mind and the Brain: Neuroplasticity and the Power of Mental Force* (New York: Harper Collins, 2002); M. Beauregard, "Mind Does Really Matter: Evidence from Neuroimaging Studies of Emotional Self-Regulation, Psychotherapy and Placebo Effect," *Progress in Neurobiology* 81, no. 4 (2007): 218-36; and M. Beauregard and D. O'Leary, *The Spiritual Brain: A Neuroscientist's Case for the Existence of the Soul* (San Francisco: HarperOne, 2008).

[7]See N. Digdon and A. Koble, "Effects of Constructive Worry, Imagery Distraction, and Gratitude Interventions on Sleep Quality: A Pilot Trial," *Applied Psychology: Health and Well-Being* 3, no. 2 (2011): 193-206. For practical tips on how to apply the latest developments in neuroscience to brain improvement, see C. Leaf, *Cleaning Up Your Mental Mess: 5 Simple, Scientifically Proven Steps to Reduce Anxiety, Stress, and Toxic Thinking* (Grand Rapids, MI: Baker Books, 2021).

[8]A. Lavazza, "Free Will and Neuroscience: From Explaining Freedom Away to New Ways of Operationalizing and Measuring It," *Frontiers in Human Neuroscience* (2016): https://doi.org/10.3389/fnhum.2016.00262.

model that explains how consciousness can integrate information detected in an energy field.[9] Hiley and Pyklkkanen (2005) also provide a quantum model that explains how consciousness can affect brains within the boundaries of known physical laws.[10] According to their model, the differences you make to your brain may start small, but small differences can add up over time.

In addition to this neuroscientific evidence, there is also everyday evidence from predicting one's own behavior. For example, I can intend right now to count to ten in my mind. If I form this intention, I can then predict that, unless something stops me or I change my mind, there is high chance I will indeed count to ten. The match between my conscious intention and my future behavior is evidence that my conscious intention can make a difference to my behavior. (We will have a closer look at how this might work when we examine the mind-body connection in chapter seven, "Your Body.")

While interpretations of these scientific developments vary, I believe our previous observations via introspection give us an independent way to evaluate certain interpretations. By introspection, we can independently verify the impact of consciousness directly within us. We are not in the dark about things we can see within us. As I argued in the previous section, I believe we can witness our own powers to intend and to decide within our own consciousness. If so, then we can interpret neuroscience as indicating conscious activity from the outside (by scientific inference), while we can detect this activity from within (by direct acquaintance).

By witnessing conscious intentions from the inside, we can gain information that is relevant to neuroscientific models of the brain. Suppose introspection can indeed reveal the reality of the power to choose, and suppose choices cannot actually occur in a deterministic system (per the nondeterministic notion of options). Then by reason, we can infer that choices do not occur in a deterministic system. This result could be a gift to neuroscience: it provides a reason to expect that, insofar as choices operate

[9]J. McFadden, "Integrating Information in the Brain's EM Field: The Cemi Field Theory of Consciousness," *Neuroscience of Consciousness* 2020, no. 1 (2020): https://doi.org/10.1093/nc/niaa016.
[10]B. Hiley and P. Pyklkkanen, "Can Mind Affect Matter via Active Information?" *Mind and Matter* 3, no. 2 (2005): 8-27.

within the brain, the brain is not a deterministic system. If one can indeed see that choices include options, then one may anticipate that studies investigating nondeterministic models of the brain will continue to bear fruit—because they are on the track of truth illuminated by another light.

As a final note, I want to share with you some reflections on the effects of my own conscious intentions. To investigate my powers, I have performed consciousness experiments in dreams. In one case, I had a dream in which I saw a blue sky. I knew I was dreaming. This knowledge inspired me to try to change the dream. So, I tried to conjure up a ball. Soon, a round image began to appear in front of the imagery of the blue sky. I then directed the round image to roll off to the right of my dream imagery. I saw the ball image begin rotating to the right. I predicted that at its rate of motion, it would exit my field of consciousness in about four seconds. I counted. Sure enough, after four seconds, it rolled out of view.

Amazingly, I was able to direct the image and accurately predict its motions without ever looking into my brain at all. I did not consult neuroscience, calculate the trajectory of particles, or check to see if the physical laws would permit my dream imagery to follow the path I determined. Instead, I collected my data by *direct awareness*. The lesson I draw is this: we don't need to wait for neuroscientists to tell us which model of the brain is correct (whether deterministic or indeterministic) for us to *directly witness* some effects of conscious intentions within us. The light of introspection is bright enough.

From my observations, then, the evidence I've seen does not reveal that intentions make no difference or that we cannot willfully do anything. It is the opposite: neuroscience points, from the outside, to a great power of the intentions you witness from the inside. By seeing this power, you can see the power you have to change structures of reality by your own conscious choices.

This analysis is just a beginning. If you continue to inspect your powers, I predict you will discover more of your powers from more angles.

HOW TO MAKE A CHOICE

We are now ready to return to the guiding question of this chapter: What sort of material could willfully make choices? So far, I have argued that you have a power to make choices; you can see this power within. But how can any material have that power? To address this question, I return to the puzzle of free will.

Recall the pieces of the puzzle:

1. You can't control events that are already determined.
2. You can't control events that are not determined (because they are random).
3. Therefore, you can't control any events (determined or undetermined).
4. Therefore, you are a puppet (i.e., you can't control any events).

This puzzle is what Bailey and I call "the puppet puzzle."[11]

I will now offer a solution to the puppet puzzle. My solution involves identifying a key assumption that generates the puzzle. The assumption is this: mindless reality pulls all the strings. This assumption is part of the mindlessness frame. According to the mindlessness frame, mindless bits of reality determine everything, including everything about you. I believe this assumption—that the mindless bits determine everything—generates the puppet puzzle. To solve the puzzle, then, I suggest that we flip the frame: you are not a puppet of mindless bits. Instead, you are a fundamentally mental reality.

I will unpack this "mind-first" solution. First, I will say more about how I think mindless bits would make you a mere puppet. Then I will explain how I think a mental reality can set you free.

How mindless bits make you a puppet. To illustrate the problem with mindless string-pullers, imagine a snowball is rolling down a hill. This snowball is rolling toward a turtle. The snowball does not have the power to choose whether to roll on top of the turtle. The snowball is a mere puppet of the forces of physics. For this reason, it has no power to choose.

Now to help us think about what it takes to have a power to choose, I want to examine a few candidate explanations.

First, maybe the snowball is a mere puppet because it is unconscious. If it is unconscious, then it cannot make a conscious decision. So, perhaps the missing ingredient is *consciousness*.

---

[11]A. Bailey and J. Rasmussen, "A New Puppet Puzzle," *Philosophical Explorations* 23, no. 3 (2020): 202-13.

But consciousness is not enough. For imagine that the snowball began to consciously think, "Who am I? Where am I going?" These thoughts give the snowball no power to stop it from rolling along its path. Its path of motion is still controlled by more fundamental things—physical laws and atoms—which are beyond its control.

Let's add, then, not merely that the snowball is conscious, but that it has a certain type of consciousness. In particular, suppose the molecular structure of the snow generates in the snowball a passionate desire to change course. Would the snowball then have the power to choose?

No. For the snowball's course is still determined by molecular activities outside the snowball's control. Whether the snowball wants to roll over the turtle or wants to stop rolling, the snowball cannot help rolling. So, the snowball is still a puppet of things beyond its control (and beyond its knowledge).

Would it help if the laws of physics allowed for alternative possibilities? It would not: even if the snowball is ultimately composed of nondeterministic quantum events, still, those events are not under the control of a snowball itself. The snowball rolls down the hill because more basic bits (atoms) determine its motions. Even if the basic bits themselves could "choose" between alternative possibilities, the ball of snow itself is a slave to these more basic bits.

The deep problem is this: the snowball has no control over its own actions. It is instead controlled by other, more basic bits of reality. For this reason, the snowball is a "puppet."

How to be free. To have real control, something must have some power to pull its own strings. For example, if the snowball could control whether it rolls onto the turtle, the snowball could then pull its own strings. It could decide for itself. Then, instead of more basic bits pulling all the strings, the snowball itself could alter its behavior.

Here, then, is what I think it would take for the snowball to be free. The snowball must acquire some power to affect its own parts. Philosophers call this power "top-down causal power." Top-down power is the power of a complex thing to acts on its parts without being determined by its parts to do so. For example, suppose a snowball decides to cause its snowflakes to melt. Then that snowball exercises top-down (from whole to parts) power over its parts.

Note that top-down causation makes sense only if the agent is at the top. By being at the top, the agent is able to be the source of its choice. It's not that the agent does what it does solely because its parts do what they do. The power goes the other way: some parts do what they do because the agent, itself, does what it does.

The picture I'm presenting here flips the mindlessness frame. Instead of the mindless bits (e.g., particles) being the basic actors, an agent with a mind is itself basic actor. In other words, a mental reality can itself pull some strings.

By flipping the mindlessness frame, we can solve the puppet puzzle. Instead of mindless controllers pulling all the strings, a conscious agent can itself pull some of its own strings. The agent pulls a string by forming an intention (within its mind) to do something among perceived options. This formation of the intention can then be a product of the *agent* (per the source condition), not mindless string-pullers.

A mental context, then, makes a difference because a mind is something that can have contents of consciousness. The aspects of free will I have identified (agency, intention, and option) are recognized in contents of consciousness. So, a mind is the recognizable context in which the aspects of free will occur. While we might speculate that free will could emerge without any mind, this speculation leaps beyond what we know and, as we have seen, lands right into the puppet puzzle. A mind provides better resources for solving this puzzle.

While mysteries remain, I hope you can see how mental resources can help. My goal here has not been to resolve every mystery about free will. Instead, I have sought to shed some light on a classic puzzle by showing how the mindlessness frame constrains our options. The mindlessness frame is a source of the puppet puzzle. We can solve that puzzle by flipping things around: instead of supposing that mindless bits pull the strings, we can recognize our ourselves (beings with minds) as string-pullers. Then we are not mere puppets.

Mindful matter. At this point, some readers may wonder how my account of choice-making "material" fits into a world made of matter. If choice-making "material" is indeed fundamentally mental, how, then, can we be fundamentally *material*?

My answer depends on what is meant by "material." If by "material" we mean something that is fully characterizable in terms of third-person properties expressible in the vocabulary of physics (shape, size, extension, mass, etc.), then I say that the power to choose is not analyzable in terms of material reality alone. For I think one can compare the first-person aspects of conscious choices with purely third-person aspects of neurological states. By this comparison, one can see some distinctions directly. For example, one can see the intention behind a choice is not the same as the shape or structure of a neuron.

Moreover, the puppet argument exposes a problem with the hypothesis that third-person material aspects of brains can, all by themselves, fully ground or determine free choices. For suppose third-person, material states of matter are not themselves first-person mental states. Then they are mindless. Suppose, furthermore, that these mindless states determine all your mental states. Then your conscious "choices" would be byproducts of mindless states. In the previous section, I argued that choices do not emerge in a mindless context alone. As a corollary, it follows that choices do not spring up primarily and fundamentally in mindless matter.

Now my goal here is not to argue that matter has nothing to do with your powers. On the contrary, I want to highlight another option: instead of thinking of matter as fundamentally *mindless*, perhaps some matter can be fundamentally mental. This matter is special. It is mindful.[12] Mindful matter is not entirely pulled along by the strings of more basic mindless bits. Instead, mindful matter is itself a string-puller. If some matter is mindful, then this matter could have the power to make choices.

In the interest of neutrality and modesty (and to avoid unnecessary dialectical distractions), I propose at this point in our journey this minimal thesis: if choices are real, they emerge in the context of a conscious mind. A conscious mind can include its own "string-pulling" power to make real

---

[12]The postulation of mindful matter is compatible with broadly materialist accounts of human persons. See P. van Inwagen, *Material Beings* (Ithaca, NY: Cornell University Press, 1990); T. Merricks, *Objects and Persons* (Oxford: Oxford University Press, 2001); and A. Bailey, *Monotheism and Human Nature* (Cambridge: Cambridge University Press, 2021).

changes to the world. So, whether matter is mindless or mindful, the material that can make choices is the material of a mind. (A fuller picture of the nature a mind will continue to emerge as we continue along our journey.)

SUMMARY

You can witness aspects of your will by your inner awareness of three intuitive elements of freedom. First, you can be aware of yourself, an agent, making choices. Second, you can be aware of your intention when you chose something. Third, you can be aware of yourself choosing something among alternative options.

It is puzzling, however, how anything could have a power to choose. There are two options to consider: (i) either everything is determined (determinism), or (ii) some things are not determined. Both options pose a problem. On determinism, you don't have control over which path to choose, since there is only one possible path. The other option adds undetermined events, but it is not immediately obvious how undetermined events help: if an event is not determined by anything, not even you, then it is unclear how you could have control over that event.

We can pull out the root of this puzzle by digging deeper into the soil of reality. The root of the puzzle, I believe, is in the mindlessness frame. According to the mindlessness frame, mindless bits determine all reality. If that's true, then mindless bits pull all strings on your behavior, and you are a puppet of their power. You are a puppet in two ways: (i) your behavior is completely controlled by things you have no control over, and (ii) you are controlled by things you have no awareness of. When mindless stuff is in control over everything, you are in control of nothing. So, you are a puppet.

To solve the puppet puzzle, we need to make room for the agent: you, an agent, must be able to have some say over your choice. If you can make your own choice, then you are a string-puller.

Here is how I think you can pull some strings. Don't start with mindlessness. Choices are not controlled by mindlessness. Instead, flip the mindlessness frame. A mind is the material in which choices can emerge. Unlike a snowball rolling down a hill, a mind is not a puppet of the motions of mindless matter. So, if a mind is present, then the motions of matter can be affected from the "top-down" (macro-to-micro) by conscious intentions, or from deeper in.

The latest neuroscience provides a second witness to this result. Empirical studies indicate that you have the power to create neural pathways in your brain by directing your mind and attention. By the power of your intentions, you make real differences to the material world, including in your brain. When you take charge over your mind, you take charge over your inner world (through gratitude, mindfulness, and intentional thinking). Taking charge over your inner world has ripple effects, through your brain and body, into your outer world.

From these considerations, I arrive at the following conclusion: your power to choose is in your hands, not in the hands of mindless matter.

■   ■   ■

You look again at the dirt wall in front of you. You see that the inscription, to your surprise, is still there. The word *mindless* stares back at you, as if presenting you with a challenge. There must be more to this wall, you think. As you hold your lantern up to inspect the wall, you notice a crevice. You slide your finger along it. As you feel the cold dirt under your finger, the dirt begins to crumble. Suddenly, the wall crackles, and another layer of dirt slides down and off the wall. You see to your astonishment another strange sight. Out of this dirt, pebbles roll into the arrangement of a new message. You place your lantern over the message. It reads clearly:

YOU ARE NOT YOUR CHOICES.

6

YOUR VALUE

*One who makes himself a worm cannot complain
afterwards if people step on him.*

IMMANUEL KANT

WE HAVE BEEN WORKING to uncover the nature of a personal being. While we still have a way to go, we have accomplished much already. We have identified a series of qualities within consciousness: feelings, thoughts, sight, and the power to choose. None of these paints the full picture, but each quality fills in something special about you.

In this chapter, I want to continue to bring into view a picture of your nature. I will highlight another quality that characterizes your nature: *value*. I want to show how value also fills in something special about you.

I also want to highlight a pattern that has been emerging in the picture of your nature. The pattern is this: each quality we have considered (feelings, thoughts, sight, and will) depends on the presence of a being with a mind. A mind provides the canvas on which contents of consciousness can organize into a first-person, subjective experience. In this chapter, I aim to show that the pattern continues: value is also a quality that depends on a mental reality. By displaying this pattern, I hope to bring into greater light the kind of reality that could have your value.

Let us have a closer look, then, at the value of a being like you.

ASPECTS OF VALUE

As usual, I will begin by collecting observations using introspection and reason. By these lights, I hope to illuminate three aspects of your value:

intrinsic, immense, and unique. I want to show how these aspects point to your great and unshakable value as a personal being.

Intrinsic value. I begin with intrinsic value. The intrinsic value of something is a positive aspect something has because of *what it is*, not because of its relation to something else.

To illustrate what I mean, consider a peaceful feeling. A peaceful feeling has a certain positive aspect. The positivity of peace is what makes it desirable: you desire to feel peace because you sense its positive aspect. The positivity intrinsic to peace is an example of something that I mean by "intrinsic value." (For the sake of neutrality and modesty, I leave open whether positivity can have a further analysis. For example, one might theorize that certain things, like love or happiness, are positive because they are what conscious beings can like for their own sake.)

We can further elucidate the concept of intrinsic value by contrasting it with *extrinsic value*. Something has extrinsic value if its value is derived from its relation to other things. A sandwich, for example, has extrinsic value. A sandwich is valuable in relation to someone who is hungry. For a sandwich has the power to give someone a positive feeling, which itself has intrinsic value. In general, things are extrinsically valuable in virtue of their relation to something that has intrinsic value.

Note that intrinsic value does not necessarily preclude disvalue. Something could have *both* positive and negative aspects. For example, if someone feels peace after forgetting about a prior commitment, their peaceful feeling might contribute to a broken promise. In this case, the peaceful feeling would have both a positive aspect (of feeling positive) and a negative aspect (of contributing to a broken promise).

I am now ready to consider the question for this section: Do you have any value? I want to share a reason I think you have some value as a person. This value is intrinsic to you. My reason is based, first, on a direct sense of my own value as a person. As a person, I have a power to think, feel, and make decisions. (My observations in the chapters on thoughts, feelings, and choices support my belief that I have thoughts, feelings, and choices.) It seems to me that these are *positive* qualities, which explains why I like them. Anything that has positive qualities has value (by my definition). So, I have value. I assume you are like me: you are a personal being too. So, I infer that you also have value as a personal being.

My reasoning here is rooted in my analysis of the aspects I think one can see by introspection. To see your value, look within. See if you sense anything positive—anything valuable—about yourself. Do you sense that you have value as a person? If so, then you sense some value in yourself.

At this point, you might wonder whether the sense of value detects real value. Could the sense of value be a mere illusion, like the sense of a tree in a dream? To answer this question, I appeal to the window theory of senses. Recall that according to the window theory, a sense is a window into portions of reality (shapes, colors, thoughts, feelings, intentions, etc.). By looking through the window of a sense, you don't just see the window itself; you also see something through the window (by direct acquaintance).

To be clear, some of the things you see may be representations that fail to match up with an *outer* reality (hence, the possibility of an illusion). Still, even a representation includes contents of reality within consciousness. These contents are themselves bits of reality. For example, the contents of a visual image in your consciousness are themselves bits of reality (irrespective of whether the image also happens to represent something external to your consciousness). So, if you can indeed sense some positive aspects within consciousness, then the positivity you sense is not a mere representation of something else (like gray neurons). Instead, the sense of positivity in consciousness is a window into a real positive aspect.

We are stepping along a narrow path. To increase the light on our feet, I will offer a few clarifications. These clarifications may help remove certain barriers to seeing the value you have right within you.

First, your value as a person is not the same as the value of your experiences. You can be sad, for example, and still a valuable person. The distinction between the value of a person and the value of their experiences is manifest in acts of compassion. When you show someone compassion, you effectively highlight their value as a person even while they are having negative experiences. There is a difference, then, between the value of a person and the value of their experiences.

Second, the intrinsic value of a person does not depend on a relation to other people's preferences or desires. Suppose everyone hated you. Still, if you have intrinsic value, then their hate would be misguided: the proper object of hate is harmful behaviors, not intrinsically valuable beings. So, if your value is indeed intrinsic to you, then your value is not rooted in anyone's preference, but in your nature as a person.

A final and key clarification: your value doesn't depend on your own sense of it. While you can sense your value within consciousness, you do not need to. In this respect, your value is like your head: just as you can have a head without consciously sensing your head, you can have value without consciously sensing your value. The *sense of value* is not the same as the *value sensed*.

This distinction between the sense of value and the value sensed is a key to unlock your window to seeing your value most clearly. To draw out the distinction, suppose you sense your own value. That sense itself has a positive aspect; it feels good. Still, the positive aspect of your sense of value is not the same as the value your sense of value senses.

To hammer down this point, consider again the value of a peaceful feeling. You sense this value by sensing a positive aspect of feeling peace. Now turn your attention to your sense of positivity. This sense of positivity also has its own positivity. It has its own value. But here is the crucial point: the positive aspect of your sense of peace is not the same as the positive aspect of the peaceful feeling itself. Again, the value a sense *has* is not the same as the value the sense is *of*.

It is easy to miss this distinction because value can also be in the sense of value. When you sense your value, you might notice the value in the sense itself. If value is in the sense, how can value be in you? Careful analytical surgery exposes my answer: the value in the sense is also in the thing you sense. It's in both. Again, while a sense of value may *have* its own value (its own positive aspect), the sense of value is also *of* value. So, while the sense of your value may have its own value, it is also of your own value.

My proposal, then, is this: you can sense some value within you. You sense your value by sensing a positive aspect of yourself as a personal being (something that can think, feel, and choose). This positive aspect is a bit of value, which is intrinsic to you.

I hope these clarifications help clear the way to seeing an aspect of your value within you. If you still have objections, hold on to them. Later in this chapter, I will address some common objections that can block one's sight of one's value (or block one from believing what one sees).

Immense value. You not only have value, but you also have a *lot* of value. How much? Well, to answer that question, I will compare the value of a personal being with the value of other things. I will argue that personal beings are the most valuable kinds of things.

To help us think about the value of personal beings, consider the following scenario. Suppose a guy named Black wants to kill some anonymous, peaceful person, Smith. Black wants to kill Smith to take his land. But Black would rather not kill Smith himself. So, he approaches an old friend, Jones.

Black asks Jones, "What will it take to motivate you to kill Smith?"

Jones answers, "I will kill Smith if you give me something that has more intrinsic value than Smith."

Jones' answer invites the question: Is there some object Black could offer that would actually be worth killing someone for?

When I think about this question, I find it hard to think of anything that would be worth killing someone for. If there are exceptions, those exceptions themselves revolve around other personal or conscious beings. For example, if killing someone were the only way to save the lives of other people, then maybe it could be worth it. But if I restrict the scope of my comparison to nonpeople (gold watches, mansions, a Corvette Stingray, etc.), then, by a direct sense of value, it is evident to me that no nonperson has the intrinsic value of a person.

In fact, as far as I can tell, everything of value revolves around personal or conscious beings in some way. Suppose you see a beautiful painting. Even if the beauty of the painting has some intrinsic value (per aesthetic realism), still, it also has value in relation to your appreciation. After all, if no one could possibly enjoy the painting, the painting would not be worth as much. Similarly, while all the houses in the world may add up to some great value, it seems to me their greatest value derives from their service to people. Without people, I am not sure there could be anything of any value. At least, when comparing people with unconscious, material objects, it is evident to me that people have the greater value every time.

People also have a value that is beyond the value of their experiences. To illustrate why I think this, suppose (contrary to what I think is possible) there could be feelings of happiness sprinkled across a sandy beach even while there are no conscious beings. These feelings are isolated from the awareness of all beings. While it stretches my mind to consider such a situation, it also strikes my mind that happy feelings would not have as much value in isolation. A happy feeling without a person to experience it is like a painting without someone to appreciate it. Even if a happy feeling has some intrinsic value (per its positive aspects), the value of an experience is not the same as the value of a personal being—who has the experience. By my lights, when I compare the value of a person with the value of non-persons (including feelings), I see more value in persons.

These observations lead me to at least this conclusion: personal beings have a lot of value. As a person, you do not only have intrinsic value. You also have immense value—a value that might even exceed the value of every other kind of thing.

Unique value. A third aspect of your value is uniqueness. To illustrate unique value, suppose someone wanted to replace an anonymous person with a clone. The result is not value-neutral, like replacing a gold coin with an equal gold coin. A personal being has a unique value that is irreplaceable.

The irreplaceability of a person's value is evident to me when I consider the terrible situation of replacing my wife with a duplicate. I admit: I don't want my wife to be replaced, not even by someone with her same look and personality traits. I want her, the individual, to stay with me. My reason is this: her value as a *particular* person goes beyond her general value as personal being. The sign of this value is the sense of disvalue (or wrongness) in replacing a person with a duplicate. I seem to witness this sense by introspection. If so, then by introspection, I witness a sign of the unique value of unique individuals.

At this point, you might wonder, what could give a person a unique stamp of value? If each person has a certain value that no one else has, why is that? What makes someone uniquely valuable? An answer to this question could help us better understand how it is even possible for something to have unique value.

Here I offer the beginning of one possible answer: unique value is grounded in a unique history. Your unique history gives you a unique personal identity, rooted in the history of your experiences. A clone might look and act like it has your life history (to an extent), but no clone would actually have your particular life history. Nothing could have your history. Your unique life history forges a unique identity. For this reason, there is no one exactly like you; nor could there be.

This proposal—that your unique value is rooted in your unique history—would explain the irreplaceability of persons. We are irreplaceable because there is something unique about each of us. There is something unique about us because each of us has forged a unique life.

If this unique history proposal is correct, then your presence in this world contributes something special to the world that no one else can contribute. On this analysis, you are truly one of a kind. The fuller ramifications of this proposal will come into view when we examine your ultimate origin (at the end of this book).

In summary, introspection can illuminate three aspects of your value. First, you have value that is intrinsic to your nature as a person. Second, your value as a person is immense—perhaps greater than the intrinsic value of any kind of impersonal thing. Finally, your value is unique: no one else has your particular value. These aspects make you very special indeed.

REMOVING OBSTACLES

While there is great value in seeing your own value, obstacles to this sight sometimes roll in. In this section, then, I will attempt to show how you can navigate around the biggest obstacles I've encountered.

Obstacle 1: Value is subjective. You might think value is only in the eye of the beholder. What is valuable to you may not be the same as what is valuable to me. After all, we can value different things. But if value is subjective (in the eye of the beholder), then people don't have objective value. And if people don't have objective value, then they don't have intrinsic value.

There is value in this objection, and indeed, it helps me bring the concept of "intrinsic value" into greater light. I offer three clarifications. First, intrinsic value does not preclude subjective value. Indeed, subjective experiences themselves can have intrinsically positive aspects. For example, consider again a peaceful feeling. The feeling has a positive aspect, which is intrinsic to the feeling itself. An intrinsic, positive aspect is what I mean by "intrinsic value." So, while some value is extrinsic (and relative), it does not follow that all value is entirely extrinsic.

Second, intrinsic value can itself be "subjective" in this sense: the value depends on a subject. For example, a peaceful feeling depends on there being a subject who can feel peace. Both the subject and the feeling have positive aspects. These aspects are intrinsic to subjective realities.

Finally, there is a sense in which subjective value actually depends on intrinsic value. Here is what I mean: something has subjective value precisely by contributing to a subject in some positive respect. To illustrate, suppose eating a sandwich makes me happy. Then the value of the sandwich is related to an intrinsically positive experience. The intrinsic positivity of something (e.g., of a happy experience) is an example of what I mean by "intrinsic value." While the causes of a positive experience may vary from person to person, the positivity of that very experience is in the nature of the experience itself. In other words, it has intrinsic value. If this analysis is correct, then something is subjectively valuable in virtue of its relation to something that has intrinsic value, such as a positive experience. In that case, something can only have subjective value (by its relation to a subject) if something can also have intrinsic value (by what it is).

Obstacle 2: Evolution explains our sense of value. We can explain the sense of value in terms of its contribution to survival. For consider this story. In the beginning of beings, some beings lack the motivation to survive. So, they tend to die off. Meanwhile, other beings have a sense of their value. Their sense of value motivates them to strive to survive, thereby leaving behind more beings after their own kind—beings like us. According to this story, there is no need to appeal to real value to explain our sense of value. Instead, the sense of value is enough to explain our evolution. Therefore, there is no reason to think that the sense of value is based on detecting real value; it could be based instead on natural selection.

I have two responses. First, I want to be careful to avoid a hasty inference. Consider that there is an evolutionary story that explains *all* our senses, including the sense that we have any senses. As a matter of logic, however, it would be a mistake to infer that all our senses fail to tell us anything about reality. On the contrary, the very story I just told presupposes that our senses detect at least something real—namely, senses.

That said, I also want to be careful not to overstate this first response. While it is true that an evolutionary story does not automatically preclude the reliability of our senses, there are ways of filling in a story that could suggest that some senses are not reliable. For example, Prakash et al. make a case for the conclusion that, in general, complex adaptive systems do not select for true beliefs about external reality.[1] If we combine this conclusion with a mindless theory of the origin of biological systems, we will arrive at the result that our senses of external reality do not likely track truths about external reality. According to this story, then, we have reason to doubt the reliability of our senses (including, perhaps, our very reasoning).

Moreover, since I am making no assumptions at the outset about whether our origin is mindful or mindless, I cannot conclude from biological considerations alone whether any of our senses are reliable (or unreliable). Maybe our senses are reliable. Maybe not.

So, I turn to my second response, which is more fundamental. This response grows out of my analysis of perception. In the chapter on perception, I made a case for a window theory of our senses. On this theory, senses are themselves windows of conscious awareness. For example, the introspective sense is a window of awareness into contents within you, including your thoughts, feelings, intentions, logical inferences, and even your very senses.

The window theory suggests a way we can see the world via our senses. Senses are windows to reality. To be aware of things, then, you do not need to *first* see your senses and then demonstrate that these senses are reliable. Your awareness is more direct. You can be aware of thoughts, colors, shapes, feelings, inferences, and so on, by direct conscious awareness. For this reason, you are not in the dark behind a veil of senses. If you were, then you could not know anything about anything, not even that you have senses. But you do know things. Therefore, you aren't in the dark. Your windows of awareness are open.

According to the window analysis of our senses, then, the sense of value is itself a window into some value, just as a sense of a thought is a window

---

[1] C. Prakash et al., "Fitness Beats Truth in the Evolution of Perception," *Acta Biotheoretica* (2020): https://doi.org/10.1007/s10441-020-09400-0.

into some thought. When you sense your value, you are not merely sensing your *sense* of value. You are sensing the value itself. Just as your sense of (phenomenal) shapes and colors in your visual field involves awareness of (phenomenal) shapes and colors, your sense of value is your conscious experience of being aware of some value. On this analysis, a sense of value within you involves acquaintance with at least some value.

As a reminder, it is not part of the window theory of perception that mistakes are impossible. You can make mistakes because you can see something even if you don't see everything with perfect clarity. For this reason, I think you can see something about your value (e.g., its being intrinsic, immense, and unique) even if you don't see everything with perfect clarity.

A final note: the sense of value goes beyond the sense of a desire to survive. While I do sense my own desire to survive, this very desire is based on a more basic sense of the value of my life. My sense of the value of my life is like my sense that 2 + 2 = 4. In both cases, I sense the reality directly. While my sense of my value may indeed contribute to my survival, that doesn't mean I don't actually have value, or that my sense of my value is not based in reality.

Obstacle 3: You can't detect value scientifically. Scientific instruments cannot detect value. You can't touch value. You can't measure it. You can't quantify it. You can't hold value in your hands. Besides, our best physics has no need for positing value as a real aspect of quarks, atoms, or anything else in the real world. So, there is no way to detect real value, whether in matter or in you.

You can probably anticipate my response. I don't think we need scientific instruments to detect value, just as we don't need scientific instruments to detect our own feelings, thoughts, or intentions. There is another instrument: the light of introspection. By the light of introspection, we can detect value by direct awareness of valuable things within us—for instance, positive experiences. So, we don't need a ruler or microscope to detect value. We have other instruments.

This response may be obvious, but I sometimes hear people suggest that we can't know that something exists unless we can detect it using a certain set of instruments. What they say casts a net of darkness over the things we can see. When one's sight of the range of instruments is limited, one's sight of reality is limited. One of my larger purposes in this book is to help people expand their range of instruments by which to see reality. By seeing more of your powers to see, you position yourself to see more of reality.

I offer a final note about the significance of the power to detect value. Suppose scientific instruments that can detect material aspects are indeed incapable of detecting value. It does not follow that you cannot detect value. What follows, rather, is that value is not a material aspect of the material world. This result matches perfectly with what you can see by direct insight into your own value. For when you see your value, you do not see a shape of a neuron or a pattern of dust—as valuable as those things might be! Shapes and patterns can be measured by instruments that detect material aspects of the world. But value cannot be measured by instruments that only detect material aspects (shape, size, structure, and so on). So, value is not a material aspect (at least not on any standard list of material aspects). If that is right, then your value, like other qualities in consciousness, sets you apart from material objects characterizable entirely in terms of material aspects.

These considerations prepare us for our next challenge, which is to see how our value could arise out of the material grains of reality.

THE VALUE PUZZLE

There is a puzzle about how anything could have the kind of value persons have. The puzzle I have in mind is about the *constancy* of a person's value. Consider that many things in the world are constantly changing. The atoms in your head are constantly changing their position. Your thoughts are also constantly changing. So are your feelings. Yet your value is not itself in flux: you continue to be intrinsically valuable every moment of every day. In this sense, your value is more stable than chemicals in your brain, thoughts in your mind, and feelings in your heart. But how? What anchors your constant value in the midst of change?

This question is about the "material" that is you. Some material must be constant in value in order for your value to be constant. What material is that?

To help us think about this question, I will present what I call "the value puzzle."[2] We can divide the value puzzle into two parts. First, there is a puzzle about the constant value of a single person *across time*. Second, there is a puzzle about the constant value *across persons*. Each puzzle has two pieces:

Value Puzzle 1 (Equality Across Time):

Piece 1 (changeless value): your intrinsic value does not change.

Piece 2 (changing states): every mental and material aspect of you changes.

Value Puzzle 2 (Equality Across People):

Piece 1 (equal value): people have equal intrinsic value.

Piece 2 (unequal states): people are unequal in material and mental aspects.

These puzzles are grounded in two observations. My first observation (by inner awareness) is this: the value of a person remains the same. For example, you have the same value as a person today as you had yesterday; I believe you can sense this value directly. Moreover, each person has this same value as a person. No one is more intrinsically valuable (as a person) than anyone else. If so, then personal value is constant. My second observation is this: everything about a person is changing. Cells in your body are dividing; thoughts in your mind are switching; feelings in your heart are fluctuating; and so on. These observations together lead me to wonder: how does a being sustain its value—and its personhood—in the midst of a changing world? I seek an answer to this question next.

HOW TO HAVE VALUE

The value puzzle draws my attention to a theme question: what "material" could have your qualities? If qualities in consciousness are the paints, I want to see the canvas. The canvas is the context for qualities of consciousness to exist.

Enter the material of *mind*. As I have argued in previous chapters, I believe qualities of consciousness do not arise in a purely mindless context, whether from grains of sand or carbon atoms. Instead, qualities of consciousness occur in the context of something that can have contents

---

[2]A. Bailey and J. Rasmussen, "How Valuable Could a Person Be?," *Philosophy and Phenomenological Research* (2020): https://doi.org/10.1111/phpr.12714.

of consciousness—what I call "a mind." A mind, then, provides the canvas for contents of consciousness.

In this section, I want to show that the pattern continues: a mind also provides the context for your value. I have three points to make. First, your value is not reducible to any aspect in any standard list of material aspects (shape, color, size, mass, etc.). Second, your value is not grounded in or explained entirely in terms of material aspects. Third, your value has its anchor in "you," something that provides a constant mental context in a changing world. Together these points suggest that mindless matter is not, on its own, a sufficient basis to explain the value of a being like you.

To be clear, my proposal here is not that mindless matter cannot produce a mental context (all at once) that has value. In the second part of this book, we will consider what it might take to make a mental context in the first place (and the prospect of making a mental context out of purely mindless bits). My purpose here is to highlight just this: some mental context must be part of the scene, somehow, for your value to be in the scene. In other words, your value depends on a mental context, not a purely mindless one.

I will expand briefly on my three points. First, you can see that your value is not the same as a shape, color, size, or any other standard material aspects. One way to see this distinction is by direct comparison. See, for example, a square shape in your mind. Notice that the square differs from your value as a person. I believe you can see the difference directly. Moreover, I believe you can also deduce a distinction based on your conscious awareness of your value. For example, you can witness your value within your consciousness, right now, even while you are not witnessing any shape, color, size, or other material aspect. By logic, that which you are witnessing within your consciousness is not the same as that which are not witnessing within your consciousness. So, your value is not a shape, color, size, or any other material aspect presently outside your consciousness.

Second, material aspects do not ground or explain your value. The value puzzle displays why. People can change in shape, size, and skin color, even while they do not change in their intrinsic value as people. So, you are not valuable just by your shape, size, or the color of your skin. Instead, you have value as a person. If people do indeed have intrinsic value, then this value remains fixed in the face of internal material changes—as organs do different things, chemical reactions take place, and atoms take new positions. As long as the person exists, none of these material changes all by themselves change the person's intrinsic value.

These first two points (that your value is not reducible to material aspects or explained in terms of them) lead to my third point: your value requires a mental context that can have consciousness. A mental context provides the context for something to have the value of a conscious being. If so, then your value depends on a mental context.

The value puzzle exposes a problem with supposing instead that mindless bits can, all by themselves, make your value. The problem, as we have seen, is about change. Mindless bits are constantly changing in their material aspects (shape, size, mass, spatial relations, etc.), whereas your value as a person remains unchanging. So, your value is more stable than mindless matter. Without a mental context, then, mindless bits of reality—whether grains of sand or carbon atoms—are the wrong kinds of things to make your value all on their own.

In response, one might wonder whether mindless matter could make value by first making valuable contents of a mind. For example, perhaps we could first make a thinking chip and a feeling chip. Then by assembling these chips into a computer, the computer could itself provide the mental context for making the intrinsic value of a person. Is that possible?

My answer is that, while we might hypothesize that mindless bits can organize into a conscious mind, there are two problems with making a valuable being by first making the contents of a mind. First, there is a circularity problem. As I have argued in previous chapters, there are reasons to think that the very contents of a mind (like thoughts and feelings) themselves depend on a mind—that is, something that can organize contents of consciousness. If that is right, then to make a mind by first making contents of a mind (thoughts and feelings) is circular. (We will have a closer look at this circularity problem when we discuss the binding problem in chapter ten.)

There is a second and more fundamental problem with making the value of a person by first making the valuable contents of a mind. The problem is that your value as a person does not merely depend on the value of your thoughts and feelings. Sure, your thoughts and feelings may have great value of their own. But you—the one who can think and feel—also have value of your own. So, to make your value, it is not enough to make the valuable contents of your mind. When I say that your value has a mental context, I mean that there must be someone (e.g., you) with a mind already in existence for your value to exist.

My proposal so far does not solve everything. In fact, one might wonder how value could remain constant even in a mental context. After all, minds are also in flux, with new thoughts coming in each moment. So, what remains constant in the mental context? This question exposes a deeper mystery. The challenge now is to see how to explain the constancy of the mental context itself. What keeps your mind in existence?

We will return to this question in the course of our investigation. For now, I will give a label for *whatever* the answer might be. My label is this: "you." The term *you* names the thing that remains constant and anchors your value. Your intrinsic value is constant, then, because your existence is constant.

So this question remains: Why is your existence constant? I will offer an answer to this question at the very end of this book. We are not ready for that yet.

Whatever you are, here I hope you can at least see—by the light of your own direct awareness—at least some aspects of your value. If my analysis is correct, these aspects are not sustained by mindless bits (all on their own), but are sustained by a mental reality: "you."

We can summarize my conclusions as follows:

1. Your constant value is not sustained by mindless bits (whether circuits or neurons).

2. Your constant value is sustained by "you," that which provides a constant mental context.

3. Therefore, your constant value is sustained by a mental context, not mindless bits.

In closing, I want to highlight a consequence of your value being anchored in you. If your value is anchored to you, then your value is firmly fixed in you. Your value does not depend on some other being (human or divine) who may like you or approve of you. No one in heaven or earth can remove the intrinsic value of a personal being. Not even the greatest conceivable being could remove your value without removing you. The way for you to have value is simply to be you.

SUMMARY

We have seen a pattern in our investigation so far: the qualities within consciousness do not exist within a purely mindless context. Instead, qualities in consciousness depend on the existence of someone with a mind.

Our observations about the value of persons fit this pattern. To see your value as a person, you do not need to see mindless motions of matter. Instead, you can see your value by an inner sense of your significance. The sense of your significance is a window into your value. According to the window theory of senses, your senses are windows into contents of reality, whether internal or external. Your sense of value is a window into your value, which is intrinsic, immense, and unique. These aspects of your value are not grounded in the changing shapes, functions, or motions of atoms. Instead, they have their anchor in a more stable reality—"you."

Of course, my proposal that you anchor your value does not answer the question of who you really are. Rather, this proposal focuses the question. Whatever you are, you are not built merely piecemeal from the elements within (e.g., from thinking chips, feeling chips, and value chips). These elements themselves exist only because you already exist. You anchor them.

The conclusion of this chapter pushes the mysteries of your existence deeper into reality. If "you" are the stable source of your value, then what is the stable source of your existence? How does a being like you sustain its existence amidst the changing clouds of atoms? What are you? We will look further into these questions as our investigation continues.

■   ■   ■

You look at the "mindless" wall again. Anticipating a pattern, you hit the dirt wall with your fist. Another layer of dirt slides down and off the wall. Sure enough, out of this dirt, pebbles roll into the arrangement of a new message:

You are not your value.

7

YOUR BODY

We are all light beings.

ALBERT EINSTEIN

*Looking for consciousness in the brain is like
looking in the radio for the announcer.*

NASSIM HARAMEIN

IT IS TIME TO CONSIDER the relationship between you and your body. What is your body? How can you move your body? How can a body affect consciousness? I will seek answers to these questions next.

THE MIND-BODY PROBLEM

I begin by drawing attention to a classic problem of mind-body inter-action. Philosophers sometimes express this problem in terms of radical differences between mind and body. They point out, for example, that a mind includes first-person mental realities (contents of consciousness)— thoughts, feelings, intentions, and the like. But a body is entirely different. A body includes third-person material realities (outside consciousness)— atoms, chemical reactions, and electrical signals between axons. In light of these differences, one might wonder how the two could go together. Can a body transfer energy into a mind, or vice versa? How could that work?

We can distinguish two questions here. First, there is a question about *specific* links between mental states and bodily states: what links a certain, specific mental state (such as, the state of wanting to move a hand) with specific neurological activities? Neurons are like levers for bodily motions. But then, how does something within your mind—a wish, an intention, a willful decision—"know" which levers to pull? The question here is about linking the content of what you want to do (e.g., "move a hand") with a specific brain state that allows you to do that very thing. If, for example, you intend to move your hand up, how might this intention generate a sequence of events leading to your hand moving up. The challenge here is to explain how a specific intention is translated into the right neurons, so that the effect has something to do with what that intention is toward (or about). In other words, the challenge is to answer this question: How can a specific intention with a specific content link with some specific target effect? This is "the specific linking question."

The specific linking question invites us to consider how our mental activities relate to the activities of smaller things, like atoms, inside our bodies. For example, suppose I intend to count to ten in my mind. When I do, I notice there is a precise match between the content of my intention (to count to ten) and the content of my subsequent experience (counting to ten). How does that work? How do atoms behind the scenes "know" to follow my intentions so precisely? Not an easy question.[1]

A second, more fundamental question is this: How can any causal link between mind and body be possible in principle? I call this question "the general linking question."

Behind the general linking question is a "wrong materials" problem. Some materials are the wrong materials for making certain effects. For

---

[1] A. Plantinga, "Content and Natural Selection," *Philosophy and Phenomenological Research* 83, no 2 (2011): 435-58 discusses some difficulties with accounting for the relationship between content and behavior, especially if reality is fundamentally mindless. One challenge is to see how to analyze content purely in terms of mindless units. For innovative work on that challenge, see teleosemantic theories (in P. Schulte and K. Neander, "Teleological Theories of Mental Content," *Stanford Encyclopedia of Philosophy* [2022], https://plato.stanford.edu/entries/content -teleological). Another challenge is to see why, if mindless units are the fundamental units of analysis, there would ever be a precise match between the content of an intention (e.g., an intention to move a hand) and a target effect (moving one's hand). For a more recent development of this challenge, see D. Crummett and B. Cutter, "Psychophysical Harmony: A New Argument for Theism," *Oxford Studies in Philosophy of Religion* (forthcoming).

example, ice cannot make a fire. Numbers cannot add up to a nectarine. Rocks can't generate rats. In each case, the materials are wrong. When the materials are wrong, some interactions call for a deeper explanation. If you saw some rats emerge from some rocks, for example, you might want an explanation of what's going on there.

In the same way, certain materials are the wrong materials for making consciousness. As we discussed in chapter two (when we discussed the sand puzzle), not just anything can make consciousness. For example, rolling rocks down a hill will not thereby cause those rocks to think that 2 + 2 = 4. Going the other way, an imaginary character in your mind cannot cause changes to a rock outside of your mind. Mental images are the wrong material for moving rocks. By the light of reason, I believe it is possible to see this causal incongruence clearly.

To further illustrate the problem, suppose you wish to turn this page. How will you do that? It might seem that you have a power turn the page using your hand. But how do you move your hand? Your hand moves by the command of neurological signals from your brain. So, to move your hand, you must cause neurological signals in your brain. But how do you do that? The challenge here is to see how something in your mind could make a difference to something outside your mind. How, for example, does a wish in your mind spark a neurological chain reaction in your brain? A wish in your mind has the wrong nature, it may seem, to move a real hand in the real world.

The problem here isn't merely that the cause is *different* from the effect. After all, different things can interact. For example, there is evidence that particles and fields can interact, yet these are very different types of things. Interaction across categories, then, is not automatically impossible. The more fundamental problem is this: the cause has the wrong nature to produce that type of effect.

On this analysis, we can see the mind-body problem growing out of the same root as the hard problem of consciousness. The hard problem is the problem of seeing how consciousness could be explained in terms of material states. For many years, I didn't see a connection between the mind-body problem and the hard problem of consciousness. These problems lived in different rooms in my mind. One day, however, while I was thinking about my own mind, I noticed a doorway that connects the mind-body problem to the hard problem of consciousness. This doorway displays a sign, which reads, "The wrong materials problem." The problem of wrong materials helps explain why the hard problem of consciousness is hard.

The root of the hard problem, it now seems to me, is in the wrong materials problem. This problem comes into view as certain causal incongruencies come into view. It is not merely that we do not see how a certain material could cause a certain effect. The root of the problem, I believe, is in things we can see (with some concentration). We can see that certain materials are the wrong materials for explaining consciousness. If so, then the problem of wrong materials is a root of both the hard problem and the mind-body problem.

To draw out this connection a bit further, consider that according to a common conception of matter, matter is fundamentally mindless and unconscious; the basic constituents of all matter are mindless particles, fields, or whatever. On this conception, brain matter is itself composed of things that are fundamentally mindless and unconscious. So, suppose for sake of argument that there is a "hard problem" with explaining mental realities (thoughts, feelings, intentions) entirely in terms of the activities of mindless molecules. Then there is precisely the same hard problem with explaining mental realities in terms of the activities of mindless molecules in brains. Whether molecules are in rocks, planets, or brains, the general hard problem is the same: the materials are wrong.

There is also a reverse problem, which is the mind-to-body side of the mind-body problem. For suppose mindless matter is the wrong material to make consciousness. Then, by symmetry, one might think contents in consciousness are also the wrong materials to make mindless matter. For example, just as sand cannot make consciousness, consciousness cannot make sand. The materials are wrong in both directions. So, if there is indeed a problem with explaining states of consciousness in terms of mindless matter, there is also a symmetrical problem with explaining states of matter in terms of consciousness. How can states within consciousness have effects in matter outside consciousness?

On this analysis, the two sides of the mind-body problem are two wings of the "wrong materials" problem. Mind is the wrong material for making states of matter, and matter is the wrong material for making states of mind. In either case, there is a problem with seeing how mind and body could possibly causally interact.

Once I saw the connection between the mind-body problem and the wrong materials problem, I realized I needed to rethink my understanding of how my own mind could possibly relate to my body. I was now in the grip of the mind-body problem.

THEORIES OF INTEGRATION

In this section, I will examine four general responses to the mind-body problem: eliminativism, epiphenomenalism, dualistic interaction, and monism. My analysis of these options will prepare the way for a fuller account of mind-body interaction, which I will give in the next section.

Eliminativism. One way to solve the mind-body problem is to eliminate the things that generate the problem. For example, eliminate mind. Or eliminate body. Then there is no problem of how mind and body interact.

I do not think eliminativism is the correct solution, however. First, as I have argued in previous chapters, I think we can have knowledge of contents of consciousness via direct acquaintance with them. I have defined "mind" as a realm of consciousness. A realm of consciousness is simply something that can include contents of consciousness, such as feelings and thoughts. On this definition, if there are no minds, then nothing can have contents of consciousness. In that case, I cannot have feelings, thoughts, intentions, or perceptual experiences that are contents of my consciousness. Yet, by the light of introspection, I see that I can have feelings, thoughts, intentions, and perceptual experience within my own consciousness. So, I think my mind is real.

Second, I also think my body is real. By "body," I mean minimally this: something that has spatial aspects, such as shape and extension. When I look in a mirror, I see something that has extension. This thing that has extension counts, then, as a body.

The window theory of perception also supports the premise that mind and body are real. According to the window theory, senses are windows into contents of reality. For example, your sense of a thought is a window into a real thought. Your sense of a feeling is a window into a real feeling. Your sense of an extended body is a window into an extended body. And so on. In each case, when you directly sense something, you are directly acquainted with it. While you may not be directly acquainted with all the aspects of the items you see, your senses put you in contact with some aspects of some items, including mental and bodily aspects.

To be clear, I am not assuming that whatever bodily aspects you sense via your window of perception are "out there" in a mind-independent world. As we saw in the chapter on perception, there are deep questions about the nature of the things we see in visual perception. For example, if you see your body in a mirror, is the figure you see able to exist apart from your conscious awareness of it? Or is the figure you see merely an image in your own mind? These questions remain on the table.

The minimal definition of "body" (as something with spatial aspects) leaves open a range of options, then. For example, an idealist (who thinks everything is in the mind) could suppose that bodies are mind-dependent spatial contents of mental images. Alternatively, one could take a certain materialist option: bodies consist of atoms, which are themselves mind-independent. In the interest of modesty, I leave these options open here. On the minimal concept of "body," we can separate the question of whether there are extended things (bodies) from the question of whether extended things are mind-dependent.

My analysis, then, is this: eliminativism eliminates too much. Through the window of perception, I see both mind (which has contents of consciousness) and body (which has extension). So, there are minds and bodies.

Still, I think the eliminativist strategy is helpful in this respect: eliminativism invites us to simplify our theory of reality as much as possible. Many concepts of mind and body add extra complexities. For example, the concept of "mind" is sometimes associated with a special type of immaterial or ghostly substance; this substance is sometimes conceived as a posit that might explain or ground consciousness. Extra concepts are a source of extra complexities. If we posit more complexity than is necessary to explain our observations, then our steps become less secure.

So, to avoid unnecessary complexities and to secure our steps, I will work with minimal concepts of "mind" and "body." These concepts will allow me to pursue the simplest theory that can make sense of our data.

Epiphenomenalism. Another response to the mind-body problem is to suppose that, while minds and bodies exist, mental realities cannot cause bodily effects. There are different versions of this idea, ranging from theories that find no causal role for the mind at all to theories that give the mind some derived causal role. On all these theories, mental states have no causal efficacy of their own.[2] In other words, minds can't do anything. This view is called "epiphenomenalism."

Here are a couple advantages of epiphenomenalism. First, epiphenomenalism takes seriously the reality of mind. Instead of eliminating first-person mental states, like thoughts, feelings, and intentions, epiphenomenalism recognizes the existence of contents of consciousness.

Second, epiphenomenalism takes seriously the puppet problem. Recall that the puppet problem is the problem of seeing how we could have any power to make choices if mindless bits of reality pull all the strings. Suppose mindless units of reality (atoms) are the fundamental actors. Then all other actors are determined by mindless actors. Actors with minds are not fundamental, then. The result is that mental reality does nothing, for if fundamentally mindless causes do all the work, then there is no room for the mental to do any work of its own. On this view, then, mental reality is like foam on an ocean wave: the foam doesn't move the wave but merely rides along it. Epiphenomenalism implies this result. For if epiphenomenalism is true, then mental reality takes a back seat, while mindless reality is in the driver's seat. The result is that you never do anything by your intentions. Instead you are a puppet of mindless bits of reality.

A major disadvantage of epiphenomenalism, on the other hand, is that it may seem to be incompatible with our experiences of our own powers. In chapter five on your will, I gave reasons (from introspective analysis in relation to recent neuroscience) why I think you are not a puppet of mindless particles. I also explained how I think you can directly see the reality of your conscious intentions and some of the effects directly in your own consciousness. While I did not yet present a solution to the mind-body problem, I gave reasons to think that whatever the solution is, it

---

[2]Many of these theories are motivated by the general problem of causal exclusion, which arises from the premise that microphysical causes do all the explanatory work. See J. Kim, *Physicalism or Something Near Enough* (Princeton, NJ: Princeton University Press, 2005).

shouldn't eliminate the role of your mind in making differences to the world.

Moreover, I believe there is also evidence of mental causation from observations of our behaviors. For example, when you feel an itch, you might observe yourself moving your body to scratch the itch. Here a causal link between the itchy feeling and the bodily movement (perhaps through a sequence of micro events) would help explain why certain bodily motions tend to follow certain itchy feelings. If instead there is no mental causation, it is mysterious how and why mental states systematically precede certain behaviors.

Additionally, a number of philosophers have pointed to a problem with explaining how mental states could *evolve* if they don't contribute anything to adaptive behavior. The problem is that evolution by natural selection works as organisms adapt to their environment. But suppose mental states have no effects on bodies. Then mental states cannot have any effects that help organisms adapt to their environment. In that case, mental function cannot evolve as organisms evolve. But then it is unexpected that any organisms would enjoy complex mental functioning.

In light of considerations like these, philosopher of mind Jerry Fodor remarks, "If it isn't literally true that my wanting is causally responsible for my reaching, and my itching is causally responsible for my scratching, and my believing is causally responsible for my saying . . . if none of that is literally true, then practically everything I believe about anything is false and it's the end of the world."[3] I share his sentiment: if mental states play no causal role in our behaviors, then many of our ordinary beliefs about ourselves and each other cannot be true.

Despite these difficulties, I think a value of epiphenomenalism is that it brings into light the challenge of explaining mind-body interaction. This challenge has deep roots, which grow out of our most fundamental concepts of mind and matter. Rather than pull out the roots, epiphenomenalism acknowledges their depth.

Consider, finally, that epiphenomenalism does not attempt to solve the body-to-mind side of the mind-body problem. One might think the two

---

[3] J. Fodor, *A Theory of Content and Other Essays* (Cambridge, MA: MIT Press, 1990).

sides of the problem are symmetrical: if first-person mental activity is powerless to explain third-person material activity (per epiphenomenalism), then a mindless noise of atoms is similarly powerless to explain mental activity. Epiphenomenalism concedes that one side (mind-to-body causation) is impossible. But then how is the other side (body-to-mind causation) possible? Epiphenomenalism doesn't answer this question.

Dualist interaction. Next, there is the theory that mental states or events (e.g., thinking, feeling, and intending) can cause material states or events (e.g., neurons firing), and vice versa. For example, the feeling of an itch may motivate you to move your hand to scratch that itch. In this process, there is a causal relationship between the feeling of the itch and brain activity that leads to the movement of your hand. Through a sequence of events, then, a mental event (an itchy feeling) causes a material event (the movement of your hand). Going the other way, changes to the material world can cause changes to your experiences, such as when changes to your skin cause an itchy feeling.

One advantage of the dualistic interaction theory is that it can make sense of our ordinary experiences of mind-body interaction. For example, feelings within consciousness often correlate with differences to the physical world, such as when feeling happy is followed by a smile. Going the other way, changes in bodily states often correlate with changes to contents of consciousness, such as when tickling someone is followed by a ticklish feeling. Dualist interaction accounts well for these experiences.

Nevertheless, this theory does not by itself actually solve the mind-body problem. On its own, it only covers the problem with the label "dualist interaction." The whole problem is about how dualist interaction is even possible. How could mindless motions in matter cause an itchy feeling? How could an itchy feeling translate into changes to a nervous system?

Our inquiry into consciousness so far brings the problem of interaction into harsher light. Each of the elements we've considered—feelings, thoughts, awareness, free choices, and intrinsic value—poses its own challenge. On feelings, there is a "wrong materials" problem with constructing qualitative aspects of feelings merely by changing purely nonqualitative aspects of bits of matter. On thoughts, there is the counting problem (revealed by the mindful thoughts theorem) with constructing all the logically possible types of thoughts merely out of configurations of matter. On

awareness, there is the perception problem with constructing visual perception without any prior mental context. On free choices, there is a puppet
problem with constructing beings who can pull their own strings out of
mindless bits that pull all the strings. Finally, on value, there is the constant
value problem with constructing your intrinsic, constant value from val-
ueless, changing materials. Each problem exposes yet another challenge
with analyzing mental activities in fundamentally mindless terms.

Reflection on these problems convinces me that contents of consciousness
are born in a certain, special type of mental context. Mindless materials are
insufficient by themselves. If so, then it is impossible (not merely puzzling)
for mindless matter in a brain to make consciousness just on its own.

In light of these sort of considerations, many philosophers consider dualistic interaction to result in very serious and perplexing problems. At the
peak of his career investigating the nature of the mind, philosopher of mind
John Searle wrote, "No one has ever succeeded in giving an intelligible
account of the relationships between these two realms" (referring to the fundamentally first-person mental reality and the fundamentally third-person
material reality). He goes on to say that the postulation of the two realms
"creates intolerable difficulties."[4] These problems motivate many philosophers
of mind, myself among them, to look further for a more complete solution.

Monism. A fourth response seeks to unify mind and body. According to
this response, the root of the mind-body problem is in a false conception
of minds and bodies as radically different kinds of reality. We can pull out
this root by conceiving of mind and body as instead comprising one fundamental kind of reality. Then interaction doesn't take place across radically
different realms. Rather it takes place within one realm.

There are two options to consider. First, there is *aspect monism.*
According to aspect monism, mental aspects (of thinking, feeling, etc.) and
material aspects (shape, extension, motion) are one and the same. For
example, the first-person sense aspect of happiness is the same as the third-
person material aspect of some neural pattern.

The other monism is *substance monism.* According to this option, there is
one kind of substance that has both mental and material aspects. A substance

---

[4] J. Searle, *Mind: A Brief Introduction* (Oxford: Oxford University Press, 2004), 131.

is something that has aspects, like a shape or a power to think. Then, instead of supposing that there are two fundamentally different kinds of substances (e.g., one kind of substance that has only first-person aspects of consciousness and another kind that has only third-person material aspects), the substance monist supposes that both mind and matter belong to one and the same substance. A single substance, then, has both mental and material aspects.

I think monism can help (as I shall explain in the next section), but there are still difficulties. First, aspect monism contradicts the results of my analysis in the previous chapters. In the previous chapters, I identified aspects of consciousness that, by the light of direct awareness, are irreducibly subjective. For example, the sense aspect of an itch feels a certain way (within introspective awareness), whereas no material aspect in a nervous system (outside introspective awareness) is itself a sense aspect. So, by direct comparison, I believe one can see these aspects aren't one and the same.[5]

Substance monism is better, but it is not a complete solution all by itself. As I've suggested earlier, I don't think the mind-body problem is fundamentally about explaining how different things can interact. At its root, it is more specifically about how certain things with certain natures can interact. Suppose we put mind (thoughts, feelings, intentions) and body (extension, shape, neural activity) into a single substance. Still, we have not explained how mind and body can interact *within that substance*. So the question remains: how can the first-person conscious side of a substance interact with the third-person unconscious side of that substance?

In the next section, I will provide a theory of mind-body interaction that draws from the accounts we have considered here. My theory will display the "mind-first" pattern we have seen in other chapters. In particular, I will aim to show how a certain substance can provide a mental context in which mind-body interaction is possible.

THE CONSCIOUS SUBSTANCE THEORY

To see how a mind and body could go together, I offer what I call "the conscious substance theory" of mind-body interaction.[6] I have organized the

---

[5]For more on the direct comparison test, see chap. 2.

[6]In A. Bailey et al., "No Pairing Problem," *Philosophical Studies* 154, no. 3 (2011): 349-60, I join two colleagues in defending the possibility of interaction between bodies and souls in response to

parts of the theory into seven "drawers." These drawers comprise a filing cabinet that stores seven parts of my theory of mind-body interaction. My goal is not to answer every question one might have about mind-body interaction. Instead, I hope to provide a framework of possibility that can help us better understand how mind-body interaction could be consistent with our first-person observations and scientific developments. Let us open each drawer in turn.

Drawer 1: Substance. I begin with the concept of a substance (*ousia*). While there are different theories of how to analyze substances,[7] for our purposes, I will work with a certain minimal, Aristotelean concept of substance.[8] On this concept, a substance is something that can have some form. For example, water is a substance that can have the form of a liquid. Water is not the form itself, but that which has its form.

To add a little more precision, let "substance" denote anything that meets following conditions:

1. The subject condition: it has (is a subject of) aspects, which constitute its form.
2. The substantial condition: it is not an event, state, or other structure, but is something that can have or be part of a structure.[9]

To illustrate this concept of substance, consider again water. Water meets these conditions of being a substance. First, water is a subject of form, for it has aspects, such as the aspect of having a molecular structure. Second, water is not the same its form, for water can change from one form to another. Instead, water is something that can be in events, states, and structures.

Jaegwon Kim's pairing argument against body-soul interaction. That defense was dialectical: we were not committed to the framework we defended. We also did not attempt to answer the deeper question of how mind-body interaction might actually work on a fundamental level. I will endeavor to answer this question next.

[7] For a detailed, contemporary analysis of substances, see J. Hoffman and G. Rosenkrantz, *Substance: Its Nature and Existence* (London: Routledge, 1996). I seek to respect the insights of their analysis in my definition below while also maintaining intuitive simplicity and ontological neutrality.

[8] Aristotle, *Categories* 1a20–4b19.

[9] This account is compatible with a range of options for how a substance may have its form. According to a relational ontologist, for example, objects have aspects by bearing a relation of exemplification to them. Constituent ontologists, by contrast, conceive of the relation in terms of constituents. Either option is consistent with my account, so long as the substance is a *subject* of its form (i.e., it is not itself a form that something else *has*).

Putting these conditions together, we can say that water is a basic subject of form—in other words, a *substance*.

The concept of a substance can explain how different things can go together into a single being. To illustrate, a substance unifies these categories: aspects, states, and events. Consider each in turn. First, an aspect is something that can characterize something. A substance can unify different aspects into a single thing. For example, something could be both red and round.

Second, a state is a structure that consists of a substance having certain aspects. For example, an icy state of water is a structure that consists of water having its icy aspects. You can think of the state of a substance as the form of that substance.

Third, an event is a state of a substance at a time (or across times).[10] So, aspects are constituents of states, while states are constituents of events. A substance binds all these constituents together by being the basic subject of these constituents. In this way, we can see how aspects, states (forms), and events can all go together into a single substance.

Armed with these distinctions, we can be more precise in our analysis of how contents of consciousness may fit together. For example, let us say that someone is consciously thinking that 2 + 2 = 4 while they also feel hungry. We can now analyze the situation as follows. This person is a substance that unifies aspects, states, and events in this way: (i) the substance has aspects (of having thoughts and feelings), (ii) the substance is in states (a state of thinking and a state of feeling), and (iii) the substance is in events (an event of thinking and feeling at a certain time). A conscious substance, then, is not itself an aspect, state, or event. Rather, a conscious substance is the material (the subject) that has aspects and states and that participates in events.

The first part of the conscious substance theory, then, is that there are substances (i.e., subjects of form) that are capable of consciousness. I call the type of substance that is capable of consciousness "a conscious substance." A conscious substance is anything that can consciously think, feel,

---

[10]This account is consistent with Jaegwon Kim's property-instantiation theory of events ("Events as Property Exemplifications," in *Action Theory*, eds. M. Brand and D. Walton, 159-77 [Proceedings of the Winnipeg Conference on Human Action, 1976]).

or have any other conscious experience. So any being capable of consciousness counts as a conscious substance.

Are there any conscious substances? The light of introspection illuminates my answer: yes. I am a conscious substance. First, I see that I am a subject (a substance) of some form because I have the form of a person. (Note that the term *form* has a minimal meaning to include any state, whether the state of being a person or the state of sitting on a chair.) Second, I also see that I am capable of consciousness. So, I count as a conscious substance. If you are conscious of these words, then you are a conscious substance too.

Note that a conscious substance may have additional capacities, too, such as to move an arm. It is not part of the conscious substance theory that you *only* have capacities for consciousness. So long as you have some capacity for consciousness, you count as a conscious substance.

Drawer 2: Mental capacities. A conscious substance has a capacity for entering into first-person states of consciousness, such as feeling, thinking, and choosing. This capacity is what I call "mental capacity," since it is a capacity to make contents of consciousness in a mind.

The substance theory can account for the existence of mental capacities. Here is how. Substances are the kind of things that can—at least in principle—have capacities. For example, if water is a substance, then water could have a capacity to boil. If persons are substances, then a person could have a capacity to think.

The substance theory can also account for the existence of *basic* capacities, which allow a being to perform actions that do not depend on more basic (prior) actions. For suppose a conscious substance can think. Then that substance could, at least in principle, think in a basic way. As we saw in the chapter on thoughts, there is a problem with supposing that mindless materials can on their own make thoughts (per the mindful thoughts theorem). Moreover, by introspection, it is evident to me that I can consciously form thoughts without first having to consciously do other things. The substance theory makes good sense of this: there can be basic acts of thinking because a conscious substance can have a basic capacity to think.

Note that in general, some operations must be basic—that is, not in virtue of other operations. Otherwise, every operation of a substance would require first performing infinitely many other operations. That's too many operations. By the twin lights of reason and introspection, one can see that one can do some things without first having to do other things (in an infinite regress). So, while we could keep asking, "How does it do that?" the answer at some level is, "That's just one of the things it can do." The operation is basic (not in virtue of its other operations).

To be clear, in saying that some operations are basic, I am not suggesting that the operations do not depend on any prior conditions or constraints. There is a difference between a basic act and an unconditioned act. To illustrate, suppose you concentrate on the thought that 2 + 2 = 4. This act of concentration may be a basic mental act in this sense: you can perform this act of concentration without first performing some more basic mental operation, like an act of trying to move some atoms in your brain. But even if the act is basic, it depends on prior conditions, such as your existence. Basic acts might also depend on certain atoms coming into certain places. So, while some mental capacities may be basic, there can still be constraints and conditions on what you can do.

There is one more thing at the bottom of this "mental capacities" drawer. Here I offer an account of how a conscious substance can have a mind. Recall that by "mind," I mean something that can have contents of consciousness. A conscious substance has a capacity for consciousness. This capacity can include the capacity for having a field of awareness. The field of awareness is the canvas (the mind) in which contents of consciousness exist. In this way, a conscious substance is the kind of thing that can have a mind by its capacity to generate contents of consciousness in a field of awareness.

Drawer 3: Bodily capacities. A conscious substance is not limited to conscious capacities. A conscious substance can also have the capacity to affect a body.

In the interest of modesty, I will continue to work with a minimal definition of the term *body* as denoting whatever has a spatial aspect. This minimal conception of a body leaves open different accounts of the nature of a body. For example, Hoffman makes an empirical case for the hypothesis that spatial objects are mind-dependent contents of

perceptual experiences.[11] On this model, your body is literally in the eye
(or visual experience) of the beholder. That's one option. Another option
is that bodies have stand-alone, mind-independent existence. In either
case, whether or not the spatial aspects of a body are entirely within consciousness, bodies exist somehow. We will have occasion to return to the
question of the fundamental nature of bodies when we consider the fundamental nature of matter (in part two of this book).

Return to the question at hand: How can you affect your body? The
substance theory empowers an answer in terms of basic capacities. As
we saw, a substance is the kind of thing that can have basic capacities.
So, just as you may have a basic capacity to form a thought, you may
also have a basic capacity to cause changes to your body. The capacities
of a substance can, at least in principle, include both mental and
bodily capacities.

The proposal so far, then, is that you are a substance with capacities,
including bodily and mental capacities. By including the existence of
capacities, we can see how it is possible—in principle—for a being like you
to have a capacity to think and move.

Drawer 4: Systematic links. I want to pause here to appreciate the power
of the substance theory to help explain how mind and body can go together.
Instead of supposing that mental states and bodily states can, all on their
own, make each other, there is another source of unity—a substance. A
substance can unite mental and bodily states by being the subject of
them both.

By introducing a common subject, the substance, we also have another
resource for analyzing causal interaction. Instead of analyzing causal interactions merely in terms of mental and material states, a substance provides
an additional source of causal power. A substance can do things that the
states by themselves cannot do.

For example, while an image in my mind cannot, all on its own, move my
body, a substance could have a capacity to form an image in my mind and
move my body. Thus, a substance can link different states together. By having
a capacity to cause different states, a substance can also have a capacity

---

[11]D. Hoffman, *The Case Against Reality: How Evolution Hid the Truth from Our Eyes* (New York:
W. W. Norton, 2019).

to cause different states *together*. In this way, a substance can—at least in principle—have a capacity to both think and move at the same time.

So, in this drawer, we combine the results of the previous two drawers. In the previous drawers, we identified a general capacity for making changes, including mental and bodily changes. In this drawer, we recognize an additional capacity to making mental and bodily changes together. By making both together, a conscious substance can establish links between mental states and bodily states. These links can then comprise programs—that is, systems of links—between mental operations and bodily operations.[12]

Note that the activities of a conscious substance need not all be *conscious* activities. A conscious substance could cause many things unconsciously. For example, it might cause microphysical states that help facilitate breathing without any conscious awareness of those states. (I will have more to say about how conscious substances may cause microphysical states later.)

The conscious substance theory supplies a bonus benefit. If mental and bodily states belong to a single subject, then we have a solution to the problem of too many thinkers. The problem of too many thinkers arises from any view on which you consist, not of a single substance, but of many different things. For example, suppose mind and body are instead two different substances that compose you. Then when *you* think, your mind also thinks—after all, it is a subject of thoughts as much as you are. But is that not too many thinkers? We don't ordinarily think of ourselves as consisting of multiple thinkers. According to the ordinary conception, when you think, there is normally only one thing that has your thoughts: *you*. While we might question this conception, the conscious substance theory can make sense of it. For if you are a single conscious substance, then when you think, your mind does not also think. Instead, your mind is a state of you (a state that includes contents of your consciousness). On this account, you think by having thoughts in the state (the field of awareness) that is your mind. In this way, there is only one subject of your thoughts. Problem solved.

---

[12]This account differs from Leibniz's pre-established harmony theory in two salient respects: first, my theory, unlike Leibniz's, does not rule out causation across substances; second, my theory, unlike Leibniz's, does not require that an original substance, God, first program all the substances to be in harmony with each other. For a discussion of Leibniz's philosophy of mind, see M. Kulstad, "Leibniz's Philosophy of Mind," *Stanford Encyclopedia of Philosophy* (2020), https://plato.stanford.edu/entries/leibniz-mind.

Drawer 5: Body-to-mind. So far, I have provided an account of how a substance could link mental and bodily states via its basic capacities. Here I want to consider how a conscious substance can thereby facilitate body-to-mind causation.

To illustrate my account, suppose you look in the mirror. As you do, you experience the visual image of a face. This experience consists in your direct awareness of a bodily figure (per the window theory of perception). Now suppose your facial expression changes (whether by your own action or the actions of things external to you). This change in facial expression results in a change in the contents of your direct awareness. For example, if your facial expression changes from straight lips to a smile, then the contents of your visual experience change: your experience changes from being a state of awareness of straight lines to a state of awareness of curves. This scenario displays body-to-mind causation: the change in geometry (straight to curve) is a bodily change resulting in a mental change in awareness.

Notice that in this case, the correlation between the mental and bodily changes depends on the prior existence of a conscious substance. Without the conscious substance, you—the subject of your consciousness—would not be consciously aware of your figure in the mirror. In that case, merely changing the shape of your face would not produce any change in the contents of your conscious awareness, for you would not have conscious awareness at all. In other words, the body-to-mind causation in this scenario depends on the existence of something that can be conscious.

This observation—that a conscious context can facilitate body-to-mind causation—is evidence for a pattern we have seen before. The pattern is this: contents of consciousness take place in the context of a mind. For example, just as swirling sand won't make that sand (or any other mindless things) aware of the sand, changing the shape of a face won't make that face (or any other mindless things) aware of a face. A spatial change, just by itself, does not make a mental change. Without a prior mental context, mindless, bodily changes do not on their own make mental changes.

The role of a mental context is easy to overlook if we are accustomed to the mindlessness frame of reality. According to the mindlessness frame, everything happens in a fundamentally mindless context—for instance, mindless motions of matter. According to this frame, all elements of mind (thinking, feeling, intending, etc.) are constructed out of more fundamental, mindless elements (unconscious molecules, physical forces, etc.). Bodily-mental causation is then interpreted as an example of mindless-to-mental causation; there is no other option. For on this interpretation, if there is a causal link between chemical reactions in a brain, say, and certain conscious experiences, the chemical reactions must provide the causal story: their motions, functions, and changes must account for conscious experiences on their own (without a mind). But this interpretation assumes that the causes themselves take place in a fundamentally mindless context of mindless forces and fields; that is, the mindlessness frame assumes that there is no mental, conscious substance in which consciousness occurs.

To illustrate my account a bit further, consider the experience of breathing. The conscious substance theory can account for this experience as follows. A substance can have a capacity to (unconsciously) cause changes in bodily states, such as changes in one's lungs. This same substance could also stimulate a corresponding feeling associated with breathing air. The key idea here is that a substance can have capacities to generate different states (whether consciously or unconsciously). In this way, a substance can link together different states, which may otherwise be unable to directly cause each other.

The conscious substance theory can also help with the hard problem of consciousness. The problem here is in seeing how merely mindless units of reality can provide an adequate explanation of mental units of reality. The conscious substance theory sheds light on how a body can affect a mind. Instead of supposing that a change in position or shape on its own causes a state of awareness (out of a sea of mindless atoms), a conscious substance can have basic capacities, including a capacity for awareness. With basic capacities, we explain how, at least in principle, a substance can link a bodily change with a corresponding mental change in one's awareness—and so affect one's experience.

In summary, the conscious substance theory provides a general framework for body-to-mind links. These links take place in the context of a conscious substance. Where there is a conscious substance, its experiences can themselves be affected by changes in the contents of those experiences, such as when the things you are aware of change shape. Moreover, a conscious substance can establish links between certain bodily changes and certain conscious experiences, such as when you experience a breath of fresh air. In short, body can affect mind when a conscious substance is present.

Drawer 6: Mind-to-body. A conscious substance can also facilitate mind-to-body causation. For example, suppose you intentionally decide to take a deep breath. As a conscious substance, you not only have the capacity to create this conscious intention, but you also have unconscious capacities to correlate this conscious intention with a package of bodily motions and other sensations. A conscious substance can actualize correlations between mental operations and bodily operations.

The idea that you have the capacity to change spatial states by mental intention corresponds with the experience of changing shapes within your visual experiences. To illustrate this power to myself, I've closed my eyes and visualized shapes. Then by an intention to rotate the shapes, I've been able to change the rotation of the spatial structure within my mental field. In this way, I witness my mental efforts result in changes in spatial things in my visual experience.

While changing the geometry of an image in my mind is not the same as changing the geometry of my body, it illustrates the possibility of changing geometries by mental intention. In this scenario, I form an intention to form an image in a basic way without first having to try move my body. The result of my specific intention is itself a spatial form ("a body") within my visual experience. Thus, I witness mind-to-body causation. The conscious substance theory accounts for this possibility, for a conscious substance is the right kind of thing to have a capacity to cause spatial changes (such as in an image) by one's intention.

Recent science of consciousness also supports the premise that consciousness can affect spatial things in measurable ways. Seth et al. analyze three ways to measure consciousness: (i) neural complexity, (ii) information integration, and (iii) causal density.[13] These measurements display the effects of consciousness in spatial brains.

---

[13] A. Seth et al., "Theories and Measures of Consciousness: An Extended Framework," *Proceedings of the National Academy of Sciences of the United States of America* 103, no. 28 (2006): https://doi .org/10.1073/pnas.0604347103.

Rather than contradict physical laws, the science of consciousness is expanding our vision of what those laws are. Hiley and Pyklkkanen provide a quantum mechanical model of conscious effects that respects known physical laws (in particular, the energy conservation law).[14] Rolls quantifies the information present at the threshold of conscious, visual perception.[15] And according to McFadden's research, consciousness integrates information as an energy field.[16] Citing various experiments to support the relationship between consciousness and observational effects, he motivates conscious electromagnetic information field theory. On this theory, consciousness can affect changes in energy fields, and these changes can propagate outward to affect systems locally and potentially far away.[17]

There may even be evidence that our consciousness can have nonlocal effects on other bodies. Research at Princeton university on consciousness has been studying effects of consciousness on remote systems. PEAR and the Global Consciousness Project report finding evidence that consciousness is linked with changes to random number generators in statistically significant ways. In a recent study of the effects of consciousness from the impact of Covid, they report that the stock market crash was nonstatistically correlated with changes to their instruments.[18] They estimate the chances at 4 in 10,000 (p = 0.0004).

Whatever we make of these studies, the conscious substance theory shows how—at least in principle—it is possible for mental activities to affect bodily changes without violating any known physical laws. By including substances with basic capacities in our theory, we can then explain mind-body interaction.

As a final note, I want to emphasize that the neuroscience of the brain leaves open different theories of how to analyze the links between mental

[14]B. Hiley and P. Pyklkkanen, "Can Mind Affect Matter via Active Information?," *Mind and Matter* 3, no. 2 (2005): 8-27.
[15]E. Rolls, "A Computational Neuroscience Approach to Consciousness," *Neural Networks* 20, no. 9 (2007): 962-82; "Consciousness Absent and Present: A Neurophysiological Exploration," *Progress in Brain Research* 144 (2004): 95-106.
[16]J. McFadden, "Integrating Information in the Brain's EM Field: The Cemi Field Theory of Consciousness," *Neuroscience of Consciousness* 2020, no. 1 (2020): https://doi.org/10.1093/nc/niaa016.
[17]E. John, "The Neurophysics of Consciousness," *Brain Research Reviews* 39, no. 1 (2002): 1-28.
[18]R. Nelson, "Global Consciousness and the Coronavirus—a Snapshot," *The Global Consciousness Project* (2020): https://global-mind.org/papers/pdf/GCP.Corona.edgescience.fin.pdf.

and material states. While empirical science provides evidence of links between mental states and brain states, the evidence of links does not by itself illuminate the nature of those links. One hypothesis is that the links are themselves grounded in mindlessness. In my view, that hypothesis leaps beyond empirical evidence into dark caves of speculation; it also leaves the nature of the links in the dark. Another hypothesis is that the links take place in a mental context of a conscious substance. This hypothesis not only fits with the empirical data but also illuminates how the mind-to-body links can happen. For then we can analyze the nature of the links in terms of the kinds of capacities we know in direct experience.

I have only begun to sketch a theory of mind-body interaction. This sketch provides contours of a picture that others may fill in with more colors and details. For example, a cognitive scientist may work to specify which specific conscious intentions correlate with which specific neurons or brain activity. The centerpiece of my picture is a conscious substance: a conscious substance with basic capacities can explain mind-to-body inter-actions by causing mental and bodily states using powers appropriate to its nature.

Drawer 7: Special options. This final drawer contains a couple additional options to stimulate your imagination and further inquiry. First, there is an idealist option, on which bodies themselves are rendered in the minds of conscious substances. On this option, you can think of your body like an avatar, which represents a deeper reality that is nothing like your visual experiences of your body.

Hoffman makes an empirical case for a version of this view.[19] Hoffman suggests that your body is like a desktop icon that represents a deeper reality. Just as a folder on a desktop computer is only an icon that represents a deeper reality of computer processes, your body is an icon that represents a deeper reality of mental processes. The spatial states you associate with your body are themselves contents of mental projections. Your conscious substance does not render these spatial contents when you aren't looking at them. The truth, on this view, is that there is no fundamentally spatial reality at all; spatial reality is entirely within

---

[19]Hoffman, *The Case Against Reality.*

contents of minds. So, the spatial aspects of your brain actually represent nonspatial qualities and capacities of a more substantial reality.

Bernardo Kastrup motivates a similar model, which he calls "analytic idealism," since he arrives at this model from a sequence of analytical deductions from what he takes to be the best account of empirical observations.[20] According to analytic idealism, spatial brains are extrinsic appearance of underlying consciousness. These appearances exist on the screen of perception, not outside one's perception. On his model, a spatial object, like a brain, doesn't generate a conscious substance (or the mind). It is the other way: a conscious substance generates spatial objects on the screen of one's perception. Spatial objects are contents of consciousness that can represent other contents of consciousness.

We can further illustrate this basic idealist option in terms of a metaphor of an ocean. A conscious substance is an ocean, with contents of consciousness rippling as waves. A body is a certain content of consciousness, like a swirling vortex in the ocean. This metaphor displays causal interactions between contents of consciousness and bodily states: waves of consciousness can affect the vortex (the body), and the vortex can affect waves of consciousness (the mind).[21]

This account may fit well with recent developments in our understanding of the nature of matter. According to Carlo Roveli, quantum field theory suggests that "matter" is not fundamentally spatial but is instead an informational and contextual field.[22] On this theory of matter, spatial bodies themselves would be contents of an underlying quantum field. Then, rather than multiply posits, a quantum field could itself be the ocean in which mind-body interaction takes place. On this model, your intentions create informational states that translate into (or are visually represented by) ripples in the quantum field. I will say more about this quantum field model of matter in chapter thirteen.

---

[20]B. Kastrup, *The Idea of the World: A Multi-Disciplinary Argument for the Mental Nature of Reality* (Winchester, UK: John Hunt, 2019).

[21]This model provides a way to reverse a certain interpretation of Aristotle's hylomorphic theory, on which a soul is the form of a body (*De Anima* 2.1). Instead, if material structures are extrinsic appearances of consciousness, then it could be the other way: a body is a form (of consciousness) of a soul.

[22]C. Roveli, *Reality Is Not What It Seems: The Journey to Quantum Gravity* (New York: Random House, 2014).

If these ideas are too much, here is a second option, which I call "shape substantivalism." According to shape substantivalism, shaped objects are themselves substances in their own right. Thus, instead of supposing that shaped objects are contents of consciousness, we suppose that shaped objects are mind-independent subjects of spatial form.

In my estimation, the best version of shape substantivalism is developed by Andrew Bailey.[23] According to Bailey, human persons are decomposable into material parts, which have spatial aspects. The conscious substance theory allows for this option, since a conscious substance could have material parts. Note that even if mental states of a conscious substance are not solely explained in terms of its material parts (per the hard problem of consciousness), it does not follow that a conscious substance cannot have material parts. A beautiful consequent of the conscious substance theory is that it can explain mind-body interaction without closing off Bailey's broadly materialist vision of human persons.

So, the substance theory gives us bonus options. On all these options, the key idea is this: a conscious substance provides a framework for mind-body interaction. By seeing how mind-body interaction could work, we have a framework for other theories that can fill in other details.

HOW TO MAKE A BODY ALIVE

The conscious substance theory not only helps explain mind-body interaction, but it can also help with another question: What explains the difference between bodies that are alive and bodies that are not? A butterfly is alive. A rock is not. What makes the difference? On a molecular scale, a rock and a butterfly consist of swarms of scattered atoms. But what makes one swarm of atoms "alive" and another not?

The conscious substance theory provides resources for explaining life. The difference between dead matter and a living organism is explicable in terms of the presence of a conscious substance. Consider that a conscious substance has the capacity for generating the activities we associate with being alive. For example, if you see a kitten chasing a cricket, this visual display provides evidence of goal-directed activity. A goal is precisely

---

[23] A. Bailey, *Monotheism and Human Nature* (Cambridge: Cambridge University Press, 2021).

something that a conscious substance could produce, along with behavioral patterns that may help it achieve that goal.

By contrast, a rock is not itself a conscious substance, or at least the evidence I have of its being a conscious substance is thin. For its atoms are not evidently caught up in any goal-directed activities. The lack of a conscious substance can explain that: without a conscious substance that can produce intentions or interests, the rock is dead. My hypothesis, then, that the difference between a dead rock and a live butterfly is the presence of a conscious substance.

This analysis also flips a certain body-first picture of your relationship to your body. The spatial aspects of your body don't make you alive. It is the other way: you make your body alive. The life of your body is a manifestation of your consciousness.

Now to be clear, it is not part of my theory that every conscious substance has the same capacities. On the contrary, the conscious substance theory can account for different levels of lifeforms in terms of different levels of consciousness. It is evident that different lifeforms display different levels of complexity of life depending on the complexity of their capacities. A plant, for example, might have the capacity for a simple positive sensation (a simple form of "interest") as its leaves come into the sunlight. A wolf has a larger range of mental capacities, ranging from simple sensations to instinctive if-then reasoning. Building up, we have the human, who has capacities not only to have thoughts and feelings but also to think reflectively about its thoughts and feelings (a basis for language). In each case, we can account for the different complexities of life in terms of different conscious capacities, ranging from rudimentary to complex. (These examples are only illustrative. I make no claims about which conscious capacities are in fact present in which lifeforms.)

The conscious substance theory can also help explain the use of a brain. People sometimes ask me what I think a brain is for. If a conscious substance can form mental operations in a basic way, free from prior material changes in a brain, then what is the point of a brain? What does a brain do?

My working hypothesis is this: brains are user interfaces for conscious beings. That is to say, brains facilitate certain conscious states in response to a certain environment. This account is a version of Paul Cisek's control model of the brain—a model he arrives at in his neuroscientific research on how brains mediate interactions with the world. According to Cisek, the brain's fundamental function is to help an organism maximize desirable states in relation to changes in the world.[24] My model includes the root idea, which is that brains are control systems ("user interfaces") for interacting with one's environment.

On this account, we can explain, on a fundamental level, why there is a correspondence between damage to a brain and alterations to conscious capacities. The reason is this: a brain is a fully immersive control system for all (or nearly all) one's conscious experiences. So, if one's control system changes, so do one's conscious experiences. Recall that on the conscious substance theory, mental-bodily interaction is not a direct relation between first-person mental states and third-person material states. Rather, this interaction is facilitated by the capacities of the conscious substance itself. So, if the capacities are affected, then so is mind-body interaction.

The user interface model also makes sense of what we see when we look at brains. When we look at a brain, we don't see a person's thoughts or feelings, at least not directly. Instead, we see spatial structures through the window of visual experience. These structures are themselves analyzable as visual icons (on the "screen of perception," as Kastrup likes to say), which represent aspects of a user interface for interacting with the world.

To illustrate further, suppose a conscious substance has a power to form an intention (per the "mind-to-body" drawer). This intention, let's say, is not fundamentally a byproduct of mindless, neural activity. Instead, suppose the intention generates informational states in a quantum field (or in some other way), which affect neural activity. In this case, there is a link between a certain mental state (the intention) and a certain bodily state (the neural activity). This link is not itself arbitrary or random: it facilitates interactions within a larger environment beyond one's immediate consciousness. Many of these mental-material links add up to a complex set of links. This complex set of links constitutes an evolving program for interacting with the world.

This user interface model can also help us understand certain unusual experiences where one's perceptions are not processed through normal

[24]P. Cisek, "Evolution of Behavioural Control from Chordates to Primates," *Philosophical Transactions of the Royal Society* B.377 (2022): 20200522.

neurological pathways. For example, in near-death experiences, people report being able to see things without their body. In extreme cases, color-blind patients even report being able to see in color for the first time.[25] We can explain such cases in terms of a transition in one's user interface.

To be more specific, consider reports of seeing outside one's body. One might wonder how one could see without using one's eyes. Do these reports suggest that a conscious substance can have visual experiences without a brain? My answer is that it depends on what we mean by "brain." If we think of a "brain" merely in terms of third-person aspects (e.g., spatial aspects), then in view of the mind-body problem, I don't think anyone sees anything just in virtue of third-person, spatial aspects of brains. Instead, on my account, seeing (as in conscious awareness of shapes and colors) is a basic operation that certain conscious substances can perform.

To be clear, it does not follow that your brain plays no role in sight. On the contrary, your brain facilitates the types of visual experiences you have in this world. To borrow Hoffman's metaphor, a brain is like a headset. A headset facilitates interactive experiences within some world. When you turn to the left or blink your eyes, the headset updates what you may see according to a program. This update requires information to describe the connections between different mental operations, the environment, and different conscious experiences. In the same way, your brain facilitates your experiences in response to your environment. On this model, while you do not literally need eyeballs to see visual images (for you can see visual imagery while you are dreaming), your eyes help to process information relevant to this environment. This coordination between your experiences and the environment depends on a complex set of capacities, represented by visual appearances of neurons and brain structures (on the screen of perception).

On this framework, an "out-of-body" experience would result from a radical change to one's user interface. The result is not that you suddenly cannot think, feel, or perceive. Instead, one's context of consciousness changes, like when one wakes up from a dream. On this model, a conscious being would still have a "brain" in the sense of having a system of capacities

---

[25] J. Long and P. Perry, *Evidence of the Afterlife: The Science of Near-Death Experiences* (New York: HarperCollins, 2010), 92.

coordinated with an environment. What changes is not the basic powers to see, feel, and think, but the environment in which one sees, feel, and thinks.

We are stepping into deep waters. Fortunately, nothing in the conscious substance theory requires that we navigate these waters. The conscious substance theory in itself leaves open what happens after a person's body dies. My purpose here has been to show how a conscious substance can illuminate the relationship between biological life and consciousness across many conceivable contexts. That's a benefit of the theory.

In summary, my theory of life is this: consciousness makes a body alive. This theory does not imply that a life can exist without a body. But it does imply that a body cannot be alive without consciousness. Consciousness fuels life.

SUMMARY

Mind and body can go together in conscious substances, which are substances that can be conscious. Conscious substances can perform basic actions, such as acts of thought, intention, and bodily actions. By performing basic actions, conscious substances can also coordinate their actions into complex patterns of interaction (i.e., programs), thereby facilitating mind-body interaction. As a bonus, the conscious substance theory empowers a theory of brains: a brain is a user interface—a system of capacities and programs—for a conscious substance.

■   ■   ■

You notice that, although multiple layers of dirt have fallen from the wall before you, the "mindless" inscription remains. How thick is this wall? Is there a way through? You wonder if answers to the mysteries of this cave lay ahead. So you push the wall with a mighty force. To your disappointment, the wall does not immediately collapse. Still, another layer of dirt slides in a compact sheet off the wall. It crumbles into a pile on the floor, and again, some pebbles from the pile haphazardly bounce and tumble along their various trajectories until they settle into slightly unnerving precision. You place your lantern over the highly ordered arrangement of shapes. You discern these words:

YOU ARE NOT YOUR BODY.

8

YOUR SELF

You are nothing but a pack of neurons.

FRANCIS CRICK

Each time you identify something you are not, it is like taking off a layer of clothing. Once you take off all the layers, then you can see that what remains is what you are.

A PLEIADIAN COLLECTIVE

THE PURPOSE OF THIS CHAPTER is to shine the light on *you*—the one who has your consciousness. Instead of viewing your outer layers, or seeing the things that you are not (your feelings, thoughts, powers, and spatial body), we will look deeper in, behind the veil of the things you are not. My goal is to identify the one behind the veil—the one who is really you.

To identify the one who is you, I will identify three arrows: (i) your oneness, (ii) your point of view, and (iii) your ability to be self-aware. Each arrow points to you from a different angle. By tracing these arrows to a common destination, I hope to bring the *who* of consciousness into clearer view. At the end of this chapter, I will seek to remove common obstacles that sometimes block people from seeing—or recognizing—themselves in this light.

FIRST ARROW: YOUR ONENESS

The first arrow is your oneness. You are someone, not some ten or some twenty. In other words, there is one of you.

But what does it mean to say that there is "one" of you? The distinction between one and many is so basic and so familiar that it is easy to miss its significance. By understanding oneness, we can position ourselves to better understand the difference between the outer layers of a being and the being itself. So, in this section, I will perform analytical surgery to expose a more precise concept of your oneness.

One substance versus many aspects. The substance theory of consciousness empowers a precise analysis of your "oneness." According to the conscious substance theory, you are a substance (i.e., a subject of form) that is capable of being conscious. In the previous chapter, I drew a distinction between the substance and states of that substance. A state of a substance consists of aspects of that substance, such as being a person, being alive, and being able to think; the substance is the subject of its states. By seeing this distinction between a substance and its states, we can see how, according to the substance theory, you are not the same thing as your states of consciousness. Instead, while you can have many different states, you can still be one substance. In this sense, you are one thing.

One being versus many parts. We can further elucidate the concept of oneness by distinguishing you from your parts (if you have parts). As far as the substance theory goes, you could have many parts, such as eyes and ears (and atoms within those parts). Here is a crucial distinction: a substance that has parts is not the same as the parts it has.

Take, for example, a butterfly. If there is a butterfly, then it is a single subject—an individual. While the butterfly may have many parts (wings, eyes, atoms, etc.), the butterfly is not the same as its many parts. For by logic, one is not equal to many. Thus, one individual can have many parts without being those many parts.[1]

Understanding this distinction between a thing and its parts can also sharpen our analysis of certain divisions within conscious beings, such as

---

[1]This distinction between the individual and its parts leaves open different ways of being related to one's parts. Some philosophers propose, for example, that organisms are more than the *sum* of their parts, since the same organism can exist with different parts. Among these philosophers, some contrast organisms with artifacts, like chairs, which they say are merely the sum of their parts. In both cases, there is still a difference between the *parts* and the *individual* that has the parts (whether it is a *sum* or more than a sum of its parts). Cf. P. van Inwagen, *Material Beings* (Ithaca, NY: Cornell University Press, 1990).

diverse personalities or divisions in split-brain patients. In each case, we can analyze these divisions in terms of distinct parts (or states of parts) of individual substances.

This analysis can also help us explain how different beings could share a single body, such as in the case of Siamese twins. One possibility is that different substances, each with their own first-person sense of self, could be united by a common body. This body could itself be an assemblage of atoms or fields united by a pair of causally connected conscious substances. Whatever the case, the more fundamental insight is this: we can distinguish the being from its parts.

Parts versus plurals. We are digging into deep distinctions. This work is not easy, but by taking the time to work through these distinctions, we are preparing ourselves for a high-resolution analysis of who you are. The distinctions will also empower us to remove certain common obstacles that prevent people from recognizing their own reality as clearly.

So, let us continue to increase the resolution of our analysis. We can further sharpen the concept of "oneness" by separating the concept of parts from the concept of a plural of things. To illustrate this distinction, consider a chair. Some philosophers have argued that we can translate our talk about "chairs" into talk about a plural of things (such as atoms) arranged in a certain chair-like way. In view of this translation, some philosophers propose that, strictly speaking, there are no chairs—at least not as individual things. Instead, when we use "chair" language, we are really talking about smaller things arranged in a chair-like way. If that is right, then, strictly speaking, chairs—as individual things—don't exist.[2]

Some philosophers go even further and suppose that, just as chair don't exist, neither do people. According to their argument, we can translate talk about people into talk about swarms of particles. If they are right, then, strictly speaking, you—an individual person—don't exist. Only the particles do.

---

[2] The philosopher P. van Inwagen is perhaps the most well known for articulating skepticism of the existence of chairs as he seeks to understand how personal beings could exist (van Inwagen, *Material Beings*). In my estimate, the best elaboration and analysis of van Inwagen's arguments—in relation to the existence of persons—come from his former student T. Merricks in *Objects and Persons* (Oxford: Oxford University Press, 2001).

To draw out this argument a bit, consider the general thesis that no complex individuals exist. This thesis is called "mereological nihilism." According to mereological nihilism, no individual thing (singular) has parts (plural). Instead, there are just the atoms, or whatever is smallest and partless. Some philosophers have followed this path to the conclusion that there are no people. For if people exist, then people have parts (i.e., we aren't partless atoms), they say. But if mereological nihilism is true, then nothing has parts. So, if mereological nihilism is true, then people don't exist. (In graduate school, I once attended a philosophy talk where the speaker argued against his own existence in precisely this way.)

I will not follow that path, however. The entire inquiry of this book is based on the premise that whatever you are, you are real. Now, to be clear, even this premise is one I don't want to take for granted. So, later in this chapter, I will show how I think you can verify your existence. For now, my aim is to clarify what it could mean for you to exist as an individual.

In the interest of modesty, I will not enter the trenches of debate over mereological nihilism. Instead, I say this: either you have parts, or you don't. Mereological nihilism by itself leaves open the option that you are a simple being. In my own view, talk about your parts is translatable into talk about parts of states of you. So, for example, your heart is "part" of you in this sense: your heart is part of a functional state of you. On this account, you have parts by having states. You could still be simple in at least this sense: you do not have *substances* as parts. Alternatively, if mereological nihilism is not true, then perhaps you do have substances as parts. In either case, we can distinguish between a thing and its parts.

My main point here is this: there is a difference between you, the substance, and mere parts of you or particles in you. As a matter of logic, talk about you is not replaceable with talk about other, smaller things that are not you. Thus, you, if you are indeed real, are not *other*, smaller things.

We may summarize this analysis as follows:

1. You exist.

2. If you exist, you are not other, smaller things.

3. Therefore, you are not other, smaller things.

People versus particles. There is one more distinction I would like to carve by analytical surgery, which exposes a significant consequence of the concept of your oneness. The distinction is this: there is a difference between an individual person and a plural of particles. This distinction follows from the previous distinctions. For we have already seen a distinction between an individual thing and a plural. From this distinction between individuals and plurals, we can deduce a distinction between individual people and plurals of particles.

This distinction between individuals and plurals can help us avoid the mistake of identifying a substance with particles that may be in it. A substance may have many particles. For example, if an energy field is a substance, then that field may contain many particles. But a substance is not the same as a plural of particles within it. For as a matter of logic, a single thing is not the same as many things. Moreover, as a matter of observation, a conscious substance can continue to exist even if it exchanges particles. So, an individual substance is not the same as the particles that may be inside it.

We can summarize this analysis as follows:

1. A person is one thing (e.g., a conscious substance).

2. Many particles are many things.

3. Therefore, a person is not many particles.

In summary, the substance theory empowers a precise analysis of your oneness. By analytical surgery, we can see how, if you are a conscious substance, you are one substance. In this way, you can be one you in the midst of many things—including plurals, parts, and particles.

SECOND ARROW: YOUR POINT OF VIEW

A second arrow that points to the being that is you is your perspective. From your present point of existence, you experience a first-person perspective. Your perspective is your point of view.

Having a point of view is so familiar that it is easy to miss its significance. I will share three significant consequences of having a point of view. Each consequence reveals something about the valuable role you play in your consciousness.

Unifies experience. First, your first-person perspective unifies many elements of consciousness into a single experience. When you pay attention to your experiences, you can see that you do not merely have many different experiences. You can also see that these many experiences are part of a single, first-person perspective.

To illustrate, consider your current experience of reading or hearing these words. This experience includes many experiences, such as your experience of your thoughts, feelings, and contents of your visual or auditory field. These experiences together comprise a unified, first-person experience.

To see the unification of your experiences, you don't have to watch molecules pack together in your brain or read the latest neuroscience. You can see this unity directly by focusing on your own unified perspective.

The unity of your perspective points to a unifying element. Without a unifying element, the many contents of your consciousness would not be unified into a single perspective. To see what I mean, suppose there were a thinking chip, a feeling chip, and an intending chip on a table. These three chips don't form a single unified perspective; instead each chip generates its own content of consciousness. While each chip may have its own field of awareness in which its contents of consciousness occur, the individual perspectives do not thereby constitute a larger perspective that includes all the contents of consciousness together. To make a unified perspective, something else is required. Without unification, the thinking, feeling, and intending are disparate contents of disparate things; they do not belong to a single perspective.

So, the unification of consciousness depends on a unifier. Third-person shapes, transitions, or functions do not, all on their own, add up to a singular, first-person perspective. A complete description of third-person states leaves out a description of *who* the conscious elements belong to. The who is the unifier of consciousness.

We can analyze the who in terms of a first-person conscious substance: the conscious substance is the who. A conscious substance can unify diverse contents of consciousness into a single perspective. For example, as a conscious substance, you can unify diverse thoughts, feelings, and images into a single perspective. You are the "point" in your point of view.

In summary, your first-person perspective unifies your consciousness. By being a conscious substance that can have a perspective, you are able to unify diverse contents of consciousness into a single perspective.

Locates your body. Second, by having a first-person perspective, you are able to discern which body in a room of people belongs to you. Have you ever wondered how you know which body is yours?

Initially, it may seem trivial to identify your body. After all, your body is the one you control, and surely, you can easily tell which body you control by simply paying attention to your conscious experience of moving your own body.

However, this method of discerning which body is yours highlights a significant premise. The premise is this: you are able to discern which *experiences* are yours. For you only know which body you control by knowing which experience of controlling a body is your experience. For example, if you experience yourself moving your finger, you can know that the subsequent motion of a finger belongs to you only if you know that the experience of moving the finger was indeed your experience. But how do you know that? Consider that there could be many conscious experiences of many different people moving a finger. How do you know which of these many experiences are yours?

To be clear, I am not asking this question to create doubts. On the contrary, I want to expose the foundation of your knowledge of your experiences. This knowledge is significant. For to know which experiences are yours, it is not enough to merely be aware of some set of experiences. You must also be aware *who* the set of experiences belongs to. In other words, you must have some knowledge of yourself as a subject of your experiences.

To draw this idea out, suppose you become aware of a state of happiness. This awareness of happiness lets you know that some happiness is real. But to be aware that some happiness is real is not the same as being aware of who the happiness belongs to. Are *you* happy? Or could you be (empathetically) aware of someone else's happiness? This question displays a key distinction: awareness of an experience is not the same as awareness of who this experience belongs to.

So, to be aware of who is having a certain experience, it is not enough to merely be aware of an experience. One must also be aware of the subject of that experience.

My reasoning here highlights an argument for the conclusion that you can be aware of the subject of your experiences. The argument is this:

1. You can know which body is yours.
2. You can only know which body is yours if you can know which experiences (of your body) are yours.
3. You cannot know which experiences are yours unless you can be aware of the subject of your experiences (i.e., the one having your experiences).
4. Therefore, you can be aware of the subject of your experiences.

This argument highlights again the role of the subject in a perspective. If this argument is sound, then when you are aware of your perspective, you are aware of yourself, a subject, having your experiences. By being aware of yourself having experiences, you are able to be aware of which point of view belongs to you.

In summary, by awareness of your point of view, you are able to tell which body is yours. Your awareness of your point of view allows you to be aware of the subject of the bodily motions you experience. This awareness in turn allows you to discern which body in a room belongs to you.

Sets you apart. Third, the experience of a point of view also sets you apart from other things that don't have a point of view. For example, you are not a rock, a spoon, or a sandstorm. Why not? Well, an important difference between you and these things is that you, unlike these things, have a point of view.

Now to be clear, I am not supposing here that a point of view could not be present in a sandstorm. Maybe some conscious substance could animate a sandstorm, for example, into a first-person perspective. In that case, we might suppose that the sandstorm composes a bodily state of a conscious substance. Still, the bodily state itself is not a first-person perspective. After all, a description of the third-person, spatial aspects of a sandstorm would not, all by itself, include a description of the first-person aspects of a conscious substance's point of view.

From these observations, we can deduce something significant about your relationship to neurons. In particular, we can deduce, contra Francis Crick, that you are not merely a pack of neurons, at least not if neurons are fundamentally characterizable in terms of third-person, spatial aspects and functions. For a pack of neurons, like a sandstorm, has no first-person perspective of its own. Yet, you have a first-person perspective. Therefore, you are not a pack of neurons.

As a final note, I want to be clear that I am not saying that neurons play no role in your consciousness. On the contrary, as we saw in the previous chapter, we can explain mind-body interaction in terms of the capacities of a conscious substance. On this account, neural states can—at least in principle—be part of a bodily state of a conscious substance.

In summary, your first-person perspective points to an integral role you play in consciousness. You not only have consciousness, but you also have consciousness that is organized into a perspective. You are a subject that organizes consciousness into a perspective. Without you, the *subject*, you would have no unified consciousness, no ability to identify which experiences are yours, and no way to distinguish yourself from things that have no perspective (like packs of neurons). But with you in the picture, you can identify yourself as the being who has your first-person perspective.

THIRD ARROW: YOUR SELF-AWARENESS

A third arrow that points to you is your own self-awareness. Self-awareness allows you to uncloak the real you. The real is you is not your thoughts, feelings, intentions, or bodily states. These things comprise your cloak. The real you is deeper in. When you look under the cloak of your consciousness, you can be aware of yourself.

There are two ways I think you can be aware of yourself: directly and indirectly. You can be aware of yourself *indirectly* by being directly aware of your own experiences. This awareness gives you an indirect view of yourself. You are aware of yourself as whatever it is that is the subject of your experiences.

But I also think you can witness the subject of your experiences *directly*. To be aware of yourself directly, focus inward. When you do, you can be aware of both your experiences and the one having your experiences. While philosophers debate different accounts of self-awareness, my proposal here is illuminated by acts of inner reflection.[3] By directing one's attention inward, I believe that one can—with some effort and concentration—be directly aware of the one who is aware. The one who has your consciousness is the real, familiar you. (We will consider a famous Humean objection to this premise in the next section.)

Moreover, I believe you can be self-aware based on your ability to be aware of your perspective. Here is why. A first-person perspective consists of three components: (i) contents of consciousness (e.g., thoughts, feelings, a visual field); (ii) a field of awareness of those contents (i.e., your mind); and (iii) the subject to whom the perspective belongs. To be aware of your first-person perspective, then, involves awareness of these components. The third component is the subject of the perspective, which is you. If you were not aware of the subject of your perspective, then you could not know that the perspective is yours. But you can know that your perspective is yours. So, you can be aware of the subject of your perspective. Therefore, to be aware of your first-person perspective involves self-awareness.

In summary, you can see yourself by looking within. To see yourself, notice first any thoughts or feelings you may be having. Then ask yourself, "Who is having your current thoughts and feelings?" If you can even ask this question, then you can be self-aware. Self-awareness gives you a window into who you are—the real you.

WHERE THE ARROWS POINT TO: SELF

The three arrows each point to you. First, your oneness points to you as one being. You are not a disparate scatter of particles; you are a single thing that unifies many things. Second, your point of view points to you as a first-person reality. Third, your self-awareness points to you as the subject of consciousness. Together these arrows point to a singular, first-person center of consciousness, which is *yourself*.

To see yourself, it is perhaps easier to first see the things you are not. See a thought in your mind. Is that you? It is not. The thought comes, and the

---

[3] B. Gertler, "Self-Knowledge," *Stanford Encyclopedia of Philosophy* (2015), https://plato.stanford .edu/entries/self-knowledge.

thought goes; the thought changes. But there is something that perceives the thought (as the thought is changing) that does not change. You are the perceiver. Therefore, you are not the thought. In the same way, you are not your feelings, your intentions, or your bodily states. Each of these come and go, while you, who perceives them, remains. So you are none of those things.

What you are, then? You are the most familiar thing in all reality. You are not your thoughts, feelings, intentions, or bodily states. You are the one who has your thoughts, feelings, intentions, and bodily states. You are the self who is always there.

I call the view that personal beings are selves "self-realism." According to self-realism, the thing that you see in first-person awareness is real; it is the subject of your consciousness. This subject is a first-person self, which you can see directly through the window of self-awareness.

By this analysis, you do not need to posit a first-person self to explain other things you are aware of. Rather, a first-person self is among the things you can be aware of directly. You can recognize the existence of your own self by your own direct awareness of yourself as the subject of your thoughts, feelings, and emotions.[4]

QUESTIONS

I will address five questions about self-realism. By addressing these questions, I hope to remove obstacles to seeing yourself by your own clearest light.

Question 1: Can I be aware of myself? Scottish philosopher David Hume famously argued that we are never aware of ourselves. Instead, we are only aware of sense impressions, like feelings, thoughts, and visual phenomena. He writes,

> For my part, when I enter most intimately into what I call myself, I always stumble on some particular perception or other, of heat or cold, light or shade, love or hatred, pain or pleasure. I can never catch myself at any time without a perception, and can never observe anything but the perception. When my perceptions are removed for any time, as by sound sleep; so long am I insensible of myself, and may truly be said not to exist.[5]

---

[4]In the next section, I will address the Humean worry that there is no "self" apart from the states of consciousness.

[5]D. Hume, *A Treatise of Human Nature*, ed. L. A. Selby-Bigge (Oxford: Clarendon, 1896), 1.4.6.

This passage poses an objection to self-realism. According to self-realism, a self is a subject of one's consciousness; the self is what *has* one's consciousness. Yet, Hume suggests that he is never aware of himself as something distinct from the states of consciousness themselves. What he apprehends instead are particular perceptions (heat, cold, light, love, etc.). As far as he can tell, then, there is not a unifying subject behind or anchoring those sense impressions. There are just the sense impressions. If that is right, then selves behind the impressions do not exist.

I have a friendly response. I will show how I think we can actually incorporate the root motivation behind Hume's thought without denying the existence of selves. Here's his motivation. Hume's skepticism of selves grows out of his analysis of conscious experiences, which he calls "sense impressions." For example, experiences of motion, causation, feelings, flowers, logical operations, and so on are all different sense impressions. So, since a self, if it existed, would not merely be a sense impression, conscious experience does not and cannot include a self.

By careful analysis, however, I believe there is a way to locate a self within certain sense impressions. To see what I mean, first recall the window theory of perception. According to the window theory, senses are themselves windows into contents of reality (whether the contents are wholly in your mind or also independent of your mind). For example, a sense of a thought is a window into a thought. In other words, when you sense a thought, you are directly aware of a thought in your mind. In the same way, if you have a sense of yourself, this sense is a window into yourself. So, for example, let us say that you have a sense impression of yourself thinking. Then this sense impression consists of your awareness of yourself thinking. Notice that yourself thinking has two parts: yourself and thinking. A sense impression of yourself thinking is a window of awareness into both. Therefore, this sense impression includes awareness of yourself.

On this analysis, Hume's own observations actually point to the reality of self-awareness. For Hume observes that every effort to witness oneself involves a sense impression, such as the impression of oneself thinking or feeling. By the window theory, these sense impressions involve awareness, which allow one to identify the contents of one's impression (thoughts, feelings, images, etc.). When you sense yourself thinking, then, you are aware of yourself thinking. Again, this awareness (of yourself thinking) includes an awareness of both your thinking and yourself, the one who is thinking. If this analysis is correct, then you are not hidden "behind" a sense impression of yourself. You are included in it.

This distinction between being *behind* an impression and being *in* an impression is the key to open the window of self-awareness. When you turn your awareness in on yourself, that very act of awareness is itself a sense impression. The sense impression belongs to you; it's yours. But the impression is also of you—that is, you are a content of the impression of yourself. For this reason, in self-awareness, you are both a content of your awareness and the subject that has your awareness. In other words, you are the familiar, common element in many sense impressions of yourself. Hume did not display this distinction between self-impressions and the self in self-impressions. If he had, I suspect he would have removed a significant barrier to recognizing his own self-awareness.

Self-realism can also explain some of Hume's observations. Hume observes that different attempts to witness himself involve different sense impressions. Self-realism can account for these differences because different impressions can provide different views of a common reality within each impression. The idea here is that different self-impressions can contain a common constituent. For just as a square image can be a common content of many different visual impressions, *you* can be a common constituent of many different self-impressions. You can be both the background behind your sense impressions (like the sky behind the birds), while also a content of self-awareness. While sense impressions of yourself are not themselves you, they are windows into you—the common content of every self-impression.

When we bring Hume's observations into closer analysis, then, they don't pose a problem for genuine self-awareness. On the contrary, they point to the many ways you can witness yourself, as one who is thinking, one who is feeling, one who is intending, and so on. Each impression of yourself is a window into a common constituent, you.

As a final note on Hume's concern, sometimes prior concepts of oneself can limit one's sight. For example, if one associates oneself with a certain bodily form, then one will not find oneself by looking inward. Or if one associates oneself with the vivacity of a sense impression, then one will not find a sense impression that uniquely picks out a self. What one finds, as Hume observes, are many sense impressions. The self is subtler, or more perhaps familiar and universal, than particular, fleeting sense impressions. Sometimes it takes a different conceptual analysis to see what could be the most clearly seeable thing.

Question 2: Does self-awareness reveal my entire nature? Not necessarily. To be aware of something doesn't necessarily involve awareness of all it. For example, I can be aware of a coin by looking at the head's side of that coin without seeing its tail's side. In the same way, you could be aware of yourself without seeing all of yourself.

Indeed, observations of mind-body interaction provide evidence that there is more to you than what you see from the first-person perspective. In the previous chapter, I introduced the conscious substance theory to provide a model of mind-body interaction. This theory predicts that you have basic capacities to cause packages of first-person states and bodily changes. Some of these capacities appear to be subconscious—that is, they operate without your conscious awareness. If that is correct, then there is more to you than you see just by your own conscious awareness.

Still, self-awareness reveals you. When you see yourself, you do not merely see a side or state of you. You see you, directly.

The premise that you can see yourself directly is a consequence of the window theory of perception. According to the window theory, you can see things by direct awareness. When you look through the window of direct awareness, you do not merely see a representation of things on the windowpane. The contents of direct awareness are themselves real—whether those realities are experiences, thoughts, feelings, or *you*.

So, I believe that direct awareness can give you clear and direct sight of the being you are. This sight is real, as is the being you see. You may be more than you see, but you are not less.

Question 3: Am I a massless, ghostly substance? My theory does not imply this. In the previous chapter ("Your Body"), I described various options for how to analyze your relationship to a body. One option, recall, was Bailey's shaped-object option, according to which you are a conscious being that can also have spatial aspects like size, shape, and location. On this account, you are not a ghost in a machine. Instead, you are a special kind of spatial machine—one that can be conscious.

A related option—which is my own current working hypothesis—is that physical aspects of you are extrinsic aspects of more fundamental, intrinsic states of you. On this account, the aspects that characterize your bodily states only characterize you in a derivative way, just as an avatar that represents you on a computer screen may characterize you derivatively. For example, if a certain shape and mass characterizes your bodily state, then, insofar as you are in that bodily state, we might say that you have a certain shape and mass (derivatively).

On either option, you are not a ghostlike entity inside a machine. Rather, you are a conscious self (substance) that operates the machinery of your body.

Question 4: How are a body, soul, and spirit integrated? Believers in souls sometimes debate whether you have three parts (body, soul, and spirit) or just two (body and soul). The first view is the tripartite view, while the second is the bipartite view. Which of these is correct?

In my view, neither one is quite right (at least not without translation). For in my view, there is technically only one substance that could qualify as you. That substance is not a mere part of you. It is you. Moreover, if there are souls, you do not *have* a soul as a mere part (or component) of you. Rather, I would say that you *are* a soul—a self.

But the term *soul* is a term of art. Here I stipulate my own minimal definition: *soul* is a label for any first-person, conscious substance, where a first-person substance is a substance that one sees when one views oneself in first-person, introspective awareness. So, if you are a first-person conscious substance, then you are a soul on this definition.

Self-realism illuminates this account of souls. According to self-realism, when you apprehend yourself, you are aware of a singular, first-person center of consciousness. In this center is a first-person self—a soul. To see your soul, then, is to see yourself, and to see yourself is to see the most familiar thing in all of reality.

Note that it is consistent with my account that you also have shape, mass, volume, and other so-called physical aspects. Self-realism leaves this open.

That said, self-realism can also help illuminate how body, soul, and spirit might go together into a single being. To illustrate how this integration might work, here is my current working model. Let "bodily state" be a state that consists of bodily aspects (e.g., shape and mass). Let "soulish state" be a state that consists of aspects associated with consciousness (e.g., sensations, thoughts). Let "spiritual state" refer to a state that consists of aspects associated with spiritual things (e.g., being capable of thinking about God, veneration, and perhaps being able to exist without a bodily state). These can all go together (at least in principle) in a single substance. For that which has bodily states could also have soulish and spiritual states. In this way, a self can unify various bodily, soulish, and spiritual states into a single being.

According to this model, the terms *body*, *soul*, and *spirit* are different ways of pointing to the same individual substance. So, for example, if you point to someone's body, you are pointing to them via their spatial expression (or representation). If you point to someone's personality, you are pointing to them via their psychological profile. And if you point to someone's spirit, you are pointing deeper into spiritual aspects of their real self (the conscious substance), which is the focal point of their spatial and psychological manifestations.

As a final note, I want to highlight the priority of a conscious substance on any of these analyses. According to the conscious substance theory, conscious *states* emerge in the context of a conscious *substance*. Without the conscious substance, there would be no conscious states or bodily states. For the states belong to the substance. In this sense, a conscious substance is itself prior to its states, whether bodily, soulish, or spiritual.

Question 5: How could a first-person, conscious self come to be? Some philosophers say there is no place for selves to enter the natural order of events. For in the natural order of events, things unfold according to natural processes. These natural processes do not include substantial selves. Instead, they include systems of particles. Systems of particles change in form and organization. Changes in form and organization are third-person spatial changes, whereas a self is a first-person reality. How could third-person realities turn into a fundamentally first-person reality? That may seem impossible.

This reflection could leave one to question whether any selves could ever exist. After all, one might think a first-person self couldn't be explained solely in terms of third-person particles. Then, if one thinks that everything is explained ultimately in terms of third-person particles, one can only infer that there is no first-person self.[6]

So, how could any first-person self ever exist in the first place?

This question points to the purpose of this book. So far, I have worked to uncover the nature of a personal being, like you. But my purpose is bigger: I want to understand how there could be any personal beings at all. The first part of this book prepares us to appreciate the significance of the existence of personal beings. Still, we have not yet identified resources for explaining the existence of personal beings. So our journey is not over. To continue our inquiry into the nature and origin of persons, I will next seek to understand how any personal being could exist in the first place.

SUMMARY

Three arrows point to you. First, the arrow of your oneness points to you as an individual. Second, the arrow of your first-person perspective points to you as a center point of consciousness. Third, the arrow of your self-awareness points to you as a self. Together these aspects point to a first-person subject of consciousness.

A first-person subject of consciousness is what I call a "first-person self." You qualify as a first-person self if you meet these three conditions: (i) you are real, (ii) your first-person consciousness is real, and (iii) a complete third-person description of material bodies is not a complete description of you. By the light of introspection, you can see that you do meet these conditions. Therefore, you are a first-person self.

While a self may have bodily states, a self is not reducible to its bodily states. When you view yourself from within, your bodily states are not the target of your awareness. You are.

To see yourself is to see a great treasure at the center of many treasures. Your thoughts are treasures. Your feelings are treasures. Your hopes are treasures. But you are greater than all of these. Without you, you would

---

[6]P. K. Unger, "I Do Not Exist," in *Perception and Identity*, ed. G. F. Macdonald (London: Macmillan, 1979).

have no thoughts, no feelings, and no hopes. You are the treasure through which all your other treasures can come into your enjoyment. You are the "who" around which all your experiences have their existence, meaning, and value.

By putting light on the "who" of consciousness, we prepare ourselves for the next question in our quest: How could a being like you come to exist in the first place? This question is perhaps the toughest and most profound question anyone can ask. Yet, it is central to our quest. To understand who you really are, we need to understand not only what you are, but also the stuff that could make you. Thus, we will investigate your possible origin next.

■ ■ ■

Your questions about the strange wall before you have become almost unbearable. "What is this wall?" you wonder. "How have meaningful messages appeared from the dirt and rocks that have slid off from it?"

The mysterious word *mindless* still remains inscribed on the dirt wall. In frustration, you kick the wall directly in the center of the inscription. This time something different happens. A final layer of dirt and rocks crumbles to the ground to reveal something smooth and shiny beneath. You wipe away some remaining clumps of dirt on the surface to see what it is. Behind the dirt is a large mirror, reflecting the light of your lantern.

As you hold up your lantern to the mirror, you see a familiar sight. It is an image of you, reflected in the mirror. You look into your eyes. As you do, you see beyond the familiar shapes and colors of your body into something deeper. You begin to see, behind your familiar eyes, your familiar self. You wonder who this familiar self really is.

Your contemplation breaks as you feel a stray pebble bump into your foot. You look down to see if there is a new message. There is!

The message reads clearly:

Proceed with caution.

Looking back toward the mirror, you notice a small gap near the mirror's edge. Using your fingers, you pull the edge of the mirror toward you. The mirror swings back like a huge door. The path forward is now wide open.

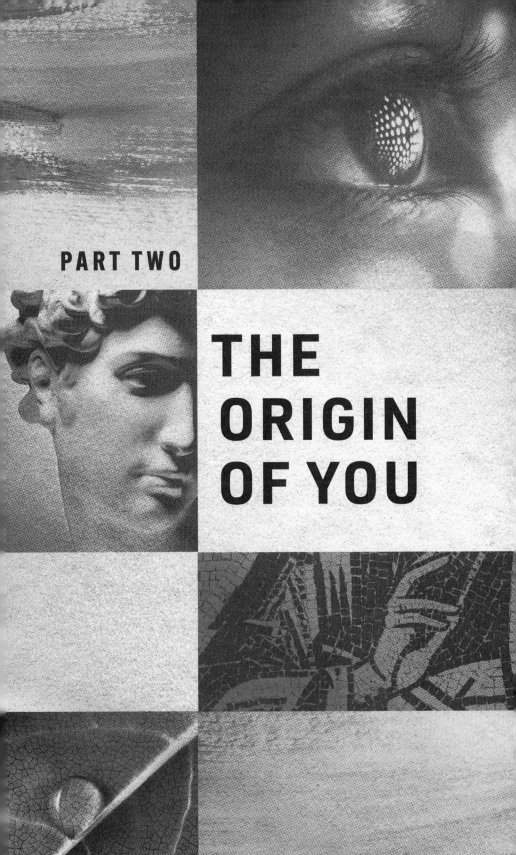

PART TWO

THE ORIGIN OF YOU

9

THE CONSTRUCTION PROBLEM

*How it is that anything so remarkable as a state of consciousness
comes about as a result of irritating nervous tissue,
is just as unaccountable as the appearance
of Djin when Aladdin rubbed his lamp.*

T. H. HUXLEY

WE ARE NOW READY to begin the next stage of our investigation. In this stage, we will consider how something like you, a conscious being, could have come to be. This stage is essential to our quest to uncover the nature and origin of a being like you. Your origin says something about what you are made of, why you are here, and the meaning of your life. If we can see into the depths of your origin, we can see into the depths of who you really are.

To proceed, we will need to move through a tight territory. This territory is dark, and few people ever even attempt to come through this place. The tightness of the territory will help guide us.

Here is a road map of what is to come in this second part of the book. We will spend the next three chapters feeling dark walls on all sides. Each dark wall represents a problem that blocks certain theories of your possible origin— from a certain angle. By blocking these options, we will be forced to crouch into an even tighter space to continue. Then, in the next two chapters, we will continue through the tight space until we reach a light at the end of the tunnel. This light will shine on the fundamental reality that makes you who you are.

In this chapter, I will seek to illuminate different parts of the construction problem. Each part exposes constraints on constructing consciousness. One constraint that will come into view is this: purely third-person, mindless materials—whether grains of sand or carbon atoms—are inadequate, on their own, to make first-person consciousness. This thesis, if true, casts a dark blanket over a purely mindless explanation of the contents of your mind: if there is any explanation of the contents of consciousness, it is not purely in terms of mindless materials. Seeing this constraint will prepare us for the next steps in our journey as we investigate the prospect of making a conscious being.

HOW TO MAKE SAND ALIVE

To help convey the general problem of constructing consciousness, I will begin by considering the prospect of constructing consciousness out of sand. By focusing on some simple and clear cases, I hope to illuminate some general principles.

To begin, suppose we are given an assignment: make some sand alive. How might we proceed? The first part of the book prepares us to appreciate the challenge of making sand alive. In chapter seven, I offered a model of how to make things alive in terms of a conscious substance. On this model, being "alive" comes from something that is capable of consciousness. Suppose that is right. Then making sand alive will involve turning some sand into a conscious substance. How might we do that?

The nature of this challenge depends on the nature of things in consciousness. In the first part of our inquiry, we examined these contents in our own consciousness: feelings, thoughts, intentional choices, perception, and value. We saw specific challenges with constructing each of these items out of purely mindless materials from scratch. Each item provides a unique window into the challenge of constructing consciousness from scratch.

Let us have a closer look, then, at the challenge of making each of these items within consciousness. For the sake of focus, I will first consider the prospect of using grains of sand to make the contents of consciousness we find in ourselves. Then, in the next section, I will identify some constraints for constructing *any* consciousness-making material.

Feelings. What exactly is so challenging about making a feeling out of sand? Some people have suggested that the challenge of making feelings out of any purely material stuff is based on a general principle of like-causes-like. The idea here is that causes must be like their effects. For example, if third-person states of sand are very much unlike first-person feelings, then third-person states of sand cannot cause first-person feelings.

I do not think the principle of like-causes-like exposes the root challenge, however. After all, causes are often quite unlike their effects. For example, fire causes smoke, but fire is different in many respects from smoke. Moreover, the conscious substance theory, which I developed in the first part of this book, predicts that causes can be categorically different from their effects. On this theory, a conscious substance can cause thoughts and feelings. Yet, a substance is itself categorically different from a thought or a feeling. So, while there may be other ways of interpreting "like" causes, the problem I want to draw attention to is not a problem of mere differences.

The construction problem is a sharper and more specific blade. It cuts away certain types of incongruent constructions. We see this problem by seeing certain incongruencies between certain natures.

To illustrate the concept of construction incongruence, consider an image in your mind. This image cannot, just on its own, be the basis for making a rock outside your mind. Why not? Because a mental image is the wrong kind of material for making (nonmental) rocks. In this case, there is a construction incongruence. You see a construction incongruence when you see, by insight into different natures, that certain things cannot be the sole basis (causal or explanatory) for certain others.

In general, some materials are the wrong materials for constructing certain things. For example, prime numbers will never add up to form a bowling ball. We do not need to check every prime number to verify this. We can see, by insight into numbers, that numbers are the wrong materials to make bowling balls. Similarly, by reason, we can see that ice cannot melt into feelings, ocean waves cannot roll into stories, and sheets of paper don't fold into sensations. In each case, the materials are wrong. Reason has the power to reveal that certain materials are wrong because reason has the power to illuminate natures, so that we can see whether one material can be constructed from another.

To see how construction incongruence can pose a challenge for constructing consciousness, consider again the project of making sand feel sad. How might we make sand sad? Suppose we try this: we pack some sand into a cubical configuration. Would the sand thereby feel sad?

It will help to separate two related questions. One question is this: could a cubical configuration by itself *create* sadness? That's my target question. We can separate this target question from another question: could a cubical configuration *contribute* to sadness? Answering this question is not as hard, especially if there is already a conscious being. To illustrate how a shape might contribute to consciousness, consider two options. First, suppose a conscious substance is present (maybe in the sand). Then perhaps changing the shape of some sand might make that substance feel sad by causing it to become aware of a shape it does not like. Here is a second option: perhaps there is a law of nature that links cubical configurations with sadness. In either case, the cubical configuration would contribute to the total explanation of why there is a sad sensation. Still, in neither case is the cubical configuration the sole basis of the creation of sadness. So even if cubicalness contributes to a sensation, it doesn't follow that cubicalness could make a sensation on its own.

By separating related questions, we can bring our question into clearer focus. The question is this: Would packing sand into a cube thereby, on its own, create sadness? The light of reason illuminates a challenge. By reason, I think we can see, via insight into cubicalness and sadness, that cubicalness does not on its own explain the creation of sadness.

To increase the resolution of this challenge, let us zoom in on the meaning of the term *explains*. We can distinguish between two translations. First, if we say a shape doesn't explain a sensation, we could mean that a mere shape does not by itself help us *see* that the sensation would occur. For example, by seeing a cubical pile of sand, we do not thereby see that sand would be sad (apart from some independent knowledge of some law, say, that links sadness with being cubical). So mystery remains: Why would *that* shape make *that* sensation? The shape by itself doesn't tell the answer. In this case, there is an explanatory gap in terms of what we can see.[1]

---

[1] For an analysis of the possible implications of an explanatory gap, see D. Papineau, "The Problem of Consciousness," in *The Oxford Handbook of the Philosophy of Consciousness*, ed. U. Kriegel (Oxford: Oxford University Press, 2020).

There is a second, stronger translation. It isn't just that we do *not see* that something with a certain shape would thereby have a certain sensation. By the light of reason, one might think we can also *see* that cubicalness is not, all by itself, the basis for sadness. If so, then sadness cannot have its sole basis in shape.

To review, I claim that packing sand into a cube would not thereby make that sand sad. This claim has two sides. First, there is the prediction side: we cannot predict, just from seeing that something is cubical, that it would thereby be sad. Second, there is the principle side: we can see, by insight into cubicalness and sadness, that cubicalness cannot in principle be the complete basis of sadness. If these claims are right, then unless the sand becomes sad without any basis at all, something else is required to make sand sad.

At this point, you might wonder why I am focused on making consciousness out of a cube of sand. Isn't it already obvious that sand, of any shape, isn't conscious? And don't we already know that consciousness arises in the context of a functioning brain? Why, then, am I concerned with shapes of sand?

I am concerned with shapes of sand because they help me focus on simple cases to illustrate the concept of a construction constraint. What I want to show here is that there are at least certain constraints on constructing consciousness. I begin with simple examples to establish clarity. For me, the problem of making feelings out of sand comes alive in my mind when I focus on examples. If I can establish clarity in certain cases, I can then expand from there to see if making the shapes or motions more complex would make a difference.

I want to emphasize that my goal here is not to argue that shapes cannot make any difference to consciousness. Indeed, I think shapes can make a difference when a conscious-capable substance is present. In chapter seven, I offered an account of how a functioning brain could affect consciousness (in terms of the capacities of a conscious substance that can link contents of consciousness with spatial brain states). My aim here is to draw out a special challenge with explaining the *original* emergence of consciousness, apart from any conscious-capable substance.[2]

---

[2]For a fuller account of how a conscious substance theory can facilitate mind-body interaction, recall chapter seven, "Your Body."

To appreciate the role of a conscious substance, suppose no conscious substance is present. Suppose instead there are only grains of sand or carbon atoms. Could consciousness then arise?

In the absence of a conscious substance, the available materials are different. For then the material in which feelings could be made is missing. For example, if sand swirls in the wind, its swirling is not itself a conscious substance, or any substance. So, if there was a time without any conscious-capable beings, we might wonder: How did the first consciousness ever get started?

My observation so far is just this: in the absence of a conscious substance, packing sand into a cube would not in itself explain (or be the sole basis of) the existence of sadness. Again, by insight into cubicalness and sadness, I think it is possible to see that cubicalness doesn't all by itself explain (predict or make) sadness.[3]

Suppose this much is right. Let us consider how we might extend these results. I take up the light of reason. Sometimes reason can reveal that some differences are irrelevant to make a difference. For example, by reason, we can see that differences between prime numbers cannot make a difference with respect to whether a prime number could become a prime minister. No prime number could become a prime minister. By reason, I think we can see that the size of the number is clearly irrelevant.

In the same way, I believe it is possible to see, by reason, that a mere difference in shape is irrelevant to make a difference with respect to making a sensation. If so, then reason can extend our sight. For example, if we can see that packing sand into a *cube* won't by itself make sand sad, then we can see that packing sand into a *sphere* won't make it sad, either. Difference in shape is irrelevant. By insight into irrelevant differences, we can then extend our sight of some constraints on constructing consciousness.

How far can we extend our sight? For example, would it make a difference if the grains of sand functioned like a brain? To test this hypothesis,

---

[3]For the sake of focus, I am leaving to the side here the prospect of a *law-like* connection between a shape and a sensation. Later in our inquiry, I will say more about how I think law-like connections could be possible (in terms of the natures and capacities of a more fundamental substance). At this stage, however, I am seeking to highlight why certain aspects, like shape, are not *on their own* enough to explain feelings (apart from a more fundamental law or explanation). Seeing this positions us to see more clearly what it might take to construct consciousness.

imagine we put the sand into a machine that causes the sand to come into a spherical configuration after being in a cubical configuration. In this case, there is an input state (spherical) and output state (cubical). This input-output pair defines a simple function. Would the sand then be sad? I don't think we need to guess here. I think it is possible to see, clearly, by insight into shape and sadness, that a mere change in shape does not, all on its own, make sadness. Adding complexity makes no difference: merely changing the complexity of the motions, shapes, or functions does nothing to reveal a relevant difference. If that's right, then making grains of sand function like a brain would not, merely in terms of their function, be enough to explain the emergence of feelings. More is required.

To be clear, I have not ruled out the prospect of emergence, where feelings emerge out of prior causes. My question here is not about whether feelings emerged, but how they might have. I will provide a positive account of how I think consciousness can and does emerge in the penultimate chapter.

So far, my proposal is this: mindless, third-person spatial changes (whether functional or structural) are not, just by themselves, enough to construct consciousness. Call this proposal, "the construction constraint." According to the construction constraint, it takes more to make consciousness than merely reconfiguring mindless matter.

To complete this section, I will offer a couple further considerations to serve your analysis. First, a construction constraint may help explain the common conviction that certain things, like sand, could not be conscious. In the chapter on feelings, we considered the problem of explaining why throwing sand into the air wouldn't make that sand feel sad. The construction problem explains the problem. The problem is not just that we have no empirical evidence that sand is conscious—for maybe sand is part of a conscious substance we don't know about. The problem is more fundamental: if grains of sand are purely third-person, mindless units of reality (without a conscious substance), then throwing sand into the air only results in third-person, mindless changes. By insight into the nature of purely third-person, spatial aspects, I think it is possible to see that third changes do not, all on their own, add up to a first-person conscious experience. If so, then we have a more fundamental explanation of the conviction that sand can't be conscious: the materials are wrong.

Second, introspection may illuminate the same construction constraint from another angle. Here is how. Consider a shape encoded in a mental image in your mind. On the window theory of introspective perception (see chapter four), you have direct access to the intrinsic aspects of this mental image. Suppose that is correct. Then by seeing the image, you can see its intrinsic aspects, including any intrinsic aspect of sadness. So, if the image includes sadness, you could be aware of this sadness just as you can be aware of its intrinsic shape and color. But do you see sadness in your images? Speaking for myself, when I attend to an image in my mind, I do not sense that the image itself has any intrinsic sadness or any other feeling. On the contrary, by introspection, I can see that the images in my own mind don't themselves have any feelings in themselves. If that is right, then a shape does not, by itself, suffice to explain or make a feeling (whether in sand or in an image).

Again, we can extend this analysis to other aspects (e.g., changes in shape, functions, and other quantitative aspects). For if one can see that shape is not sufficient for feelings, then in the same way, one can see that other purely quantitative aspects are not sufficient for feelings.

As always, see what you can see for yourself. When you consider a shape, do you see that this shape would of itself make a sensation? Or do you have the sense that more is required? Only you are in position to answer these questions for yourself.

For our purposes, and because we are in deep territory, I want to proceed extra carefully. For this reason, while it does seem evident to me that shifting shapes are not enough (on their own) to make sensations, I will not rest my analysis on this premise alone. Instead, I will proceed with the minimal premise that, at least, when I consider a shape, I do not see how that shape would, of itself, make a sensation. I see only dark.

Thoughts. Even if we could somehow make some sand feel, another task would be to make the sand think. How might we do that?

I will highlight three different construction problems with making some sand think. First, there is again the problem of wrong materials (i.e., construction incongruence). Sand is composed of third-person, mindless materials. A thought is another kind of reality: a thought is an organization of first-person conceptual materials. For example, when you think about trees, this thought contains a concept of trees, a concept you experience in first-person consciousness. The challenge, then, is to see how third-person, non-conceptual materials could construct first-person, conceptual materials. Here we have the same problem we have just considered, which is the problem of constructing first-person "sense" materials from purely third-person "nonsense" materials. This first construction problem, then, is another instance of the general problem of construction incongruence.

Second, there is the counting problem. To review briefly, this problem arises from analyzing the building power of logical links between thoughts. In the chapter on thoughts, I argued that logical links allow the construction of more types of thoughts than types of thoughtless material states. From here, I deduced the mindful thoughts theorem, which states that purely mindless states—like the scattering of sand—cannot be the sole determiner of every type of thought.

We can solve the counting problem with mental resources. The mindful thoughts theorem does not rule out a mental basis of thoughts. Indeed, according to the conscious substance theory, all thoughts can have a mental basis. To illustrate how, suppose you are contemplating some mathematical propositions. In your contemplation, you perceive—by direct awareness, perhaps—an abstract landscape of numbers and equations. This perception of abstract structures can then be a basis for the formation of certain thoughts about those structures, such as the thought that $2 + 2 = 4$. You can be aware of thoughts forming in your mind in precisely this way. Thus, if there is a mental framework already in existence (a conscious substance), then we can account for the origin of thoughts in terms of that framework.

Without a mental framework, things are different. Making mindless sand think is not like making yourself think. Making yourself think is easy: just think of something. But making mindless sand think is hard—actually, impossible, if my counting argument is sound.

In addition to these construction problems, here is a third challenge: How do we construct rational thoughts from nonrational, mindless materials?

The challenge here is to show how mindless materials could, all on their own, be a rational basis for rational thoughts. This challenge arises on all the major theories of rationality (e.g., reliabilism, evidentialism, and proper functionalism). For on every theory of rationality, rational thoughts have some rational basis. But suppose a thought has a nonrational, nonmental basis. For example, suppose some cancer cells produce the thought, "I am a living being." Then that thought would not be rational. The problem, then, is to see how any of your thoughts can be rational if they are based (both currently and ultimately) in the motions of mindless, nonrational units of reality.

To draw out the problem, consider again some sand. Suppose that wind somehow causes some sand to think (if that were possible). For example, as some grains sprinkle into the air, they collectively think, *A leaf falls on a stone*. This thought is random. Even if the thought happens to be correct, it is correct only by accident. The sand does not arrive at this thought by any fundamentally rational processes (e.g., by following principles of reason in one's mind), for the motions that caused the thought are fundamentally mindless (according to this story). The challenge, then, is to see how to construct a rational thought from purely mindless materials.

One way we might try to meet the challenge is by appealing to a process of evolution by natural selection. Perhaps rational beings are more likely to survive and have offspring. Irrational beings are less likely to survive and so die off. Hence, over time, the surviving beings tend to be relatively rational, at least in contexts relevant to their survival.

This evolutionary account, while helpful, still leaves the critical piece unexplained, however. It leaves unexplained the very mental context in which someone could form rational thoughts. Consider that an evolution could spawn self-replicators that either have no thoughts or have no thoughts that could contribute a difference to their behavior (i.e., a difference not already determined by tinier mindless causes). A deeper, more fundamental question, then, is about how any thinking powers could—in principle—come to exist in a purely mindless context in the first place. Can chemical reactions acting randomly—without direction from any mind—give rise to thought?

The question here is not an appeal to mystery. It is a question that points to what we witness clearly in our own minds. We witness ourselves forming thoughts on the basis of reasons, which in turn are reliable if they are based on sight (acquaintance with aspects of reality). But if these reasons are instead based entirely on mindless motions of cosmic debris, which themselves see nothing, then the reasons are blind; they are not based on any real insight into reality.[4]

Hasker expands upon the problem of making sound reasoning out of fundamentally mindless matter.[5] He points out that according to a certain physicalist paradigm, all our behaviors are determined by lower-level, nonmental states of matter (e.g., mindless molecules moving about). On this picture, the mindless is the fundamental determiner of everything that happens. But then, argues Hasker, principles of sound reasoning play no explanatory role. Sound reasoning is like foam on an ocean wave; the foam floats along the wave, but it makes no difference to reality, including to what we think. The fundamental problem, then, is that in a fundamentally mindless world, principles of sound reasoning make no difference to what thoughts we actually think. Instead, all thoughts are determined by a mindless noise of nonreasons. But nonreasons don't make rational thoughts.

To be clear, we could accept this result if, in addition to blind (mindless) bits, we suppose that a conscious substance with a mind is in the scene. For a conscious substance could have causal powers over what happens. In that case, it is not that mindless chemicals (say) provide the basis for rational thoughts, wholly apart from a mental context. Instead, there is mental context, a pool of awareness, in which rational thoughts can emerge.

To illustrate how a mental context can make the difference, consider this "reason-based" model. On this model, personal beings have a mind that includes a power to reason. For example, a person can use reason to explore abstract structures in a logical landscape of ideas. In this way, a person can see (by direct awareness) a difference between logical and illogical inferences. The sight of logical inferences can then form a rational basis for rational thoughts. In this way, rational thought can have a rational basis in a mental context, where someone has the power to see logical links in their mind.

But without a mental context, this rational basis for rational thought is not available. In particular, there is nothing about grains of sand, say, that

---

[4]I owe the reference to cosmic debris to Bill McClymonds.
[5]W. Hasker, *The Emergent Self* (Ithaca, NY: Cornell University Press, 2001), 117.

would, by themselves, predict a rational thought. Instead, one can see, by insight into rationality, that mindless grains of sand are insufficient, in principle, to make a rational thought just by themselves (absent a mind). If so, then there is a problem with constructing rational thoughts purely out of mindless grains of sand.

I believe the root problem, then, with making sand think rationally is that sand doesn't have a mind. If we could make a mind out of sand, then perhaps we could solve the problem. But how do we make a mind out of sand? Without a mind, a pile of sand has the wrong materials for thoughts, let alone rational thoughts (based on reason). That's the problem.

Introducing mental materials pushes the construction problem deeper into reality. The obvious question now is this: How can there be a mind? If sand can't make rational thoughts (on its own), how could sand make a rational mind (on its own)? So far, we have transformed the problem of constructing rational thoughts into the more fundamental problem of constructing a mind.

For the sake of modesty, I will again seek to lean on the side of caution. So, while it does seem evident to me that thoughts cannot come out of a purely mindless context (on their own), this premise is not essential to my larger analysis. Instead, I will proceed with the more minimal premise that, at least, when I consider any third-person mindless, material things, I do not thereby see how they could, of themselves, make a real first-person thought. So, I don't see how mindless matter could make thoughts. I see only dark.

The power to choose. In chapter five, we considered various puzzles about free will. These puzzles each reveal a problem with finding free choices in a world that is fundamentally mindless.

As I argued, mindless causes present a puppet problem. If mindless things pull the strings on all our behavior, then we don't pull any strings by our own powers. Particles make us puppets.

However, I also argued that we are not merely puppets of particles. By the light of introspection, you can witness yourself directing your thoughts and actions. You can witness yourself pulling strings by your own power. You can also successfully make predictions about what you will do later based on your current intentions, which is further evidence that you have a real power to do things by your intentions.

If we are not puppets, then we have an additional construction problem. The problem is now is the problem of constructing a being that can make its own choices. If we use particles to construct a being, how can that being be free to choose a path that the particles were not already headed down?

As far as I can tell, there is only one conceivable way for any being to make a free choice: that being must be able to make choices directly by its own power to choose. As we saw in chapter five, the concept of freedom includes the concept of an agent, who is the source of a choice. Otherwise, something other than the agent pulls the strings. No one else, and nothing else, can ever make your choices for you. For you to make a choice requires *you* to make a choice.

For this reason, it seems to me that the only way to give sand the power to choose is to first convert the sand into a real agent (a conscious substance) who can make its own choices via its own intentional actions. Otherwise, the sand is a mere puppet of other things, such as the atoms composing its crystals.

We arrive then again at a fundamental problem with constructing consciousness. The foundational problem is in constructing the *being*—the substance who is capable of forming elements of consciousness. It is not obvious how we could construct a conscious being out of sand. The sand is composed of individually mindless grains. Can individually mindless grains add up to a first-person, conscious being? Reason pressures me to think not, just as reason pressures me to think that a wooden Pinocchio will not spontaneously become alive (ever).

In general, the power to choose is not derivable from purely mindless units of reality (apart from a conscious substance). Whether we construct a sandman or assemble chips into a robot, our construction does not make a power to choose. We can change the shape, size, mass, and other third-person aspects of things. But as far as reason reveals, these changes don't by themselves add up to a first-person agent with a real power to choose. So, it is unclear how free will could ever arise out of mindless grains of reality.

Awareness. Next, there is the problem of constructing conscious awareness. Consider how we might give sand awareness. We could try carving the shapes of eyes into the sand. But shapes won't give the sand sight. Shapes are blind.

Of course, there are ways to construct sophisticated imitations of sight. As with the other conscious elements (feelings, thoughts, and free choices), we might try to create something that functions *as if* it has that element. For example, we might create a computer that translates visual information from a camera. This translation of information could then be used to cause the computer to function as if it has conscious awareness. But that is not enough: to act like you are aware is not the same as actually being aware. You could *act* like you are aware of a spider without actually seeing any spider at all. So, while a simulation of awareness is possible, actual awareness is another thing entirely.

Consider, moreover, that unlike actual conscious awareness, computer functionality is entirely describable in terms of third-person facts about inputs and outputs. Blind chips do not—and cannot—add up to a field of awareness. What is left out is first-person awareness (the real thing).

On this analysis, the construction problem is a problem of category, not complexity. Everything about complex systems—whether a system of transistors, a system of stars, or a system of cargo ships—is describable entirely in terms of third-person facts (about shape, size, extension, pixels, motions, function, etc.). Yet, none of these third-person facts add up to real, first-person conscious awareness.

Leibniz illustrates this problem of constructing first-person, perceptual awareness by zooming in on mindless mechanisms. He offers the analogy of a mill:

> Supposing there were a machine, so constructed as to think, feel, and have perception, it might be conceived as increased in size, while keeping the same proportions, so that one might go into it as into a mill. That being so, we should, on examining its interior, find only parts which work one upon another, and never anything by which to explain a perception. Thus, it is in a simple substance, and not in a compound or in a machine, that perception must be sought for.[6]

This is the right time in our inquiry to appreciate Leibniz's illustration. His illustration makes use of two premises: (i) perceptual awareness is real, and

---

[6]G. Leibniz, *The Monadology and Other Philosophical Writings*, trans. R. Latta (Oxford: Clarendon, 1898), 228.

(ii) the first-person aspects of awareness are irreducible to third-person aspects of matter. In the chapter on perception, I explained why I think these premises are discernable via introspection. My argument was that, by introspection, you can be aware of your own field of awareness; so, awareness is real. Furthermore, by introspection, you can see first-person aspects of contents of your awareness (including thoughts and feelings), which you can see are not identical to third-person aspects of material reality. If so, then there is a challenging construction question here: How can purely blind, nonaware elements of reality construct, ground, explain, or produce first-person awareness?

In summary, here is the challenge. Conscious awareness exists. Yet it is not obvious how, in principle, to construct something that has conscious awareness out of unconscious bits of matter. We are not entirely in the dark. There is something that is known to generate awareness: you. You provide the mental context for awareness. The deeper question, then, is about how to generate you. If generating awareness from mindlessness is a problem, then generating a mental context from mindlessness is no less a problem.

Other aspects. You also have other aspects that contribute to the construction challenge. For example, you have intrinsic value as a person, emotions, desires, hopes, and perhaps even a sense of purpose. But grains of sand have none of those aspects. Could grains of sand gain value, emotions, desires, hopes, or a sense of purpose. It is not obvious how. Grains of sand, whether taken individually or collectively, change in spatial or quantitative aspects, like shape, motion, or structure. Yet, as with the other qualities of consciousness, mere spatial or other quantitative changes do not, by themselves, explain a change in intrinsic value, emotions, desires, hopes, or a sense of purpose.

Once again, I believe it is possible to see a construction incongruence in each case by insight into the relevant aspects. For example, by insight into quantitative aspects of sand (shape, motion, etc.) and qualitative aspects of you (intrinsic value, desiring affection, etc.), I think one can see that the quantitative aspects do not, by themselves, explain the qualitative aspects. If that is right, then sand cannot, all on its own, explain all the aspects of you. More is required.

THE PROBLEM OF MIND-MAKING

In this section, I will further draw out the challenge of constructing a being like you.

The materials problem. Each of the construction problems we have considered have in common a fundamental problem: the problem is that third-person, mindless materials seem to be the wrong materials for making first-person elements of consciousness. Grains of sand, for example, are the wrong materials for constructing consciousness. This isn't because grains have the wrong shape or move too slowly. We equally cannot make consciousness (where there is none) by piling up hammers, throwing a baseball fast, or blowing dust. To make consciousness, we need the right materials. Grains of sand, hammers, baseballs, and dust are the wrong materials. They are third-person, nonsensing states of reality. Third-person, nonsensing materials do not of themselves add up to—or explain—first-person consciousness.

Again, it is possible by reason to see that certain constructions are impossible. For example, we can see that numbers don't add up to nickels, feelings cannot transform into flowers, third-person facts don't add up to first-person facts, and so on. The materials are wrong.

I am focusing on what I think can be clear cases to emphasize that my argument need not rest on vague intuitions. It rests on construction constraints that I think one can see clearly by insight into certain natures, just as one can see clearly that 2 + 2 does not add up to a dragon. While the things I am highlight take careful analytical surgery to see, once we position ourselves in the right way, I believe at least certain constraints can come into clear view.

So, on reflection, I think it can be clear that imagination is not the product of mindless materials. Without the presence of a mind (or some field of awareness), there is nothing in the sand in itself that would have the contents of an imagination. As a matter of logic, the imagination of a mind does not consist solely of grains of sand outside a mind.

Fortunately, we are not entirely in the dark about how consciousness could come to exist. We have already identified something that can construct consciousness: a conscious substance can do it. A conscious substance is the right material. By definition, a conscious substance has the capacities to make consciousness. So, a conscious substance could, in principle have the capacities to feel, think, choose, and see. If there is a conscious substance, then there can be many different contents of consciousness.

Recall that a conscious substance is something that is capable of generating the elements of consciousness in a basic way. It doesn't generate consciousness by first having to generate third-person states. Rather, generation can be direct: the conscious substance directly forms thoughts, feelings, and intentions (within the constraints of its nature, rules of reality, and prior conditions).

Problem solved? No. Introducing a conscious substance pushes the problem deeper in the fabric of reality. Suppose feelings, thoughts, intentions, and awareness come from a conscious substance. Still, where does a conscious substance come from? From a certain perspective, introducing conscious substances may seem to only make the problem worse. If it were difficult to see how to make consciousness, it is all the more difficult to see how to make a consciousness-maker. We have pushed the problem deeper in.

The deeper problem. To illustrate the deeper problem, suppose a Mars rover discovers what looks like a large, functioning clock outside a cave. Scientists wonder where the clock came from. So, they direct the rover into the cave to find more information. Inside, the rover video captures a large factory. We now know where the clock came from. But we have a larger mystery: Where did this clock-making factory come from? Explaining a clock in terms of a clockmaker pushes back the mystery: What explains the clock-maker?

In the same way, explaining consciousness in terms of a consciousness-maker pushes back the mystery. What explains the consciousness-maker?

The mystery of consciousness is more puzzling than the mystery of a clock. For in the case of a clock, we can at least conceive of a kind of material that could be organized into a clock. The clock and a clock-maker are both made of the same kind of material after all. So we could imagine that a clock factory is itself assembled by someone operating through their body.[7]

---

[7]For details on how a first-person being may operate through a body, recall the seven drawers of the conscious substance theory in chap. 7.

The deeper problem, then, is in explaining how there could be any first-person conscious substance. How is that possible? I mean, seriously. What materials could conceivably construct a first-person conscious self, like you? Not leaves. Not sand. Not stardust. Then what?

As I have thought about this question long and hard, I have found myself pressing against dark walls. Every material I can conceive of seems to be the wrong material. All materials are either first-person (e.g., elements of consciousness) or third-person materials (elements of unconsciousness). Both kinds fail to explain how a first-person substance could exist.

Think again about the first-person elements of consciousness. By the light of introspection, you can witness yourself forming first-person elements, such as thoughts, feelings, intentions, and mental images. Yet, forming these elements of consciousness is not the same as forming a whole being (a substance) who can have its own elements of consciousness. Is it even possible to form a being? Whatever the answer, this much is as obvious as anything in the world: one cannot construct a conscious substance just by thinking or feeling a certain way. Thinking and feeling, on their own, are insufficient for constructing a conscious substance.

The other option is to use mindless, third-person materials. Can we turn them into a conscious being? I don't think so. We've already seen the many problems with using mindless, third-person materials to construct the elements of consciousness (including feelings, thoughts, powers to choose, the imagery of a dream, and so on), let alone the first-person selves that organize the elements into a perspective. On my analysis, mindless materials are also the wrong materials for constructing first-person, conscious realities.

So, I am still left with a deep problem of consciousness. My inquiry so far deepens the problem. Whether we use first-person elements of consciousness or third-person mindless materials, it is beginning to appear to me that there is no way to construct a conscious substance. To construct a conscious substance takes something else, if it is even possible at all.

Yet, here we are. How is our existence possible?

RESPONSES

Let us consider a few possible responses to the construction problems. I'll look at three.

Brute fact. Maybe there just is no explanation of first-person conscious substances (selves). Explanations must stop somewhere, one might think. Perhaps explanations stop with conscious substances.

This response admits defeat. If we cannot explain consciousness, we can always turn back. At any moment, we can head back out of the cave of consciousness. There is no shame: most people do not come even this far.

I am not ready to turn back. The light of reason compels me to look deeper. By reason, I see that if conscious substances were inexplicable, then there would be no explanation for why you or I exist or continue to exist. But then what keeps us alive? Nothing? Reason resists this result.

Besides, if conscious substances can exist without any explanation, then why don't conscious substances spontaneously appear from nowhere, uncaused, randomly wherever I go? Conscious substances don't spontaneously appear from nowhere, uncaused, wherever I go. So, I expect there is some explanation of conscious beings, even if it is hard for me to see what it could be.

Divine power. Perhaps God can help. After all, if God exists, then God is omnipotent. An omnipotent being would have the power to do anything, including make a conscious substance.

Unfortunately, this response solves nothing. The whole question is about how it is even possible—in principle—to make a conscious substance. Omnipotence doesn't answer that. Suppose it is impossible to construct conscious beings. Then it is impossible for any being, whether omnipotent or not, to construct conscious beings.

To draw out the point, suppose an omnipotent being exists. Then, by the light of reason, an omnipotent being is a possible being. A possible being can have possible powers to do possible things. But no possible being can have impossible powers to do impossible things. Some things are impossible (full stop): for example, it is impossible to construct square circles, shapeless computers, and sandy thoughts. No possible power, then, not even the greatest possible power, could construct any of these things. For no possible power could construct something that is impossible to construct.

The question remains: How can any conscious beings come to exist? Is constructing conscious beings impossible? If so, then no being can do that.

Emergence. Maybe conscious beings are made possible by certain states of matter. While we cannot see how matter does it, perhaps matter just does it somehow. After all, we don't see how the molecular structure of water makes water feel wet to us. Yet wetness emerges somehow.

You can probably anticipate what I'm going to say about this "emergence" response. Sure, conscious beings may have emerged somehow. The whole question is, how? Later, I will devote a chapter to investigating how emergence can work. At this point in our inquiry, however, we have not seen the light. We have only seen dark walls that block options on many sides. The term *emergence* labels the mystery.

In this respect, the emergence response on its own is like the divine power response. It solves nothing. It is no better than appealing to omnipotence or magic.

I should emphasize here that the construction problem is not an appeal to ignorance. I am not making inferences from what we don't know in the dark. Rather, the construction problem brings into the light certain construction constraints I believe one can see. For example, blowing sand into the wind will not—and cannot—by itself make the sand consciously aware. The materials are wrong. I believe one can see this by insight into the nature of the materials.

On a final note, brute, unexplained emergence generates an additional problem, which I call the problem of "cheap consciousness." If consciousness can emerge without any explanation, then some form of consciousness might, for all we know, emerge from any shape, including the shape of your ear or the shape of a sand crystal. But consciousness is not that cheap. We can see by our awareness of spatial structures in our imaginations that images with those structures are not thereby conscious—they are *in* consciousness, but they don't *have* consciousness. So, there are constraints on what can be conscious.

SUMMARY

In the first part of the book, we arrived at the following thesis about your nature: you are a first-person conscious self. This thesis sets us up for the second part of this book, which is an inquiry into your ultimate origin: How might a first-person conscious self ultimately come to be?

In this chapter, I sought to identify some constraints on constructing consciousness. I focused on four elements we find in our own consciousness: feelings, thoughts, the power to choose, and awareness. Each of these requires the right material. Feelings depend on the sort of thing that is capable of feeling. Thoughts depend on the sort of thing that is capable of thinking. The power to choose depends on the sort of thing that is capable of choosing. Awareness depends on the sort of thing that is capable of awareness.

On my analysis, each element of consciousness is a window into a certain type of material. This material can feel, think, choose, and be aware. This is the material of a conscious being. One constraint on constructing consciousness, then, is this: consciousness depends on the existence of a conscious being.

This constraint pushes the mystery deeper into reality. To explain consciousness, we must now explain how there could be a conscious being. Apparently, purely third-person, mindless materials, like grains of sand, are not enough. Third-person facts do not by themselves explain first-person facts. But then what could be enough?

Moreover, there are also constraints on using first-person materials, like thoughts, feelings, and intentions. You can't make a conscious being just by thinking of a conscious being. No thought, feeling, or intention is capable of generating a first-person self on its own. These materials are also wrong.

So, while first-person selves exist (by the light of the first stage of our inquiry), it is unclear how they could. The construction problem constrains our options. There is still space to continue head, but the journey forward is tight. The constraints will guide us as we go deeper in.

■ ■ ■

You step through the open door to go deeper into the cave. Suddenly, your lantern's flame goes out. It is pitch black. You pull a dimming flashlight out of your back pocket. As you shine the light at your feet, you see that the cave floor ahead of you drops steeply. To continue forward, you will have to climb down.

10

THE BINDING PROBLEM

Maybe it is wrong to think of consciousness
as made up of parts at all.

JOHN SEARLE

THE TASK OF THIS CHAPTER is to identify another constraint on the origin of a conscious being. To explain the existence of conscious beings, it is not enough to explain the individual contents of consciousness (feeling, thinking, intending, etc.). For suppose we could convert some dead materials into contents of consciousness. Still, there remains a further question about how to organize these contents into a single, unified being. What unifies your consciousness? How do diverse experiences come together to make one unified experience of a single subject? These questions point to the problem of the unity of consciousness.

In this chapter, I will consider how the unity problem can challenge us to rethink what it might take to construct a conscious being. This challenge is an extension of the general construction challenge I described in the previous chapter. The general construction challenge is about how to construct consciousness (and its contents) in general. The unification challenge is more specific: How does anything construct the unification of consciousness? What binds consciousness together? I will seek to show that, at minimum, it takes a conscious being to unify consciousness, and that therefore a unified consciousness cannot be constructed from scratch (apart from the presence of a conscious being). This result will provide an additional constraint on any theory of how you could have come to be. Seeing this constraint will further constrain our path forward.

THE UNITY OF A CONSCIOUS SELF

I will begin by making some observations about the unity of consciousness. As usual, I will take up the light of introspection. By shining this light on my own consciousness, I will seek to identify aspects of the unity of my consciousness. I invite you to do the same as you follow along.

Two types of observations reveal two types of unity to me. First, by introspection, I observe my first-person perspective, which unifies many elements of consciousness within my perspective. For example, in this moment, I experience epic trance music (that conveys a feeling of curiosity and excitement), visual imagery of text, my intention to continue writing in a flow state, and a sense of contentment. I notice that these diverse experiences come together in a single, unified perspective. For example, my visual imagery is not separated into its own perspective, while my experience of contentment occupies a different perspective. Instead, these different experiences occupy the same perspective. Call this unification of consciousness into a single perspective "perspectival unity."[1]

There is also a second type of unity. I observe that this unity is rooted in *me*, the one who has my perspective. Call this second unity "subject unity."

Subject unity is the unity provided by the subject (or bearer) of consciousness—what I call a "self." In chapter eight ("Your Self"), I traced three arrows to the center of your consciousness. At this center is not just a perspective, but that which has a perspective. I identified this center as a first-person self (i.e., that which you can witness directly in self-awareness). If there is a first-person self, then this self can be a subject of many different states of consciousness. As a single subject, a self unifies the consciousness that belongs to it.

Subject unity can also unify different perspectives over time. Suppose you can change your perspective. For example, suppose you change from seeing one page in this book to seeing a different page in this book. Then there are two different perspectives at two different times. Yet, the perspectives are related, because you were the subject of them both. In this way, subject unity goes beyond mere perspectival unity. While a perspective

---

[1] For an elaboration on different theories of perspectival unity, see A. Giustina, "Conscious Unity from the Top Down: A Brentanian Approach," *The Monist* 100, no. 1 (2017): 16-37.

unifies different contents of consciousness into a single perspective, a subject unifies different perspectives into a single subject.

Without subject unity, there would be no perspectival unity. Here is why. Perspectival unity is a unity of consciousness into a single field of awareness, which has many contents (images, sounds, feelings, etc.). Yet, a field of awareness does not exist on its own. As I sought to show in the chapter "Your Self," a field of awareness exists by belonging to a subject of that awareness. If awareness belongs to a subject, then without a subject, there is no field of awareness (no perspective)—and so no contents within a field of awareness. So perspectives depend on subjects.

Your consciousness, then, is unified in two ways. You have a unified perspective, and you are a single anchor of your perspectives over time.

Once again, I believe you can witness these unities of consciousness by introspection. Introspection brings them into direct light. If you could not see these unities directly within your own consciousness, then what I have been proposing would be mere theory. But what I am proposing is not a mere theory: it is rooted in data you can see directly within your own mind. When you do the work to see into your own mind, you bring a theory of consciousness out from the dark and into the light of your own direct awareness.

Here, specifically, is what I think you can see. By your light, you can see yourself having a perspective. This sight involves awareness of three things: (i) yourself, (ii) your perspective, and (iii) the contents of consciousness in your perspective. By seeing these things, you can also see the two unities of consciousness. First, you can see the unification of your contents of consciousness (in a perspective). Second, you can see the unification of perspectives (as being yours). In this way, you can see the unities of consciousness within you. (As always, test everything I say by your own light.)

INTEGRATING CONSCIOUS ELEMENTS

How can there be unities of consciousness? While awareness of your own consciousness may reveal that unities exist, this awareness does not reveal how there can be any unities of consciousness in the first place. Why are there unities? Could sand blow into a unity of consciousness?

In this section, I will examine the problem of constructing unities of consciousness piecemeal. My goal here is not to solve the problem, but to expose its toughness. (My solution will come later.)

To illustrate the problem, suppose some neuroscientists work to create a conscious machine that can think, feel, and form mental images of dragons. To divide their labor, they create three task teams. The first task team works on creating thinking chips. The second works on creating feeling chips. The third makes the imagination chips.

These teams each encounter the general construction problem of constructing these contents of consciousness from unconscious materials. Put that problem aside here. For sake of argument, let us suppose that each team somehow succeeds in their task. Together, they create the thinking, feeling, and imagination chips.

Now it is time to put the chips together into a single being. How might they proceed?

Here is what they do. They put all their chips on a table. More specifically, they place two thinking chips, two feeling chips, and one imagination chip on a table. The project leader then piles these chips on top of each other. The leader points to the pile of chips and announces, "Behold, there is our conscious machine!"

You may think something is missing, however. Do the chips form a single conscious being? Presumably not. First, there is no perspectival unity that unifies the thoughts, feelings, and imagination into a single perspective. Second, there is no single subject of consciousness that has a perspective. In this situation, the chips on the table do not comprise a single conscious being with a single conscious awareness of thoughts, feelings, and an imagination all together. There are many chips with many states of consciousness, but not a single being.

The deep problem is that, in general, putting things together (whether chips or brain parts) does not thereby make those things form a single conscious thing. While a thinking chip thinks, the pile of chips together does not think. If a pile thinks just in virtue of containing something that thinks, then piling books on my head would yield a thinking pile just in virtue of containing me (a thinking thing). But that is not how thinking works. A pile of things that includes a thinker is not itself thereby a thinker.

We have here a combination problem. The problem is to see how, in principle, combining things could form the unities of consciousness. Clearly, merely putting conscious things closer together doesn't make a single conscious thing. After all, when friends get together, conscious beings get closer together. But *collecting* conscious beings together is not the same as *constructing* a new conscious being. When you get together with friends, you may generate new conscious experiences, but it takes something else to generate a new conscious being.[2]

The challenge of constructing a conscious being reminds me of conversation I had with my son, Micah, when he was two years old. I asked him where he thought he came from. He answered immediately, "Mommy's tummy." I then asked him where he thought mommy came from. He paused for a second. Then he said, "From daddy!" Naturally, I proceeded to ask him where he thought daddy came from. He looked at his mom and then back at me. Then he replied, "You came from mommy!" His cosmology was circular.

A similar circularity arises if we attempt to construct conscious beings from scratch. For as we have observed, conscious beings involve unities of consciousness. So, if we want to construct a conscious being, then we will need to construct a unity of consciousness. How do we do that? The problem now is that unities of consciousness depend on the prior existence of conscious beings. After all, conscious beings are themselves integral to what unifies consciousness into fields of awareness (per the subject and perspectival unities). Therefore, we are caught in a loop. To construct a conscious being (from scratch), we must construct a conscious unity. But to construct a conscious unity, we must first construct a conscious being. We have entered a construction circle.

The circularity problem is deep and categorical. It arises from basic principles, which I believe anyone can verify by immediate experience of one's

---

[2]David Barnett ("You Are Simple," in *The Waning of Materialism*, eds. R. Koons and G. Bealer, 161-74 [Oxford: Oxford University Press, 2010]) draws out this same problem in his Simple Argument. His argument begins with what he takes to be an uncontroversial datum: pairs of conscious beings cannot themselves be conscious (cf. A. Bailey, "You Needn't Be Simple," *Philosophical Papers* 43, no. 2 [2014]: 145-60). While I think he is correct about this datum, in the interest of modesty, I do not assume even that much. My observation is that, at the very least, assembling conscious beings is insufficient on its own to *explain* the unification of consciousness.

own consciousness. By directly witnessing your own contents of consciousness, you can see their unification into a single perspective of a single being. By this sight, you can see the conscious unities and the impossibility of a circular construction of them.

On this analysis, conscious unities present a special construction challenge. This challenge goes beyond the general construction challenge of constructing contents of consciousness. The challenge here is to see if we can explain the specific unities of consciousness. The problem of explaining the unities of consciousness is sometimes called "the binding problem" (alternatively, "the combination problem"). By understanding this problem, we prepare ourselves to see another constraint on possible theories of the origin of conscious beings.

To further clarify what is at stake, I will next examine a few proposals for how we might attempt to solve the binding problem.

RESPONSES

Causal connection. Maybe causal connections can help. For example, maybe we can link together a pile of conscious chips to form a unified conscious being. Sure, the pile on its own is not enough to constitute a conscious unity. But perhaps many conscious chips could be unified if they interact with each other in a certain way. Given the right causal interactions, perhaps the conscious chips could form the perspectival and subject unities of consciousness.

However, when we increase the resolution of our analysis, problems come into view. Here I will highlight three challenges for the causal integration proposal. First, causal connections between conscious things are not, on their own, sufficient to explain conscious unities. To illustrate why, suppose the neuroscientists synchronize a thinking chip with a feeling chip. Specifically, they program the thinking chip to think, "I am Bob." The thinking chip then sends a signal to the feeling chip to cause the feeling chip to feel a sensation of happiness. These chips are now causally connected. However, despite their causal connection, it does not yet follow that a new being is experiencing *both* the thought "I am Bob," and the feeling of happiness in a single, unified conscious experience. What we have here are two causally connected conscious chips. The unification of the thought and feeling in a single first-person perspective remains to be established.

To elaborate, linking conscious chips together is like getting together with friends. You might shake your friend's hand, but that isn't enough to form a third being who has its own unified consciousness. The problem here is general. Take any two conscious things (whether they are chips on a table, individual people, or sections of a brain). No description of their interactions depicts, just by itself, a single, unified field of awareness. For example, vision scientist Stephen Palmer provides a detailed account of causal processes in vision, but nothing in that account of causal activities depicts a unified awareness.[3] A complete description of the causal interactions leaves out a description of the unified conscious awareness by a single being. In short, causal interaction is not by itself enough for conscious integration.

There is a second problem: causal connection is not only not *sufficient* for unities of consciousness, but causal connection is also not *necessary* for unities of consciousness, at least not logically. For, by paying attention to your own visual field, you can see a unity of diverse contents of consciousness awareness, and you can see this unity directly without logically deriving any causal connections. By direct awareness of your total experience, you can see that the relationship between the total experience and its parts is tighter and more immediate than any external causal relations.

For example, at this moment, there are many phenomenal qualities (of thoughts, shapes, colors, sensations, etc.) unified within your own field of awareness. You are directly conscious of this unity. Your conscious awareness of this unity does not include any conscious awareness of causal relations between the contents, whether in your brain or somewhere else.

Instead, there is a more immediate unifier: your awareness. To see the unifying power of your awareness, you do not need to see parts of your visual field *causing* other parts. While the parts may indeed be causally connected, their causal connections are not by themselves what make them unified. Instead, your own awareness unifies different contents of consciousness together (in perspectival unity), which in turn is unified by you (the subject

---

[3]S. Palmer, *Vision Science: Photons to Phenomenology* (Cambridge, MA: MIT Press, 1999).

of your consciousness). If so, then the unity of consciousness does not consist in causal connections, but in the awareness by a single subject.

Finally, in addition to these two problems (that causal links are neither necessary nor sufficient for conscious unities), here is a third problem. The causal account of unity implies too many thinkers. The problem of too many thinkers, recall, is about demarcating you as a single thinker. In this context, there is a bizarre multiplication of thinkers if you consist of thinking parts, one for each thought. For example, suppose a region of your brain has a conscious thought, while another region of your brain has a feeling. And suppose these regions interact to form you, a single being who has both a thought and a feeling. Then in addition to your own thinking self, there is also a little thinker inside of you. If this thinker is itself composed of particles, then there many overlapping clouds of particles in its vicinity, with many of these clouds being no more or less qualified to count as a thinker. The result is that there are many overlapping thinkers inside of you every time you have a thought.

The thesis that you contain many thinkers has striking ethical implications. For example, if you were to sacrifice your own life to save a friend, you would be taking the lives of all other thinkers inside of you. In that case, self-sacrifice would be murder. Moreover, if you change your mind about something, you risk annihilating a little thinker within you—for example, by changing out cells or neurological activities that were having your previous thoughts. I suspect most people will not find these results to be signs of the truth, for we don't ordinarily think that we can annihilate other beings in this way.[4]

But even if we accepted these ethical implications, there is a more fundamental reason not to multiply thinkers. The reason is that the posit is unnecessary. Your awareness of yourself having thoughts consists in self-awareness, which allows you to witness the unity of your consciousness directly. When you witness your consciousness, you can tell directly that you are having your thoughts without appealing to some other, causally connected things. So causal connections don't constitute the unity you see directly. This analysis, if correct, would also explain why causal interactions between

---

[4]For a further analysis of some ethical implications of containing other subjects, see D. Crummett, "What If We Contain Multiple Morally Relevant Subjects?" *Utilitas* (2022): 1-18.

friends don't, on their own, form a third thinker composed of them. That would be too many thinkers.

Functional integration. Maybe function can help: perhaps if we caused some conscious chips to be functionally integrated in a certain way, then they could form a conscious unity. Could that work?

Unfortunately, I don't think function, just on its own, is enough. A functional account of unity inherits the first two problems we saw with the causal account. First, functional unity is not sufficient for conscious unity. Searle famously seeks to support this premise using his Chinese nation argument.[5] The gist of this argument is that, while a Chinese nation could simulate the function of neurons in a brain, the nation would not *thereby* be a conscious being. To draw out the idea, Searle conceives of a situation where the people of China interact with each other to simulate the interactions of neurons. For example, just as neurons communicate by sending signals through neurotransmitters, people can communicate with each other by sending signals to each other's phones. Searle then suggests that these causal connections are not enough for consciousness. For Searle thinks the implication is absurd: it would be absurd to suppose that the billions of individually conscious beings would themselves constitute a first-person conscious being just by acting a certain way.

Searle's argument is not without controversy. One type of reply is that if consciousness is analyzable in terms of functions, then perhaps a Chinese nation actually would constitute a conscious being if it functioned like a brain. This reply comes from those who reduce consciousness to functional states. Suppose consciousness is a functional state. Then if the Chinese nation instantiates that functional state, the Chinese nation would be conscious.

However, previous steps in our inquiry help us navigate this controversy. In particular, the observations we have made about particular contents of consciousness (feelings, thoughts, perception, etc.) bring into view certain

---

[5] J. Searle, *Mind: A Brief Introduction* (Oxford: Oxford University Press, 2004), 87. Searle is also famous for his Chinese Room argument ("Minds, Brains and Programs," *Behavioral and Brain Sciences* 3 [1998]: 417-57), which appeals to the same type of considerations. The general strategy is to set up a scenario in which certain aspects of consciousness (e.g., consciously understanding Chinese) are missing from a functional simulation of those aspects.

aspects of consciousness. By these observations, I think one can see that, while there are functional aspects of consciousness, not all aspects of consciousness are functional aspects. Recall, for example, these aspects: first-person qualitative aspects of feelings, logical links between thoughts, intending, intrinsic value, and so on. According to the window theory of awareness, your own sense of these aspects is itself a window of awareness into their reality. By seeing their reality, you can see directly that they are not the same as a function of inputs and outputs. You can sense your own happiness, for example, without sensing some set of inputs and outputs correlated with happiness.

More fundamentally, even if there is a purely functional way to analyze consciousness, we still have the additional challenge of seeing how to construct a first-person self, which is the subject (the bearer) of consciousness. We do not solve this problem just by organizing a bunch of individual things, whether chips or people. For even if individual things work together to function like a large brain, mere function is not sufficient to explain the generation of a real, first-person self. On the contrary, I think it is possible to see, by direct insight into our own selves (via self-awareness), that function does not by itself explain the emergence of first-person selves.

My first objection to the functionalist solution, then, is that function is not (by itself) enough. Many thinkers could coordinate and function like a large brain of a large thinker. But that would not thereby reveal the existence of a real, first-person thinking self composed of little thinkers.

Second, the conscious unity of a field of awareness does not consist in a functional integration between its constituents—that is, function is also not necessary for unity. Awareness is. Again, I believe we can see this directly. Just as we can be acquainted with the unity of consciousness within a field of awareness without being acquainted with any causal interaction between its elements, we can also be acquainted with this unity without being acquainted with functional integration. If so, then the unity of consciousness is something we can witness directly and immediately. By the light of my own direct acquaintance with my conscious unity, I infer, then, that functional integration cannot be the whole story.

Emergent unification. When all else fails, try "emergence." Perhaps the team of neuroscientists could generate a conscious unity by trial and error. According to this suggestion, we can simply grant that neuroscientists cannot predict when a conscious unity will emerge. No one can. Still, perhaps they could cause a conscious unity to emerge by flipping the right switch, even while they couldn't know ahead of time which switch that is.

I am not actually opposed to this proposal. In fact, I will give a theory of emergence in chapter twelve. However, I am opposed to impossible constructions. Some constructions are impossible, as we have seen. The challenge on the table is to see how, in principle, emergence could be possible. While we can say that the unities of consciousness emerge, the deeper question is, how?

To further highlight the challenge, let us consider a case of unification involved in seeing a painting. In this scenario, there is a large painting of an ocean with sky above. The painting is cut in half and sent to two people, Bob and Sue. Bob sees the top painting and thereby forms a visual image in his mind of a sky. Sue, on the other hand, only sees the bottom painting. She forms a visual image of the ocean. Between the two of them, every part of the larger painting is seen. Yet, here is the critical point: the whole painting is still not seen in any single unified state of awareness. For Bob only sees the top half, while Sue only sees the bottom half. No one sees the whole thing. How, then, can individual visions by individual things (whether people, chips, or brain parts) combine into a unified awareness by a single being? It may seem impossible.

My point here is not to suggest that there cannot be an answer. I think this question is answerable. But I want to sharpen the question so that we do not rush to easy answers that don't solve the deeper problem. The deeper problem, on examination, is that certain constructions cannot work. For example, you cannot construct a conscious unity by stacking people together. If Bob sits on top of Sue's head, there are still two visual images in two fields of awareness. Bringing their bodies closer together brings us no closer at all to explaining how there would be a single field of awareness of the whole scene.

So, if there is a way for a single awareness to emerge, the question remains: *How?* Emergence isn't the answer. Emergence invites the question.

SUMMARY

There is more to constructing a conscious being than constructing individual contents of consciousness (feelings, thoughts, intentions, images, etc.). Even if we could make all the contents of consciousness from scratch, it doesn't follow that we could assemble them into a unified conscious being. There remains the challenge of seeing how to unify conscious bits into a conscious unity—that is, the binding problem.

The binding problem comes to life from direct observations about our own unities of consciousness. We examined two unities. First, there is the unity of consciousness within one's field of awareness (perspectival unity). Second, there is the unity of consciousness that belongs to you, the subject of your field of awareness (subject unity).

These unities present a problem with building a conscious being from scratch. For if we build a conscious being from scratch, then we cannot *start* with a conscious being. But a conscious being is precisely what creates subjective and perspectival unities. The conscious being provides the conscious center of the conscious unities. From a single conscious center, there is a single field of awareness, which unifies many little bits of consciousness into an organized whole. Without the conscious center, then, there would be no awareness, and so no conscious unities. But how does a conscious center ever come to be?

To construct a center of consciousness, one would need to construct a conscious being, since the being is the unifying element. This construction project is like constructing a house all at once, without first constructing or assembling its parts. Is that even possible?

Despite the construction challenges, we have made progress in seeing how *not* to construct you. This progress narrows our steps forward.

■　　■　　■

The flashlight in your hand flickers as you evaluate the best path down the descending rocks before you. You carefully climb down the steep decline, deeper into the cave. You wonder how deep the path will take you.

11

THE IDENTITY PROBLEM

The "I" in the mind has to be numerically identical over time.

ALEXANDER ROSENBERG

THE ENIGMA OF YOUR EXISTENCE is even greater than we have seen already. In the previous two chapters, we saw two types of problems with the production of you: (i) the problem of constructing your contents of consciousness (feelings, thoughts, perception, etc.), and (ii) the problem of binding these things together into a single perspective of a single being. But there is an additional mystery. Even if the world can construct your consciousness and bind it together, there is still the problem of constructing the specific individual who is you. How does the world make you in particular, at this moment, and from moment to moment?

This question is more profound than it may appear on the surface, and it is often overlooked. It is not trivial to account for your specific existence, as we shall see. I call the problem of accounting for the specific thing that is identical to you "the identity problem."

The identity problem is different from the construction problems we examined in previous chapters. Those problems were about constructing the general kind of thing you are—that is, some first-person self. The identity problem is more specific: it is about constructing a certain, specific self.

In this chapter, we will unpack the identity problem. We will begin with a famous thought experiment to bring the problem into focus. Then we will examine three standard solutions and some classic problems with them. My goal is to show why I think the standard solutions fail to pull out the root of the identity problem. Seeing these failures will position us to see another tight constraint on how any specific conscious being could have come to be. This constraint, like the other construction constraints we've encountered, will further narrow our path forward.

THE TRANSPORTER EXPERIMENT

To begin our inquiry into your identity, I present the classic transporter experiment. In this experiment, you are invited to step onto a transporter in the starship *Enterprise*. The transporter will annihilate your body on the ship and recreate it on a planet. The scary part of this experiment is the question it inspires: will you survive the transportation?

Here is how the transporter works in more detail. First, it makes a molecular copy of all your atoms. Then, it destroys all your original atoms on the ship. Meanwhile, an energy field creates new atoms on the planet and arranges them according to the blueprint of your exact makeup. Once the process is complete, a copy of your body will be located on a planet. The transporter operator assures you, "It works every time."

Do you step onto the transporter?

Here is a reason to worry. You might wonder whether you will be truly *you* on the planet. Will the production of a replacement of your body on the planet be sufficient to produce you, the same individual? Or, will replacing your body merely replace you with a clone?

From a third-person, external perspective, it is impossible to tell for sure. For suppose you go through with the transporter process. Then the person on the planet acts like you. To everyone else, it is you, at least functionally. Their knowledge of external actions, however, does not give them knowledge of the specific, internal self that you are.

But your own perspective puts you in a different position. If the transporter works, you will be able to see for yourself whether you exist on the planet. You can see, "Here I am!" If instead you are annihilated, then you'll simply never know what happened. You'll be gone.

What is at stake here is an identity question: What makes you specifically you? When you step on the transporter, will the thing that is you survive the transportation? If so, what exactly is it that survives. Atoms? Which atoms? Suppose external, third-person truths about atoms do not determine your first-person identity. Then what does? What determines the specific identity of the specific individual you are? In short, what makes you, you?

To increase the resolution of the question, I will now add a twist to the story. Suppose you step onto the transporter, but instead the transporter malfunctions. This time, the transporter fails to annihilate your body on the ship. Thus, your original body remains intact. Meanwhile, the transporter still makes the duplicate of your body on the planet. In this scenario, the body on the planet is atom-per-atom the same as the body on the ship.

What happens to you now? Are you now on the planet? Or, are you still on the ship? Or, are you somehow both on the planet and on the ship, experiencing a split awareness of being in two places at once?

Once again, from an external, third-person perspective, no one has direct knowledge of where you are. From the operator's perspective, you might still be consciously aware of yourself on the ship, or you might find yourself on the planet. The operator might speculate that you remain with your original atoms (on this ship), but this speculation is a matter of philosophical debate.

Still, from your own perspective, you do not need to speculate about where you are. You have inside knowledge that others don't have. From the inside, you can tell where you are. Suppose you find yourself on the ship. Then, even while you may wonder whether you are the same person who stepped onto the transporter, you can at least see where you are now. For you can see yourself on the ship. Even if the person on the planet claims to have your body, your memories, and your name, these claims do not incline *you* to think you are actually on the planet at this time. You know where you are by your own conscious awareness.[1]

I want to emphasize the role of first-person awareness in illuminating the identity question. Without first-person awareness, we would have no access to first-person truths. In that case, asking what makes you, *you*, would be like asking what makes a plurb a plurb. The term *plurb* by the way, refers to the contents of a box that no one could ever open or see into. First-person awareness allows us to open the box of first-person truths. When you open the box of your own first-person truths, you can see that

---

[1] We will return to the question of how you could verify your identity across time.

your first-person perspective is real. This sight of first-person truths allows you to understand what it would mean for you to find yourself still on the ship, irrespective of third-person truths about atoms.

So here is the identity question: What makes a certain first-person you, *you*? This question has two wings. First, there is a question about your identity across time: What makes you the same person today as yesterday? This is the diachronic wing. Second, there is a question about your identity at a given time: What makes you, you right now? This is the synchronic wing. I will consider some possible answers to both wings of the identity question next.

THREE VIEWS OF SELF IDENTITY

To gain deeper insight into your identity, we will examine three standard accounts of your identity. The accounts are as follows:

1. The body view: a body determines your identity.

2. The psychological view: some psychology determines your identity.

3. The soul view: a soul determines your identity.

Let us examine each in turn.

Body view. According to the body view, a material body makes you, you, at a given time and across time. So, for example, you are the same person you were this morning because you have the same body you had this morning.

The body view transforms the identity question into a question about the identity of your body. What explains the identity of a body?

The transporter case reveals a problem with accounting for which body is yours. As we saw, in the transporter case, there can be two bodies that look alike in every bodily respect. Yet only one is yours. Which one? According to the body view, we can account for which body is yours solely in terms of third-person truths about a body. Yet, third-person truths about bodies leave out your own first-person experience of yourself. So, we cannot account for which body is yours solely in terms of third-person truths about a body.

The problem here is not that you cannot have (or even be) a body. The problem, rather, is that the body view does not by itself account for your identity. No matter what your relationship is with your body, there remains this question: how can third-person bodily facts account for the particular, first-person self you are?

To draw out the challenge further, I'd like to highlight three more specific problems with accounting for your identity solely in terms of bodily states. First, there is the boundary problem. The boundary problem is about accounting for which atoms (or spatial objects) belong to your body. Suppose we zoom in on your body. We find a scatter of atoms in mostly empty space (or fields). Some atoms may be close to the "edge" of you. But what determines the "edge" of you? The problem is that there is no nonarbitrary answer.

To solve the boundary problem, perhaps we could say that the atoms that belong to your body are the ones under your influence. Then we can identify your body in terms of what you can control.

But this response brings us back where we started: What makes something under "your" control? We can answer this question if we can identify what makes you, you. But now we are moving in a circle: if we explain your identity in terms of your body, and then explain the identity of your body in terms of its relation to you, we have effectively explained your identity in terms of your identity. How does that help? It doesn't.

Second, there is the atom replacement problem. We already considered the case where all your atoms are replaced. The problem is that atoms cannot determine your identity if you could still exist without them. Suppose atoms in your body determine your identity. Then you go wherever some atoms go. But, if you can survive the replacement of some atoms, then you do not go wherever some atoms go. Instead, your body's atoms could be swapped out for other atoms, while you remain in the same place.

The problem here is that as your body changes, you still remain you, the same you. While you change in various ways, you are still the same conscious substance. If so, then even if all the atoms in your body were exchanged with new atoms, you would still be you. Here we encounter the diachronic question: what accounts for your identity across time? As your body changes, you remain you. What accounts for that?

Note that it will not help to suppose that your identity is maintained by a certain arrangement of atoms. For if arranging some atoms were sufficient to make you, you, then the duplicate body on the planet would become you (not another version of you), just by having a certain arrangement of atoms. By first-person awareness, however, you can verify that your identity is not determined by arrangements of atoms. As we observed in the transporter experiment, third-person facts about atoms and arrangements of atoms leaves out the first-person fact about who is you.

There is a related (more technical) iteration of this problem. To illustrate, suppose you clip your fingernails, and you survive! In this process, some atoms separate from your body. Call the original atoms that remain in your body, "the Originals." Do these Originals determine your identity? Well, they are the only atoms in your body. So, if any atoms determine your identity, presumably they do. But how could they? A moment ago, the Originals were merely part of your total body. So, they were not sufficient on their own to determine your identity then. How, then, could they determine your identity now? The fundamental problem here is that, in general, if something is sufficient to determine your identity at one time, then it would be sufficient to determine your identity at any other time it exists. If that is right, then since the Originals didn't determine your identity a moment ago, they don't determine your identity at any time. In other words, no particular atoms determine the identity of your particular, first-person self. From all this it follows that if you can indeed survive the clipping of your fingernails, then your identity isn't determined just by the atoms in your body.[2]

In addition to these challenges (from the boundary problem and the replacement problem), there is also the problem of loose identity. This problem depends on the premise that you can continue to be you from moment to moment. The problem, then, is that your bodily states are only loosely the same from one moment to the next. For example, a body of atoms at one time is only approximately the same as a body of atoms at another time. By contrast, you are not merely approximately you from moment to moment. You are one and the same you.

We are in difficult terrain. There are many thorny concepts by our feet. To help us step carefully, I want to have closer look at what it might mean to be the same you.

---

[2]T. Merricks, *Objects and Persons* (Oxford: Oxford University Press, 2001) provides a detailed analysis of these, and other, replacement puzzles. His conclusion is that the identity of persons is not grounded in material parts or anything else.

Two clarifications are in order. First, when I say that you are the same you, I mean you are the same underlying substance. As a self-substance, you are capable of changing states, such as when you change from happy to sad. To change in states is not the same as changing from one self to another self. In fact, the very concept of something changing states presupposes that there is something that remains the same—the subject of change. So, if you can change states, then you are the same subject of those changes.

The second clarification is about how to see that you are the same self. Here is how I think you can do that: you can witness yourself continuing to be. You do this by direct awareness of yourself across time. For example, you can be aware of yourself continuing to think about the ideas of this book.

Self-awareness puts in you in a special position. If you are aware of yourself, you can apply the direct comparison test to see that you are you. With respect to other individuals, by contrast, you do not have the same access to them. Instead, you can only be aware of them as they appear to you. For this reason, it is always an open question whether a thing external to you maintains its exact identity; you can't see sameness of an individual directly from the outside.

In self-awareness, you are not on the outside. You have inside access to yourself. For this reason, you are able to be aware of yourself as you are, as opposed to only your aspects or appearance. In this way, I believe you are able to recognize yourself as the same individual self, not just at a single time, but also across time.[3]

Suppose this analysis is correct: you are the same person today as you were yesterday. Then the "loose identity" problem is that this sameness of your first-person self is not accounted for merely in terms of bodily states. Facts about bodily states are third-person facts about motions, shapes, functions, and so on. These facts do not include the first-person fact about which self you are. So, there is a problem in seeing how third-person facts

---

[3]This account does not, by itself, rule out the possibility of error. For example, suppose you were created one minute ago with all of your memories. Then your memories could trick you into thinking you existed longer than you have. Still, in the absence of a reason to think you are a recent duplicate of someone else, your own direct experiences of yourself continuing supplies evidence of your continuing (at least while you are having those experiences). Thanks to Brianna Bode for drawing my attention to the possibility of false memories.

about a body could, all by themselves, account for your first-person identity across time.

Finally, underneath these three problems (the boundary problem, the replacement problem, and the loose identity problem), there is also a more fundamental problem. The problem is that even if we could explain your identity in terms of a body, we still only relocate the mystery. We are left with the question of how to explain the identity of a body. We might be tempted to say that what makes your body the same across time is that it belongs to the same being, you. But then to explain your identity in terms of your body's identity is to explain your identity in terms of your own identity. That's circular: it explains your identity in terms of itself. A circular explanation is no better than no explanation.

Therefore, if we are to illuminate what makes you, you (across changes in your states and environment), I do not think it can suffice to simply identify you with a body. There is still the question of what makes certain atoms in a certain body "yours."

Psychological view. Let us try another account: psychological identity. According to the psychological identity hypothesis, you maintain your identity by having certain psychological states. Instead of having the same body, you remain you by having enough of the same psychological states.

One version of this view is in terms of your memories. As long as you have enough of the same memories, then you are you. So, for example, if you have enough of the same memories you had yesterday, then you are the same person you were yesterday.

The memory view can help makes sense of body-switching cases. It is conceivable for a conscious self to have a different body than the one it has. One way to make sense of switching bodies is in terms of the continuity of consciousness. For example, suppose you take on a new body. You still count as "you" so long as you continue to have enough of the same memories you had in your previous body.

The memory view is incompatible, however, with previous steps in our inquiry. In particular, the conclusion of the first part of the book is that you are a being capable of consciousness—what I call "a conscious substance." You are the same conscious substance from moment to moment. By contrast, your psychology is only loosely the same from moment to moment, for you can forget things or change your thoughts. The problem here is that you are not merely approximately you. You are exactly you.

Your exact identity differs from the loose identity of your psychological profile. Exact identity is a transitive relation: if A is identical to B, and B is identical to C, then A is identical to C. Yet, "psychological continuity" is not transitive. Thus, while you might have enough of the same memories to count as "loosely" identical, eventually the changes will add up too far. Psychological continuity, then, does not by itself explain your strict identity as a first-person self that can exist throughout many psychological changes.

The psychological view can be tempting because we naturally associate ourselves with a set of psychological traits, such as our likes, dislikes, and core values. This psychological profile is our "ego" self. We associate with our ego self when we identify with certain qualities we have. In this sense, we could say that our psychology is part of our "ego" identity.

But strictly speaking, you are not your traits. You are the thing—the substance—that has your traits. Your traits can change, while you remain the same individual. For example, you can gain new knowledge. As long as it is *you* who has changed, then even while your traits are not the same, you are still the same you.

To draw out this distinction a bit further, suppose two people, Jerry and Barry, have the same personality. They act the same way in the same circumstances. In describing their traits, we could say they are the same person. But they are not the same individual person. If they were the same individual person, then any changes to Jerry would be a change to Barry. But that makes no sense: Jerry could change personalities without affecting Barry's personality at all. The point is this: there is a difference between a personality and an individual who has that personality.

So, to be clear, the identity problem is about the identity of the individual, not of its personality. An individual can change in personality without being swapped out for a different individual. For this reason, having the same personality is neither necessary nor sufficient for being the same individual.

The question remains: what accounts for the identity of an individual?

Soul view. Some readers may suspect that my ambition is to show that souls solve the identity problem. After all, if your identity isn't explained by your body or by your psychology, then only one option remains: your identity is explained by your soul. So perhaps you are the same being because you have the same soul.

I do not endorse this solution, however. Whether or not you are a soul, the soul-identity account does not pull out every root of the problem. A mystery remains: to say that a soul maintains your identity is to translate the mystery of "your" identity into the mystery of the identity of a soul. What accounts for the identity of a soul?

This question points to the same circularity problem that the body account faces. Regarding bodies, we saw a problem with accounting for which body is yours without already presupposing references to your body. Regarding souls, we have a similar problem: How do we account for which soul is yours? Suppose we say that your soul is the one that has your psychological states. This solution brings us back where we started. The problem remains: What makes certain psychological states *yours*?

The big challenge, as I see it, is to avoid relocating the mystery. Suppose we account for your identity in terms of the identity of something, X, whether a body or a soul. We then relocate the mystery: What explains the identity of X? We could posit another item, X*, to explain the identity of X. But then what explains the identity of X**? To complete the explanation, we need some item whose identity is not explained by the identity of anything. Its identity is just basic and underived. So, if we say that X's identity is basic and underived, then this is no better (or worse) than saying your identity is basic and underived.

I am not suggesting that souls can play no role. In chapter eight, I offered a minimal account of a "soul" on which you count as a soul (in virtue of being a first-person self). On that account, a soul can mitigate other problems (e.g., the atom replacement problem, the boundary problem, and the loose identity problem). So, my purpose is not to remove souls.

Rather, my point is that souls don't, on their own, solve every problem of identity.[4] They push the problem of explaining identity deeper in.

---

[4]In this respect, I agree with J. Berger's analysis ("A Dilemma for the Soul Theory of Personal Identity," *International Journal for Philosophy of Religion* 83 [2018]: 41-55), according to which the soul view leaves open certain questions about identity. For I think identity is at some level *basic* (without further analysis or grounding).

So, if we want to make use of souls in our theory, we should give them a different job.[5]

YOUR IDENTITY IS PRIOR

We are deep in the cave of consciousness. In this place, we are seeking to see what could explain the identity of a first-person self. When we look at classical explanations, however, we see dark walls. Is there a way past the darkness?

Fortunately, we have light with us. First, the light of logical analysis exposes a root of the puzzles of identity. The identity puzzles grow out of a certain "dusty" picture of reality. In this picture, certain bits of reality exist prior to you and then, in the unfolding of time, come together like a dust cloud to determine your identity. These bits may be atoms, psychological states, or even other conscious beings. Whatever they are, on this picture they existed prior to you, and no particular bit is required for your continued existence. The result is that the things that determine your identity can, paradoxically, exist without you, and you can exist without them. That's the problem.

Previous observations in our journey prepare us to step past this problem. In a previous step, we observed the unifying power of a first-person self: a self at the center of consciousness can organize a dust cloud of diverse contents of consciousness into a unified experience. This observation reveals a way to paint a different picture. Instead of starting with a dust cloud of diverse bits and then organizing them into a single self, there is another possibility. A first-person self can organize diverse bits of reality (contents of consciousness) into a unified reality. In this picture, a dust cloud does not determine the identity of a first-person self.

To step past the identity problem, then, I recommend that we flip the picture: instead of supposing that replaceable bits come together like a dust

---

[5]There are other jobs available. For example, something like souls (or their equivalent—e.g., substantial first-person selves) could play the role of the *bearer* (or subject) of consciousness, which can endure through psychological and bodily changes. And one could argue that a soul theory (or something equivalent) provides an account of *how* one can be a subject of change by anchoring one's identity to something that exists *prior to* (independently from) the particular changing states and parts. I will say more about the prospect of a prior identity in the next section.

cloud to make you who you are, suppose instead that your identity is prior to any replaceable bits. That is to say, no replaceable bits determine or explain your identity. Call this proposal, "the prior identity hypothesis."

The prior identity hypothesis brings to light a different picture of your relationship to your bodily parts. Instead of supposing that your bodily parts determine your identity, it could go the other way. Perhaps you determine the identity of (at least some of) your parts. For example, your heart may have its identity in virtue of its functional service to your whole body, which in turn has its identity as a certain state of you. On this account, your heart is yours by its functional relationship to you. In this way, your bodily parts could derive their identity by their relationship to you, as a whole. Then, as they say, the whole would be prior to the parts.

Whether or not you are a whole who is prior to your parts, the priority hypothesis entails at least this: your identity is not derived by assembling some parts together. Your identity is prior.

The prior identity hypothesis, if true, implies something special about your origin. It implies that you are not a byproduct of an organization of parts. Unlike a house, which can be constructed by assembling certain materials, you cannot be constructed by assembling certain materials. There is no way to take materials and organize them to produce you.

While these implications are far-reaching, they are perhaps unsurprising given the replacement puzzles we have seen. For suppose your atoms were replaced, one by one, with duplicate atoms that do the same thing. Suppose, next, that someone takes your original atoms and assembles them to form a duplicate of your body. Have they thereby made you? They have not. By your own awareness of yourself, you can see that you are not identical to a duplicate of your body.

If, on the other hand, your identity were derivable from changeable, atomic parts, then your original atomic parts would constitute you so long as they come into the exact same arrangement and function as before. But they don't. A duplicate of your body is not you. Therefore, your identity is not derivable from atomic parts.

The prior identity principle also frees us from the particular problems we have seen with the theories of personal identity. Those problems arise from attempts to account for your identity in terms of prior items. If we suppose instead that your identity is not determined by prior items, then those problems go away.

In this chapter, I have not attempted to provide a full account of your identity. On the contrary, I have worked to show that accounting for your identity is a great challenge. The result of my inquiry so far shows that this challenge is not solvable by appealing to souls, bodies, or psychological states alone. Perhaps your identity is basic, or perhaps there is an explanation deeper in. In either case, your identity is prior to (not determined by) your changeable parts.

As a final note, I would like to show how the prior identity principle relates to the question of your origin. The prior identity principle blows against the dusty picture of your origin. A common view about origins is that whatever determines a being's origin also determines its identity. So, for example, if a dust cloud of atoms determines your origin, then those atoms also determine your identity. But, as we have seen, the transporter thought experiment and the replacement puzzle challenges the premise that atoms can, all on their own, determine your identity. A fundamental problem, as we have seen, is that third-person truths about atoms leaves out the first-person truth about which first-person self you are. Hence, on the view that origin determines identity, it follows that third-person truths about atoms do not, on their own, determine your origin. In other words, a dust cloud of atoms could not have determined your origin.

But then what could have determined your origin? That question remains.

SUMMARY

You are a first-person self. Which self are you? You know which one. You are not me (over here) or your neighbor (over there). You are you (right where you are).

What makes you, you? Not atoms: you can be same first-person self and swap all your atoms for different atoms. Not psychological states: you can change psychological states and still be the same first-person self. Not a soul: a soul, conceived as a first-person self, is what you are, not what makes you what you are. If instead we say that what you are is what makes you what you are, then we run into circularity: what you are then makes itself. Running in a circle solves nothing.

The identity problem, then, exposes another constraint on your origin. Your origin is not determined, all on its own, by components (whether atoms or psychological states) that can exist apart from you. While you might determine the identity of your parts, no separable parts can, on their own, determine your identity.

These constraints on your origin constrain our path forward. There is only a small opening ahead.

■　■　■

You reach the end of the steep decline, and you follow the narrowing path ahead. The further you walk, the lower the ceiling of the cave gets. You duck your head and feel the walls closing in on either side of you as you continue to inch forward. The pathway tightens, and you feel pressure to turn around and go back. Just as you begin to wonder whether you will be able to continue any further, you notice a glowing light ahead.

12

HOW CONSCIOUSNESS CAN EMERGE

Truth is in the depths.

DEMOCRITUS

SO, HOW COULD YOU HAVE COME TO BE? The purpose of this chapter is to put light on the materials for a possible answer.

We have come into difficult terrain. The cave is dark, the terrain is rocky, and the walls are narrow on all sides. Few people make it this far. Voices of doubt call them back. Meanwhile, those who do make it this far make different claims about what you can find ahead. These conflicting claims fill the cave with a cloud of controversy that make it hard to see any clear steps forward. Is it possible for anyone to see the truth through the mist?

Despite the challenge, we are equipped to continue. We have tools in hand to illuminate more steps ahead. Until we find that we are blocked by immovable walls, we will continue to press forward to see what we might see.

To take the next step, I will begin by presenting a theory of a mind-first ontology. This theory takes off the mindlessness frame. Instead of positing a mindless floor of reality from which all our hopes and dreams emerge, we can open new options with a mind-first ontology. The big idea in this theory is that consciousness emerges within a mental framework.

I will develop the mind-first theory over the next two chapters. In this chapter, I will focus on the emergence of consciousness in general. I will show how I think consciousness can emerge from a consciousness-making substance. Then, in the next chapter, I will tackle the hardest question of this book: How can there be a conscious-making substance? I will show how previous observations put light on a resource for answering this question in terms of a foundational substance of the right kind. My theory will also cast new light on the nature of matter itself: I will share how I think a foundational substance of a certain sort could give rise to certain mind-dependent aspects of matter, which are evident in both first-person experience and recent scientific theories of the nature of matter.

TYPES OF EMERGENCE

Let us begin by clarifying the meaning of "emergence." We can distinguish three types of emergence: weak emergence, strong emergence, and incongruent emergence. I will describe each in turn.

Weak emergence. Something weakly emerges if its existence can be derived from an analysis of prior things. To illustrate, suppose there is a traffic jam. The traffic jam "emerges" from many individual vehicles. By analyzing the positions and relationships of vehicles on a road, we can determine whether the collection of vehicles, in total, constitutes a traffic jam. The state of being a traffic jam, then, is derivable from an analysis of prior things—vehicles and their positions. In this sense, a traffic jam counts as weakly emerging from vehicles and their positions.

Weak emergence does not require an actual deduction, but only a possible deduction (in principle). For example, in a complex system, we might not see everything that is derivable from that system. Nevertheless, our own current lack of sight does not automatically imply that there couldn't be a derivation from prior states. As long as a derivation is possible in principle, the derivable thing counts as emergent in this "weak" sense.

The concept of weak emergence can help us specify certain reductive theories of consciousness. For example, suppose a feeling of love reduces to a chemical reaction in a brain. Then, insofar as the chemicals themselves consist of mindless molecules, we could say that mental state (feeling love) is analyzable in terms of mindless states. In other words, the mental is ultimately mindless. On this reductive account, the feeling of love can be seen (by reason) to derive from molecules. In that case, love weakly emerges from molecules.

In part one of this book, I shared reasons I doubt that every aspect of consciousness reduces to molecular motions or aspects. A root reason, as I argued, is that reductionism leaves out first-person aspects of consciousness. That is to say, a complete description of third-person aspects of unconscious things (whether grains of sand or chains of carbon) does not include all first-person aspects of content of consciousness. We can sharpen this reason in terms of weak emergence. To illustrate, consider a spatial configuration of some grains of sand. Is it possible to derive, merely using reason, a first-person feeling of love from a spatial configuration of sand? If not, then a feeling of love does not reduce (in this weak emergent sense) to a spatial configuration of sand. The idea generalizes: if felt aspects of consciousness are not derivable, merely using reason, from the functions, patterns, or motions of mindless bits of reality, then felt aspects do not weakly emerge from mindless bits. If that is correct, then a feeling of love does not, just by reason alone, weakly emerge from mindless molecules. So, I think we need more than weak emergence if we are to explain consciousness.

Strong emergence. Next, there is strong emergence. Something strongly emerges from some prior things when it is *not* derivable from a mere logical analysis of those things. To illustrate, suppose wetness arises from a certain molecular structure. Then, if an analysis of the molecular structure cannot by itself predict the emergence of wetness, we could say that wetness strongly emerges on the molecular structure.

Note that while strongly emergent states are not *derivable* from a mere analysis of prior things, they may still be *determined* by prior things. For instance, some people think first-person consciousness is determined by prior states, even if consciousness is not logically derivable from prior states. Here the determination is a relation that links the natures of things.

Determination opens an interesting possibility. Suppose nonsensing materials do not allow us to see, by reason alone, that first-person sensations will arise. Still, there is another option: perhaps, as a matter of reality, certain third-person states deterministically make first-person sates of consciousness (whether or not we could predict this just by logic). In that case, consciousness would be strongly emergent on unconscious states. (I will say more about the prospect of strongly emergent consciousness in a moment.)

Incongruent emergence. A third type of emergence is incongruent emergence. This type of emergence is not just impossible to predict; it is impossible to produce. This emergence can be seen to be impossible by reason itself. It is not just that we don't see how to make the number twelve out of a triangle. We can also *see*, by reason, that twelve cannot emerge out of a triangle. The nature of a triangle is incongruent with the number twelve, and therefore, an emergence of twelve from a triangle is impossible.

Many of the chapters in this book have been devoted to bringing into the light cases of incongruent emergence. For example, we considered the prospect of constructing these things: sensations, thoughts, sight, the power to make choices, the intrinsic value of persons, the unity of consciousness, and the identity of conscious beings. In addition to these constructions, we also considered the prospect of constructing a first-person self by assembling contents of consciousness (without the presence of a mind). My argument has been that we are not entirely in the dark. When we hold our lights up to molecules, for example, we can see that certain constructions are impossible without additional resources. For just as it is possible to see that a triangle cannot emerge from the number twelve (on its own), I believe it is possible to see, by careful attention and analysis, that certain constructions of consciousness cannot emerge from certain materials (on their own).

I want to emphasize that incongruent emergence goes beyond a mere explanatory gap between things. Many philosophers recognize that there is an explanatory gap between mindless matter and consciousness: that is, merely seeing mindless matter does not, all on its own, give one insight into consciousness. Explanatory gaps, while mysterious, are not necessarily problematic.[1] But incongruent emergence is more dangerous: incongruence throws mystery into the furnace of impossibility.

A disclaimer: I don't claim one must see everything with equal clarity. Some things can be clearer than others. In the chapter on thoughts, for example, I provided a complex deduction. While the deduction has been independently reviewed, it has many steps, and I don't claim to have equally clear sight of each step. In general, some deductions may be clearer because they are simpler or depend on easier sight.

---

[1] D. Papineau, "The Problem of Consciousness," in *The Oxford Handbook of the Philosophy of Consciousness*, ed. U. Kriegel (Oxford: Oxford University Press, 2020) proposes ways we might live with explanatory gaps.

In fact, I believe that one of the reasons debates over the nature and basis of consciousness are so entrenched is precisely because it is not immediately obvious which aspects of consciousness can or cannot be constructed from which materials. In general, it is easier to *not see* something than to *see* something. Suppose we look at some unconscious things, like some grains of sand. Then we consider consciousness in general. Seeing sand and thinking about consciousness may not immediately give us any clear insight into whether a construction of consciousness out of the sand could be done. If there is a problem, we need to look closer to see it.

This sight takes work. It takes work for a mind to gather up the conceptual pieces required to zoom in on the specific constructions we have examined. To see a construction incongruence, one must enter the forest of concepts and turn over specific leaves. From a distance, some construction constraints on consciousness may not be so clear. But when we look closer at specific aspects of consciousness, certain constraints can come into clearer view. The work we have done in this book positions us to see many things that cannot be seen without doing this work.

In our quest, we have zoomed in on specific contents of conscious (feelings, thoughts, perception, intentions, etc.); my goal has been to gather up the relevant concepts and trace relevant inferences so that we see certain, specific construction problems (e.g., via the deduction of the mindful thoughts theorem).

Let us review, briefly, the big picture of the construction constraints we have encountered. In the previous three chapters, three general types of constraints came into view. First, we saw the "materials" constraint when considering how we might convert sand into a conscious, feeling, and thinking being. Reflection on the details delivered a general constraint on constructing first-person materials from purely third-person materials. The problem here is that purely third-person materials (grains of sand, snowflakes, or chains of carbon atoms) are the wrong material, on their own, for constructing a real, first-person conscious self. Turning third-person molecules into a first-person self is like turning numbers into nickels, growing thoughts on trees, or making feelings out of flour. The materials are wrong.

Second, we saw an additional constraint on constructing conscious unities. By paying attention to aspects of consciousness, we see not just that there is conscious stuff in general, but we see that conscious stuff is organized into conscious unities. We considered two types of unities: (i) the unity of consciousness in a single field of awareness and (ii) the unity of consciousness that belongs to a single subject of awareness (a first-person self). Both unities call for special construction constraints. For example, we saw that first-person materials (thoughts, feelings, intentions, etc.) do not on their own unify themselves into conscious unities. So if conscious unities emerge, something else is involved.

Third, we saw constraints on constructing your specific identity. By paying careful attention to your first-person self, you not only witness your consciousness and your unities of consciousness, but you also witness yourself as a particular, enduring individual. If so, then there is an additional challenge. How can your specific identity be constructed out of the identities of atoms that can move in and out of bodily parts? On my analysis, we can avoid incongruent emergence if, instead, the emergence of your identity does not depend entirely on changeable atoms.

Again, I want to emphasize that these particular problems with particular cases of emergence require specific and concentrated inquiry. Without this inquiry, we are not in position to distinguish incongruent emergence from congruent, strong emergence. The difference here is subtle and easy to miss. To sharpen the distinction, consider the difference between seeing that some mathematical conjecture can be disproven versus not seeing how to prove it. Until one sees the disproof, one is in the dark—and one cannot say whether the conjecture is true or not. But if one sees a disproof, whether faintly or clearly, one then has a positive reason to doubt the conjecture. In the same way, if one sees the incoherence of some construction, whether faintly or clearly, one then has a positive reason to doubt the possibility of such construction.

When I consider construction constraints myself, I find that some constraints are clearer to my mind than others. For example, it is evident to my mind that throwing sand into the wind will not—and cannot—generate thoughts. This clarity is not based on what I don't see. It is based on a sense that sand is the wrong material for constructing thoughts (and my deduction of the mindful thoughts theorem further sharpens the resolution of this sense). Still, it is even more evident to my mind that throwing sand into the wind will not construct a first-person, thinking self. For it takes more to make a self than to make a thought.

I can also say that in the course of writing this book, the construction constraints have grown in severity in my mind. Before I began this inquiry, the prospect of constructing consciousness out of unconscious materials struck my mind as strange, like the prospect of a ghost coming from a brick wall. After closer inspection, however, the prospect appears not merely strange but manifestly impossible. In fact, if I may display the fullness of my conviction, the prospect of making first-person selves out of mindless debris now appears to me even more problematic than making contradictions, like square circles. In the case of contradictions, I only have one root reason to think that a contradiction is impossible: that is, it seems impossible for an attribute A and its negation to go together in one thing. But, unlike constructing a contradiction, which has a single root of incongruence (A and not A), constructing conscious selves solely out of mindless blocks of reality has many independent roots of incongruence. The many construction problems each point to construction incongruence from a different angle.

It remains for me to draw my application: incongruent emergence never actually happens. Here is my argument for that:

1. Incongruent emergence is impossible.
2. Whatever is impossible never happens.
3. Therefore, incongruent emergence never happens.

This argument is illuminated by the light of reason. By reason, I see that incongruent things (that, by definition, contradict necessary principles of reason) are impossible. And by reason, I see that whatever is impossible never actually happens. Therefore, I infer—by reason—that incongruent emergence never actually happens.

The next question I want to consider, then, is this: How could consciousness emerge?

SUBSTANCE EMERGENCE

Substances can help us in our inquiry. In this section, I will share how I think consciousness can emerge from substances of the right kind.

Recall from chapter seven (on the mind-body problem) that a *substance* is something that has some form, like the form of rock or a person. A substance can also have basic capacities, such as a capacity to move or think. A basic capacity allows the substance to do something directly—without having to first do something else in that same act. For example, if a substance has a basic capacity to think, then the substance can think without first having to do other things, like move its arms. We also saw that basic capacities can still depend on prior conditions, such as when a basic capacity to have a certain thought depends on prior experiences.

By including substances in our ontology, we can give an account of the emergence of consciousness in terms of the capacities of a substance. Conscious states can emerge in a substance, like ocean waves emerging in an ocean. Recall that a *conscious substance*, by definition, is a substance that has a capacity for consciousness. So, if there is a conscious substance, then its consciousness can emerge within that conscious substance. Call this emergence from a substance "substance emergence."

To illustrate substance emergence, suppose a conscious substance forms a conscious intention by a basic action. Then, the substance itself is a source of the intention. While other states of the substance could motivate or influence the intention, the states are not the whole story. The substance itself forms an intention in response to its states. In this way, an intention can "emerge" from (or in the context of) a conscious substance.

The emergence here differs from other, classic types of emergence. Classic cases of emergence involve emergence in terms of states of things. For example, a state of wetness emerges on certain molecular states. In this case, *states* are the whole story. The emergence I am proposing, by contrast, is not from a mere state, on its own, but from an underlying substance. A substance supplies an additional resource.

To be clear, I am not suggesting that states could never emerge from other states alone. I think state emergence is indeed possible. For example, as we saw, a traffic jam could emerge from the positional states of individual cars. My suggestion, rather, is that in some cases, emergence involves more than mere states. That's where substance emergence can help.

I see several benefits of the concept of substance emergence. First, substance emergence can give us deeper insight into strong emergence. To see how, suppose an image emerges in your mind. We say this image "strongly emerges" if its emergence could not be predicted merely by a logical analysis of prior states. Suppose so: nothing prior predicts the image. Still, while nothing predicts the image, something could still produce the image. If you, a substance, have a capacity to produce images in your mind, then you have a capacity to cause images to strongly emerge. So, substance emergence provides a deeper account of strong emergence.

A second benefit of substance emergence is that it can help us avoid incongruent constructions. For example, while it may be incongruent to construct first-person aspects of feelings out of a field of shapes, it is not incongruent for a conscious substance to form feelings. A conscious substance is the right material to be a fountain of feelings by its basic capacities.

Third, substance emergence also unlocks a new solution to the hard problem of consciousness. The hard problem is hard—indeed, impossible—if we have the wrong materials. For example, states of cosmic debris do not, all on their own, give us explanatory resources to see how or why consciousness would ever emerge. So how can consciousness emerge? The substance theory answers this question by suppling the right material: consciousness is not impossible if there is a substance that has a capacity to produce consciousness. This production is not in virtue of other unconscious states (per the construction problems) but is instead in virtue of causal acts of a substance of the right kind.

My solution, then, is to flip the frame. The hardness of the hard problem, it seems to me, is rooted in the mindlessness frame. It is indeed hard to see how to derive consciousness from purely mindless units of reality. But we can flip the frame: if conscious substances are themselves units of reality, then we have recognizable materials for making consciousness.

Fourth, substance emergence also unlocks a new solution to the binding problem. That problem, recall, is about explaining how disparate things can come together to form a unified consciousness, such as a visual field. Substance emergence can account for the two types of unities of consciousness we identified in the previous chapter. First, a conscious substance accounts for subject unity (the unity of a single subject of consciousness), for a conscious substance is a single subject of consciousness. The substance itself unifies the consciousness by being a unified self at the conscious center.

Second, a conscious substance accounts for perspectival unity (the unity of contents of consciousness into a single perspective), for a conscious substance can have a single perspective by a basic capacity to be aware of many things at once. The material fits.

Finally, my own self-reflection seems to independently support the existence of substance emergence. When I reflect on myself, I notice the emergence of such things (or states) as thoughts, feelings, intentions, emotions, and desires. So, whatever I am, I appear to be a material that can make contents of consciousness. A material that can make contents of consciousness is what I mean by "conscious substance." So, it appears to me that a conscious substance is the right material to make contents of consciousness, and that such a material actually exists.

My theory, then, is that, like ripples emerging in water, unified consciousness can emerge in a substance. This unification is not derived from an organization of bits of reality, whether conscious or unconscious. The unification of consciousness, rather, is something that a first-person, conscious substance naturally produces.

If you have followed me this far, you can probably anticipate my next step. My next step is to look deeper in. Suppose consciousness comes from a consciousness-making substance. Still, the question remains: How do you make a consciousness-maker? Apparently, you and I are consciousness-makers. But what makes us? Could a first-person substance explain the emergence of other first-person substances? How might that work? I will examine this question in the next chapter.

SUMMARY

Previous chapters reveal severe constraints on the emergence of consciousness. For example, consciousness cannot emerge merely in virtue of spatial changes (apart from any deeper law or explanation). Something else is needed.

To develop a theory within the constraints, I make use of the concept of a first-person, conscious substance. A first-person substance can help us see how a certain kind of thing might produce organizations of consciousness. A first-person substance can also be the center of consciousness in every conscious being. In this way, all consciousness could emerge in the context of first-person substances.

■   ■   ■

Knowing there is something ahead, you decide to push forward. You can only move forward now by crawling. You crawl toward the light ahead. Finally, the narrow passageway opens into a large room. In the back of the room is a colorful, sparkling ball of light.

13

YOUR ULTIMATE ORIGIN

I am seated in the heart of all living entities.

BHAGAVAD GITA 20:10

In him we live and move and have our being.

ACTS 17:28 NIV

WE ARE NOW READY for the hardest question. If the challenge of explaining consciousness were not hard enough, we have now arrived at an infinitely harder challenge: How could a first-person conscious substance come to exist? This question is the hardest question of this book. It is also the hardest question I have ever considered in my career as a philosopher.

Dark walls block me from many proposals. They block me from proposing that conscious beings emerged from the motions of mindless atoms. They block me from proposing that conscious beings emerged from thoughts or feelings, for you cannot just think or feel someone into existence. Dark walls also block me from proposing that something created you out of absolutely nothing. These proposals don't just seem hard for me to accept; they seem to me impossible.

A glimmer of light leads me forward. I am ready to offer my theory of the "stuff" that makes you, for your consideration. I will share how I think conscious beings emerged. It is the only way I can see they could have emerged.

SOURCE SUBSTANCE

In this section, I will develop what I call "the source substance theory." This theory has four sides, like four sides of a window. Each side is part of a framework of possibility through which to see how conscious beings could possibly emerge.

Side 1: Source substance. The foundational side of the theory is about the foundational side of reality. According to the source substance theory, there is a foundational side of reality, which is a most fundamental type of substance. This substance is not itself derived from other substances of other kinds. Instead, this fundamental substance exists at the ground floor of reality. I will call this fundamental substance "the source substance."

By introducing a fundamental substance, we have a resource for providing the deepest possible explanation of things. A fundamental substance is itself a basic component of reality, for it does not derive its existence from any prior reality. As such, the source substance can be the deepest, original source of all emergent things.

You might wonder how the source substance might itself exist without emerging from prior things. Here is a classic idea: a substance can be non-emergent by having a *necessary nature*. A necessary nature is a nature of something that cannot not exist—that is, it cannot come to be, cease to be, or fail to be under any possible circumstance. On this account, we can see why a source substance would not emerge from anything prior, since nothing could exist prior to (without) it, since it has a necessary nature.[1]

It is not essential to my theory, however, that the source substance have necessary existence. I mention this account to give one idea of how a substance might, in principle, be able to exist at the ground floor of reality. Whether or not the source substance has a necessary nature, still, the key idea is this: the source substance is a fundamental type of substance, which does not itself emerge from a prior type of reality.

Side 2: Conscious capacity. The next side of the theory is about the nature of the source substance. Rather than multiply kinds of substances unnecessarily, we can analyze the source substance in terms of the kind of substance we already identified. This is the first-person kind of substance,

---

[1]A. Pruss and I offer a defense of a necessarily existent thing in A. Pruss and J. Rasmussen, *Necessary Existence* (New York: Oxford University Press, 2018).

which one can know via inner awareness of oneself. If the source substance is a first-person substance, then it could, like us, have a capacity to generate consciousness.

This account has a great explanatory benefit. By working with a common kind of substance, we can explain a link between the contents of consciousness within us and contents of reality outside. Some contents of our consciousness include structures of shapes and colors. These same structures can also occur "out there," such as in a mountain landscape. A conscious substance explains how that is possible, for a conscious substance could be capable of creating the same type of structures we witness directly in our own mental imagery. In this way, we have an explanation of how the contents of consciousness in our minds might, at least in principle, match the contents of a larger field of consciousness generated by the source substance.

This benefit is a bonus. My more fundamental motivations for appealing to a common kind of substance will become apparent in the final part of my theory.

Side 3: Emergent unities. The third side of this theory is about how the source substance could fit with the rest of reality in a unifying way. There are two roots of unity. First, as the foundational substance (per side 1), the source substance can unify things that depend on it, just as a seed unifies a large tree that grows up from it. Second, and related, the source substance is the right kind of material (per side 2) to make the kind of unities "out there" that we know in consciousness.

To elaborate on the value of unification, consider that reality exhibits patterns. For example, throughout the universe, objects move and act in similar ways, whether they are near us or far way. We can describe these patterns in terms of principles of reality, such as principles of motion, principles of psychology, and even principles of logic.

The patterns, though familiar, point to a certain mystery: Why do any patterns occurs throughout the cosmos? For example, why do flowers come up from seeds? Presumably, nowhere in the universe do flowers come up from massless, blue cubes. Why not? Is there a deeper explanation?

The source substance supplies a deeper explanation in terms of a common source: from the source substance emerges certain common kinds of things. These things have natures and capacities that set the stage for certain patterns throughout reality. For example, flowers spring from seeds according to the natures and capacities of seeds. Seeds, in turn, emerge from more basic ingredients (e.g., atoms) that exist throughout the universe. These ingredients themselves have certain common natures and capacities because they are common effects of a common origin. For this reason, we have reason to expect that any flowers on any planet in the whole universe would come from seeds (not blue cubes), according to the same patterns.

The source substance is also the right kind of substance to unify reality. Recall that, per the second side of my theory, the source substance can generate contents of consciousness. This capacity is key. The capacity to generate contents of consciousness unlocks the possibility of informational contents (i.e., conceptual structures) we witness within thoughts. This information can then allow the source substance to structure states of reality according to general patterns that match these intentional structures. For instance, the source substance could generate states of matter that conform to patterns, encoded by certain informational states.[2]

On a more fundamental level, a capacity for consciousness also unlocks a power to make the unities of consciousness. For example, by a power of visualization, the source substance could form the imagery of the universe within a universal (quantum) field of awareness.[3] In this way, a single fundamental substance could unify reality via the same unities we already recognize in consciousness.

In the interest of modesty, I want to emphasize here that there are a range of options for how a source substance could structure reality. For example, it is not a required part of the conscious substance theory that conscious

---

[2]We can divide laws into *necessary* laws (that cannot not hold) and *contingent* laws (that can fail to hold). Necessary laws may include laws of logic and any necessary truths about any necessary things. Necessary laws could be grounded in the source substance's necessary nature or in other natures of its effects. This account fits well with a correspondence theory of truth, on which truths correspond to prior realities. If truths correspond to prior realities, then necessary truths may correspond to prior necessary realities. Meanwhile, all contingent (nonnecessary) laws that hold throughout the cosmos could be grounded in the source's contingent acts, or in cooperation with the acts of other things that emerged from the source. In this way, the source can be a root of all the laws that organize all reality. I will say more about this informational account in the next section when I discuss the informational theory of matter.

[3]For a recent development of this account, see. M. Longenecker, "A Theory of Creation Ex Deo," *Sophia* 61 (2022): 267-82.

substances do everything intentionally. In chapter seven, I pointed out that first-person substances can (at least in principle) include subconscious capacities, such as a capacity to make one's heartbeat. While these capacities may be organized by prior informational states (which in turn may arise out of the source substance), they need not depend on intentional states for their continued operation. As far as this theory goes, the source substance may be able to organize informational states by intentional actions, non-intentional actions, or basic states of its nature.

Finally, there is a bonus benefit of the source substance theory. By explaining the unity of consciousness, this theory can also help solve (or sidestep) the combination problem. The combination problem, as we have seen, is about how tiny units of reality can combine to form conscious unities, such as you and me. Many theories of consciousness fall prey to this problem because their basic building materials are either mindless or diverse. As we have seen, there is a great mystery in seeing how disparate items could, in principle, construct the first-person perspectival and subject unities of consciousness. The source substance theory rolls away the clouds of mystery. For if fundamental reality is a single substance, then fundamental reality does not consist of many disparate things (whether conscious or unconscious). Then, rather than suppose that we are made via combinations of things, we can walk along another path (more on that soon).

Side 4: Emergent selves. I now arrive at the most difficult question: What could explain your ultimate origin?

The challenge is to see how any power could make you. It takes more than thinking and planning to make someone like you. For while someone could think of a character as if it were real, thinking so doesn't by itself make it so. Another power is required.

I am now ready to answer this challenge. Within the narrow constraints we have identified, I see one option: you emerged out of a fundamental, first-person substance. On this account, the fundamental substance does not think or feel you into existence; nor does the fundamental substance convert dust into a self-aware being. Instead, the fundamental substance makes use of itself. It is the reality out of which you are made.

I use the term *out of* loosely to allow for a few interpretations (but not many). Here I offer three possible interpretations (which are not exhaustive):

(i) the source substance forms you by entering into a certain form; (ii) the source substance grounds you (in the way an ocean grounds its waves); (iii) the source substance makes you with its substance via a basic power.[4] On all these accounts, the source substance is not external to you, but is—in a certain significant sense—*within* you.

My proposal, then, is this: the fundamental source is the true center of all beings. Self-awareness involves awareness of the fundamental self. The fundamental self is the deepest part of you. The fundamental self is the deepest part of all beings.[5]

Now to be clear, I am not suggesting that there is no distinction between you and the source substance. You are not all of the source substance, and the source substance is not all of you. There is distinction.

However, on this account, we are closer to our ultimate source than many people conceive. We are closer than I had conceived before I began this investigation. Our connection to the source substance is not a mere causal link, like the connection between striking a match and starting a fire. Our connection to the source is more intimate, like the connection between a flame and a fire. Like a fire that forms flames, the fundamental substance forms conscious beings out of its own substance.[6]

The connection here is conceptual: to even conceive of yourself (your first-person self), you conceive of your center point—the deep self within you. While you may not realize the deepest nature of your center point (just as a baby doesn't realize the nature of the mother who holds her), still, you cannot be consciously aware of the center of yourself without, in fact, also being consciously aware of the substance in all things.

---

[4]A related idea is that, just as we have a basic power to make new thoughts in our minds, the fundamental substance has a basic power to make new beings in its substance.

[5]I use the term *part* in a broad way. When I say the source substance is part of you, I do not mean that it is a *spatial* part that is located within an interior part of you. Nor do I mean that it is a separable part that could be replaced by another part of the same type. Rather, your relationship to the source substance is more like the relationship between you and your own field of awareness. In a sense, you are "in" your field of awareness, like the ocean is in a field of waves. In a sense like this, the source of all is the "I" *in* you. (This sense of "in" allows there to be another sense in which we are also *in* the source. For a development of this account, called "cosmopsychism," see P. Goff, *Consciousness and Fundamental Reality* [New York: Oxford University Press, 2017].)

[6]This analysis may remind some readers of Neoplatonism, as there are some similarities in terms of the unity of fundamental reality and its intimate connection to everything else. My theory has independent roots, however. Any intersections with that school of thought are coincidental.

On this picture, a vision of your ultimate origin is a vision of the ultimate self. To make you, a fundamental self enters a unique and special form. The fundamental self is the fire, and you are the flame. This fire animates you, as you animate your many forms. Unlike a real fire, the fire within you gives you freedom to explore, think, and move by your intentions. The fire gives you power to decide on a path. Your explorations extend your path. As your path extends, you bring the fire within you into new places.

This theory has a practical ramification for our relationships with each other. For if the fundamental substance comprises all beings, then all beings are deeply, deeply connected. When we attack each other, we actually attack the deepest part of ourselves, which affects our conscious experiences. This attack is not merely metaphorical. It is metaphysical. To attack someone is to attack their inmost center, and to attack their center is to attack your own inmost center. For, on this account, all centers of all conscious beings are one and the same fundamental Self, the great "I Am," in whom all beings live and have their being.

So, at this place in the cave of consciousness, the stuff that made you comes into the light. Your ultimate origin is right within. It must be. As far as I can see, no other construction of you is possible. If this theory is too much, what can I say? Constrained by walls on all sides, my inquiry leads me here.

And we are not done.

MINDFUL MATTER

A mind-first ontology can also provide insight into the nature of matter. Matter is commonly conceived of as the "stuff" out of which the world is made. What is this stuff? In this section, I consider how a mind-first ontology can shed light on the nature of matter in view of recent physics.

I begin by considering, first, a purely mindless account of matter. To be material, on this account, is to be made of atoms, which are fundamentally mindless units of reality. This account grows out of the mindlessness frame of reality. According to this frame, mindlessness comes first in all things.

For reasons I've shared, it seems to me that the mindlessness frame is a root of all kinds of construction problems. I have not found that these problems resolve on closer examination. On the contrary, the more I've studied the problems of consciousness, the more trouble I find with the mindlessness frame. Zooming in on these problems only exposes the problems in greater detail.

However, my goal is not merely to identify problems with the mindlessness frame. I want to offer a positive account of the foundations of consciousness. In this section, then, I want to show how a mental framework can account for whatever the mindlessness frame was supposed to account for, plus more. To do this, I will propose how I think we can flip our picture of the material world: instead of seeing first-person mental reality as emerging from third-person mindless reality, I will seek to show how all the aspects of material reality could emerge from first-person mental reality.

Developments in physics point the way to a mental analysis of matter. The prospect of a mental analysis was anticipated by Nobel prize–winning physicist Max Planck, who remarked, "I regard matter as derivative from consciousness."[7] More recently, physicist Richard Conn Henry concludes his analysis of more recent experiments by saying without qualification, "The universe is mental."[8] According to this analysis, the fundamental nature of matter is itself specifiable in terms of things we know in consciousness (such as informational and perspectival states).

Let us have a closer look at this analysis and what may motivate it. For our purposes, I am interested in whether a mind-first analysis of matter is at least conceptually possible and explanatorily fruitful.

One motivation for a mental analysis comes from explanatorily deep models of the fabric of the cosmos. For example, the pioneering quantum field theorist, Carlo Roveli, reports that on our latest models, matter is most fundamentally analyzable in terms of informational states, which are contextual and relational.[9] We may call this theory "the informational theory" of matter.

Previous steps in our inquiry position us for greater insight into the informational theory of matter. In our analysis of thoughts, in particular, we observed that thoughts have structural contents. For example, the thought that for every action, there is an equal and opposite reaction has this structural content: that for every action, there is an equal and opposite reaction.

---

[7]Interview with M. Planck, *The Observer*, January 25, 1931.

[8]R. Henry, "The Mental Universe," *Nature* 436, no. 29 (2005).

[9]C. Roveli, *Reality Is Not What It Seems: The Journey to Quantum Gravity* (New York: Random House, 2014), 244-88.

This content is a bit of information. Bits of information in thoughts empower a realist interpretation of "information." On this interpretation, informational states in matter are not different in nature from informational states we witness in thoughts. In both cases, these states are structural contents of thoughts.[10]

I would like to highlight four benefits of a realist interpretation of informational mater. First, informational matter allows us to cut away extra complexity in our theory. We already recognize informational contents in our first-person data (per my analysis in the chapter on thoughts). So, rather than posit a new kind of entity, we can instead understand "informational" matter as consisting of things familiar to us in consciousness. This result, then, simplifies our theory, which contributes to its intrinsic plausibility.

Second, a realist interpretation of informational matter can help explain the contextual aspect of matter. While interpretations vary, Roveli suggests that "a quantum mechanical interpretation of a certain system cannot be taken as an absolute observer-independent reality."[11] This interpretation is known as Relational Quantum Mechanics (RQM). According to RQM, properties of physical systems are themselves relative to observer-dependent contexts. What explains these contexts? Some theorists point to a familiar material: first-person (perspectival) beings. First-person beings are paradigm cases of observer-dependent contexts. For instance, a chair appears one way to you and a different way to me. Of course, appealing to first-person beings will not help if physical reality is fundamentally impersonal. But suppose a first-person substance exists at the foundation of reality (per the source substance theory). Then we have an independently recognizable resource to explain observer-relational properties of matter. Instead of positing a new kind of observer-dependent context, we might understand the contextual aspects of matter in terms of contexts defined

---

[10]My proposal here is compatible with (though does not require) a Platonist account of *propositional contents*, which are ungrounded, abstract entities. On my model, even if abstracta are ungrounded, propositional contents can still enter consciousness (as contents of consciousness). Thus, for example, the source substance can "entertain" abstract informational contents, which thereby constitute the informational aspects of matter.

[11]C. Roveli, "Relational Quantum Mechanics," *International Journal of Theoretical Physics* 35, no. 8 (1996): 1648.

by fundamentally first-person perspectives.[12] This possibility is open. One way to fill out the contextual aspect of matter, then, is in terms of first-person centers of informational of reality.

Third, the informational theory may also help us make sense of the mathematical foundations of matter.[13] Matter behaves according to certain patterns, which we can analyze mathematically. The mathematical analysis reflects a law-like, informational aspect of matter.

Fourth and finally, an informational theory of matter displays the explanatory power of the source substance theory. According to the source substance theory, the source substance can form contents of consciousness, like informational states. By forming informational states, this fundamental substance can create organizations of spatial aspects within fields of awareness. These spatial aspects could then change and act according to the functional nature of "matter." If so, then the possibility is open that spatial structures of matter grow out of the organizations within a (quantum) field of awareness produced by the source substance.

In summary, the informational theory of matter fits a mind-first ontology like a hand in a glove. For if the source substance has the powers of a mind, then it has powers known to generate informational states. Thus, the mind-first ontology can give a deeper explanation of the nature of matter in accordance with recent physics.

My proposal, then, is that all aspects of material reality can have an analysis in terms of informational, contextual aspects of mental reality. I call this account of matter "the mindful matter account," which I believe grows out of the most realistic and parsimonious interpretation of recent physics. On this account, the stuff of "matter" is conscious substance viewed extrinsically (from the outside).

I would like to close this section with a note on classification of views. I appreciate Ludwig's observation that we have diverse conceptual resources

---

[12] A. Oldofredi, "The Bundle Theory Approach to Relational Quantum Mechanics," *Foundations of Physics* 51, no. 1 (2021) provides a realist account of relational quantum mechanics in terms of bundles of properties and relations. While this "bundle-theory" account is contrasted with substance approaches, its main points are consistent with my main proposal—which is that the fundamental properties of matter vary in relation to observational contexts.

[13] S. Schneider, "Does the Mathematical Nature of Physics Undermine Physicalism?," *Journal of Consciousness Studies* 24 (2017): 7-39; cf. P. Goff, "Is It a Problem That Physics Is Mathematical?," *Journal of Consciousness Studies* 24 (2017): 50-58.

to describe the world in different ways.[14] For this reason, I am keen to provide a theory of consciousness that is conceptually flexible. In this section, I have considered how we might retain a materialist's set of concepts without falling prey to the problems of the mindlessness frame. My point, then, is not to flip materialism but to fill it—with mind. In other words, fundamental reality is mindful, whether or not we also classify it as "material." We may classify all such accounts that emphasize the primacy of mentality "mind-first" ontologies.

In the end, my goal here is not to commit to the existence of mindful matter. Rather, my goal is to show how a mind-first ontology can, at least in principle, give us greater insight into the nature of matter. In my view, the most parsimonious account of matter is in terms of mental contents known in consciousness (information, spatial imagery, etc.). But the prospect of other accounts of matter are also possible, as is the prospect of an ontology that does not include what we think of as "matter." A mind-first theory is consistent with a range of options.

I will next consider the prospect of what I consider the best alternative to a mind-first ontology.

MINDLESS MATTER

In this section, I will compare the mind-first theory with an alternative— that reality is fundamentally mindless. On this theory, the floor of reality consists entirely of mindless building blocks, which have no capacity to make contents of consciousness. Or, if reality has no floor (because each layer of reality depends on a prior layer in a bottomless regress), still, mindless reality comes first, prior to all mental reality.[15] Call the theory that mindless reality comes first "the mindlessness theory." (The theory that reality is fundamentally both entirely mindless and mental is contradictory. So, I set that theory aside.)

I will give three reasons why I favor the mind-first theory over the mindlessness theory. My first two reasons are about probability. My third reason is about possibility. Together, these reasons weave together to

---

[14]D. Ludwig, *Pluralist Theory of Mind* (Berlin: Springer, 2015).
[15]Thanks to Zach Blaesi for helping me consider different ways reality might qualify as being fundamentally "mindless."

reinforce in my mind the thesis that mentality is a fundamental aspect of reality.

Reason 1: Complexity. A mind-first ontology simplifies my vision of reality. If reality has a mental root, then we can explain both (i) contents of consciousness and (ii) contents of matter in terms of a single kind of substance. Consider, first, that a conscious substance would have the power to produce contents of consciousness within its mind; by producing contents of consciousness, the source substance explains their existence. Second, as I have sought to show, the general aspects of matter are analyzable in terms of informational states of an underlying mind. So, I do not think we need to posit any fundamentally third-person mindless substances to explain the existence of matter. If that is right, then a mental analysis of fundamental reality reduces complexity.

The simplicity of a theory is related to its probability, for simpler theories have fewer ways to go wrong. For example, a theory that posits one kind of substance has fewer ways to go wrong than a theory that posits more kinds of substance. For this reason, a theory that posits fewer kinds of substance is more probable, other things being equal.

In response, it is sometimes suggested that the mind-first theory adds complexity. Behind this suggestion is the premise that positing a fundamental mind adds a new kind of substance, one that is *immaterial*. According to this argument, we have experience with material things, but no experience with an immaterial thing. Therefore, positing immaterial things multiplies complexity beyond necessity.

However, this argument depends on certain concepts of "matter" and "mind." In particular, it assumes (i) that we don't have direct, first-person experience with minds, or (ii) that matter is itself decomposable into fundamentally mind-independent things. As you know, I have reason to challenge both premises. For as we have seen, I think we can be directly aware of mental realities via introspection, and I think mental realities can provide a basis for a mental analysis of matter itself.

Here I want to offer a couple more notes about the mental analysis of matter. While this analysis reaches to the edges of human inquiry, it is not without empirical underpinnings. Hoffman and Prakash independently motivate a mind-first account of matter from their analysis of the science of perception.[16] In their article, they propose a precise and way to formally define "particles" in terms of interacting conscious agents. According to their analysis, then, we can interpret "physical properties" in terms of aspects of consciousness. Aspects of consciousness are, according to their model, the ingredients out of which physical reality is analyzed. Whether we adopt their particular account or not, their analysis suggests that a mind-first analysis of matter is at least available.

Second, when we step out of the technical weeds, we can also see the explanatory power of a mind-first analysis from a bird's eye perspective. Here is how. We can classify all observable contents of reality into three types: (i) spatial (shape, motion, spin, etc.), (ii) informational, and (iii) experiential. We can explain each of these contents without positing fundamentally mindless things. Instead, these contents are all explicable in terms of the effects of conscious substances. Consider each in turn. First, the source substance can form spatial forms within visual fields, just as we can form spatial forms in the contents of our own visual fields. Second, the source substance can generate informational states by generating thoughts (or thought-like structures) in a universal field of awareness. These informational states can then give "matter" its structure and predictability, which is consistent with what certain quantum field theorists are proposing. Third, conscious substances can generate experiential contents. In this way, a mental framework has the resources to make everything intelligible.[17]

Whether one accepts this analysis or not, my point here is that a mental analysis can simplify our theory. Suppose instead we posit mind-independent things. This posit adds complexity. Instead of dividing reality

---

[16]D. Hoffman and C. Prakash, "Objects of Consciousness," *Frontiers in Psychology* (2004): https://doi.org/10.3389/fpsyg.2014.00577.

[17]We can also account for a popular, pretheoretic conception of "matter" in terms of the phenomenal aspects we witness in first-person awareness. Two aspects are relevant to defining this concept of matter. First, there are geometric aspects, like extension and spatial relations. Instead of supposing that these geometric aspects we see in our visual fields aren't real, we can treat these phenomenal aspects realistically. In other words, the geometries we see in a field of conscious awareness are real. Matter also has *mass*. What is mass? We can characterize mass functionally: mass is a relationship between an object's force and acceleration. Force and acceleration in turn have functional analyses in terms of input states and output states. So, a fundamental account of matter will include a fundamental account of the fundamental input and output states of matter. These functional states are then analyzable in terms of propositional (informational) contents of a fundamental mind.

into the material and immaterial, we can unify reality by conceiving of "matter" as an extrinsic state of an intrinsically mental reality. According to this vision, we can work with a single, basic kind of thing, which is the kind of thing we know directly in first-person experience of ourselves.

Consider, moreover, that the simplest theory of fundamental reality, whatever it is, does not posit extra quantities or parameters. Elsewhere, I have suggested that the simplest positive account (description) of the nature of fundamental reality is in terms of qualities (e.g., value, mind, power) that do not add arbitrary, fundamental (unexplained) quantities or limits.[18] On this analysis, a fundamental substance would have capacities to produce or ground the rest of reality without fundamental limits or boundaries. If that is correct, then, on the simplest theory, a fundamental substance would have the capacity to construct thoughts and feelings—for without that capacity, its fundamental nature would have an unnecessary, unexplained limit in possible capacity. For this reason, it seems to me that the simplest theory of the foundational substance independently predicts that the foundational substance is a substance capable of generating contents of consciousness.

Finally, as a bonus consideration, a mind-first ontology can simplify our theory of perception. As we saw in chapter four, every theory of perception faces the challenge of explaining how we can see an external world. To meet this challenge, I developed the window theory of perception, according to which perceptual experience is a window into reality. This theory implies that we can see at least some things directly. The only things we see directly, however, are within consciousness, such as thoughts, feelings, and visual imagery. Therefore, if we can see an external world (per direct realism), then the external world itself consists of the same kinds of things we see via internal awareness—that is, contents of consciousness. That's the simplest account. In other words, the window theory of perception predicts that your internal world consists of the same kind of things you see in the external world: both are contents of consciousness. This result is possible if the contents of reality (internal and external) are contents of consciousness.

---

[18]J. Rasmussen, *How Reason Can Lead to God* (Downers Grove, IL: InterVarsity Press, 2019), 62-74, 136-51.

We can summarize this idea as follows:

1. The contents of internal perception (e.g., visual images in dreams) are mind-dependent.

2. The contents of external perception (while awake) are the same kind of things as the contents of internal perception. (You can see this commonality by direct acquaintance with contents in dreams—e.g., images—and comparing them with contents you see while awake.)

3. Therefore, the contents of veridical perception are mind-dependent.

If we suppose instead that in addition to the contents of consciousness, there are bits of reality in a freestanding, third-person, fundamentally mindless world, then we multiply categorical complexity. A complete theory of reality is simpler (and thus intrinsically more likely) if it instead leaves out additional, unnecessary complexities.

Reason 2: Chaos. A first-person substance would have capacities to organize the world by creating informational states, as we have seen. This organization can explain why the world is not chaotic.

A mindless substance, by contrast, would only organize the world by accident. An accidental world does not have the same resources to predict recognizable organization, let alone beings capable of recognition. Sure, mindless substances might randomly organize a world, just as rocks might randomly roll into a meaningful message. But a mindless foundation has less resources to predict that meaningful organization would be probable. There is nothing about a mindless reality that, by itself, predicts that any mental reality would ever emerge. This lack of prediction reduces its probability. A simpler theory that makes better predictions is more probable.

In response, we could pick up predictive power by positing additional mindless things. Then perhaps we could develop a theory that predicts (with some reasonable probability) the emergence of a unified world with conscious beings. For example, we might suppose that while mindless substances have no capacity to be conscious, some mindless substances do have the capacity to generate first-person conscious selves. By adding complexity to our base theory, the theory gains predictive power.

I think this response is the best type of response on behalf of the mind-lessness frame. Still, there are a couple mitigating factors to keep in mind. First, by adding to the base theory, we also complicate the theory. The extra complexity diminishes its probability of being true compared with a simpler alternative.

Second, positing mindless foundations compounds the construction problems we have seen. For suppose there are mindless substances at the base of reality. These substances cannot cause themselves to have thoughts or feelings (because they are mindless). Yet, some of them can supposedly still produce whole thinkers and feelers, since here we are. How? If the building blocks of reality cannot produce thoughts and feelings (because they are mindless), how can they have the greater power to produce thinkers and feelers? To answer this, we might posit a mysterious power, but this posit adds to the complexity of our theory.

It seems to me, then, that mindlessness multiplies mysteries—beyond necessity. A simpler way to explain the organization of the world is in terms of the kind of thing already known to provide organization—a mind.

Reason 3: Construction. Finally, and most fundamentally, there are the many construction problems we have seen. My analysis leads me to think that these problems present the most difficult challenge for the mind-lessness theory. The challenge is to see how mindless materials could, in principle, construct (cause, form, or turn into) first-person conscious selves, all on their own.

I suspect an inchoate, if not explicit, form of this problem is at work in motivating some philosophers to become skeptical of the existence of first-person selves.[19] The worry is that mindless third-person substances (e.g., point particles) do not predict, produce, or turn into any genuine, first-person selves. By this analysis, a scatter of mindless particles will not produce first-person conscious beings any more than raking leaves will

---

[19]P. K. Unger, "I Do Not Exist," in *Perception and Identity*, ed. G. F. Macdonald (London: Macmillan, 1979); A. Rosenberg, "Disenchanted Naturalism," *Kritikos* 12 (2015): https://intertheory.org/rosenberg.htm; K. Frankish, "Illusionism as a Theory of Consciousness," *Journal of Consciousness Studies* 23 (2016): 11-39. Unger, *All the Power in the World* (Oxford: Oxford University Press, 2006) later argues in a reverse direction: instead of offering reasons to doubt that first-person selves exist, he argues from the existence of people to the conclusion that reality is not exhaustively physical.

produce a ghost or a goose. So, if mindless substances are the ultimate producers of all that exist, then selves do not exist. Removing selves removes the construction problem.

But I am not in position to remove selves. For reasons I gave in the first part of this book, I think first-person selves exist. For example, I am a first-person self. I think I can verify my existence directly in self-awareness. So, despite the ramifications, I think there are first-person selves.

The deep problem I have, then, is to see how first-person selves could exist purely in terms of third-person, mindless causes. Is that even possible?

In preparing this part of the book, I've turned over this basic idea—that first-person selves cannot come from third-person materials—in my mind many times and in many ways. There is something intuitive about it. I admit, however, that I am at the edge of my thinking here. Could a third-person, mindless blob have a basic capacity to make a substantial first-person self? My mind wants to says no, but I also want to be careful. I admit I do not see with perfect clarity the capacity limits of every conceivable unconscious substance. While it is clear to my mind that certain things, like sand and songs, cannot make first-person selves, it is more difficult to talk about materials whose natures I have no insight into. In the spirit of modesty, I can say at least this: it seems to me that conscious reality is more apt to sprout from a prior conscious reality than from any known unconscious reality.

I want to say a little more about the nature of the problem, as I see it, with mindless construction materials. The problem of generating selves is especially pressing if selves are real subjects of consciousness (per the previous steps in my analysis). For then to produce a self requires more than merely moving around some atoms. It requires the generation of a new substance (i.e., a subject of psychological form).

To illustrate what it would mean to generate a new substantial self, imagine there are some black blobs. These blobs are moving around until they reach what I'll call "the special state." In the special state, these blobs produce a brand-new substance. Specifically, they produce a conscious, thinking self.

How?

One idea is to posit basic causal capacities. Perhaps, for example, some mindless blobs (atoms, fields, rocks, or whatever) could make a self by some basic causal act or event. Then while the blobs cannot themselves be conscious, they could produce something that is conscious by a basic act.

On the other hand, positing mindless causal capacities does not supply nearly the same construction resources as the source substance theory. Consider, first, that third-person, mindless matter cannot, just in virtue of its mindless states, generate contents of consciousness. For example, grains of sand cannot make thoughts or feelings in their own mind (for they have no mind).[20] Yet if the grains of sand lack the resources to produce a thought or feeling, how could they acquire the greater resources to produce a whole thinker or a feeler? If there were sand that could produce a first-person self, that would be very special sand, indeed.

A principle at work in this analysis is a "greater than" principle: greater capacities include certain lesser capacities. To illustrate what I mean, suppose some materials have a capacity to make a whole fire (all on their own). Those materials would also have the capacity to make a flame. The capacity to make a fire is greater than, and includes, the capacity to make a flame. For example, if striking a certain match cannot even make a flame, then striking that match cannot make a whole fire, either. A greater resource is required.

In the same way, one might think that any capacity to make a first-person, thinking self would include a capacity to make thoughts of its own. Just as the capacity to make a fire includes the lesser capacity to make a flame, the capacity to make a whole thinker would, one might think, include the lesser capacity to make a thought. Going the other way, if some materials lack the capacity to make even make a thought (on their own), those materials would not have the greater capacity to make a whole thinker. A greater resource is required.[21]

---

[20]Here I am considering materials that can, all on their own, produce thoughts and feelings. The paradigm examples of things that can directly produce thoughts and feelings are themselves conscious, and so capable of having thoughts and feelings within their own field of awareness. In other words, the paradigm example of things that can make thoughts and feelings can also make thoughts and feelings within their own mind.

[21]A related idea is in W. Hasker, *The Emergent Self* (Ithaca, NY: Cornell University Press, 2001). Hasker proposes that some things could somehow produce a conscious, thinking self even if those same things do not have thought-making capacities themselves. Still, on Hasker's view, the foundational reality itself has thought-making capacities (and is a conscious being). Thus, he has resources to explain why there are any thought-making capacities in the first place. The explanation is this: the fundamental substance has the *basic* capacities of its effects, including

Moreover, we have seen many specific problems with making minds out of mindless ingredients. We can classify the problems into five types. First, there is the general construction problem, which is about how mindless materials could, in principle, construct thoughts, feelings, desires, intentions, and all the other contents of consciousness (whether directly or indirectly). Second, there is the combination problem, which is about how to organize contents of consciousness into the unities of consciousness. Third, there is the identity problem, which is about how to make something that has the specific identity of your own first-person self. Fourth, there is the puppet problem, which is about how you could do anything via conscious intentions (if mindless bits pull all the strings). Finally, there is the prediction problem, which is about how to predict mental reality solely from mindless ingredients. These problems, individually and collectively, support the premise that fundamentally mindless, impersonal reality would never include first-person conscious selves—or at least that the emergence of first-person selves would be highly unexpected.

So, here is where I am at. I have reasons to doubt that third-person materials would produce first-person selves. If, instead, a first-person self is in the very foundation of reality itself, then there are mind-making resources at the ground level of reality—and the problems with making minds out of mindless materials evaporate. These considerations suggest to me that reality does not consist of a fundamentally third-person, mindless reality.

A big thesis, then, that emerges from my inquiry is this: reality is deeply personal. Indeed, if my analysis is right, personal reality seeps to the foundation of all reality. In other words, reality is fundamentally personal.

To my interest, many scientists and philosophers have been approaching this general thesis from a variety of different conceptual schemes, including cosmopsychism, idealism, panentheism, varieties of theism, and mindful materialism.[22] The common thread in all these theories is that

---

the capacity to think and feel. This idea is also supported by a related greater-than principle: in the absence of any prior consciousness-making capacities, the greater capacity to make an entire conscious being would never arise. In short, the basic capacities for consciousness seep to the bottom of reality.

[22]Some recent examples include D. Chalmers, "Facing Up to the Problem of Consciousness," *Journal of Consciousness Studies* 2, no. 3 (1995): 200-219; P. Goff, *Consciousness and Fundamental*

mindless, impersonal reality is not the base of reality. It is the other way: the ultimate origin of personal, conscious reality, according to these theories, is itself personal.

We can summarize these final considerations as follows:

1. You exist.
2. If reality were fundamentally mindless and impersonal, you would never exist.
3. Therefore, reality is not fundamentally mindless and impersonal.

At this place in our journey, I want to offer a note of appreciation for following me this far. We have traversed difficult terrain, with complex ideas on all sides. Whether or not you agreed with me at every step, I hope that our journey to this point brings into greater view the significance of constructing a being like you. If there is a single idea I hope all readers will be able to take away, at least, it is this: you are a significant kind of reality, the construction of which is no trivial matter.

SUMMARY

This chapter completes my theory of the emergence of consciousness by showing how any conscious beings could ultimately exist—thus answering the guiding question of the second part of this book. A key idea in this chapter involves flipping the mindlessness frame. Instead of positing mindless units beyond all experience, I propose that a first-person, personal reality is fundamental to all other realities. This mind-first picture is simpler and has greater explanatory power than the mindlessness-first picture, or so I argue. The mind-first picture also provides resources for solving the many construction problems, explaining the nature and formations of matter, and explaining how there can be any beings like us. For these reasons, I arrive at this theory of your ultimate

Reality (New York: Oxford University Press, 2017); B. Kastrup *Why Materialism Is Baloney: How True Skeptics Know There Is No Death and Fathom Answers to Life, the Universe, and Everything* (Winchester, UK: Iff, 2014); B. Kastrup, *The Idea of the World: A Multi-Disciplinary Argument for the Mental Nature of Reality* (Winchester, UK: John Hunt, 2019); B. Rickabaugh, "The Primacy of the Mental: From Russellian Monism to Substance Dualism," *Philosophia Christi* 20, no. 1 (2018); D. Hoffman, *The Case Against Reality: How Evolution Hid the Truth from Our Eyes* (New York: W. W. Norton, 2019).

origin: your origin is not based in impersonal, mindless stuff but in the "stuff" of a personal foundation.

■   ■   ■

The ball of light you see before you transforms into a radiant figure. The figure glows with vapors of light that flow gently toward you. As you stand in the presence of this light, you experience the specialness of your own being.

You begin to hear a voice that seems to come from within you. This is what you hear:

There is a great light within you. By the light within you, you have sought to see past the shadows to see your true self. Your persistence to see more has positioned you to see more. Whenever you look into a place, you always see more in that place. As you have looked within, you have come to see more of who you are within.

When you see yourself, you see that you are more than stardust. What you call a "body" is a shadow produced by you in your current state of limitation. A shadow may represent you, just as this figure of light represents us. But your shadow is not you. Your shadow follows you.

Your uniqueness is forged by the uniqueness of your path. Your path did not begin with a state of nothingness. Your path did not begin with a state of mindlessness. Your path began with a unique state of majesty. This unique state is stamped into you and no one else. The origin point of your path is a jewel that belongs only to you. You have a uniqueness that no one else has or could have.

Yet, every being is united by a single, great reality, which unifies the world. The reality in the center of you is the same reality in the center of me. Every person is a face of this one, fundamental reality.

So, we tell you, every being contains a special piece of original reality. Without original reality, you would not be here; without you, original reality would not be extended by your unique perspective. You are indispensable to the original reality, just as original reality is indispensable to all beings.

What we tell you is not hidden behind speculation or revelation. See for yourself whether what we say is true. Look within. By your own light, you can see your true self. When you see yourself, you do not see shapes or sizes. You do not see a mere shadow of yourself. You see your own first-person self. That is who you really are.

There is still more to see. In states of limitation, even the clearest lights are dim. In dim light, familiar things appear as unfamiliar forms and shadows. In dim light, our connection to one another is dim. We perceive distinction, which distorts our awareness of our unity. We see each other as shadows and shapes. This is why we struggle to perceive who we really are. It is part of the state of limitation we are in to perceive our true identity through a lens of limitation. We tell you, you are more special than you understand.

Suddenly, the figure of light scatters into many figures of light, which flicker away.

You stand still, awestruck at what you just encountered. After a while, you realize there is nothing left to see in the cave. So, you begin to head back. As you make your way back out of the cave, you wonder, "Can I believe what I have seen?"

CONCLUSION

In this concluding chapter, I want to summarize the primary results of our inquiry and then show a surprising application.

PERSONS ARE PRIMARY

An idea that emerges from this book is this: you are rooted deep into reality. How deep? All the way down to the deepest layer of existence. The ground floor of reality is the "stuff" of persons.

On this picture, personal reality is the primary reality. There are three aspects of this primacy. First, persons are primary in the order of nature—to explain how consciousness can emerge. Second, persons are primary in the order of knowledge—to explain how rational thoughts can emerge. Third, persons are primary in the order of value—to explain how your value can emerge and be sustained in fields of change. In this picture, then, mindless grains of reality are unnecessary to explain who you are. Instead, it is the opposite: without personal roots of reality, there would be nothing— no consciousness, no matter, no reality at all.

Here is a recap of the main steps we took to reach this viewpoint. First, we began by shining the light of introspection on contents of consciousness. When I shine this light on my own experiences, I notice contents of consciousness that emerge within me. For example, I notice feelings, intentions, imaginations, and spatial structures within my field of awareness.

Second, we saw problems with producing contents of consciousness without a conscious substance. Consciousness does not come from kicking over rocks, throwing up sand, or organizing computer chips. So how do we construct consciousness?

The problem with constructing consciousness from unconscious materials goes beyond the hard problem. The hard problem of consciousness is about what we *cannot see*: we cannot see how to derive consciousness in principle from rocks, sand, or computer chips. But there is another, more fundamental problem—the construction problem. The construction problem is about what we *can see*: we can see that certain constructions are impossible. For example, it is possible to see that mere third-person aspects of sand alone are insufficient for the construction of the first-person experience of thinking.

Third, we identified a material for constructing consciousness. This material is familiar. You know this material when you look inward to witness your own self. The material that can make consciousness, I argued, is a personal substance with basic consciousness-making capacities.

On this analysis, the knowledge of the construction materials does not come from looking at brains or computer chips. Instead, we can know what makes consciousness by looking within at our own selves. By inner conscious awareness of ourselves, we can see the kind of thing that can construct thoughts, feelings, and other contents of consciousness. We can see that *we*, conscious selves, can construct contents of consciousness.

Fourth, we looked at the hardest question of this book: what constructs a conscious self? Not nothingness. Not mindlessness. Not even first-person states of consciousness. Then what? My answer is that the only thing that could conceivably construct a conscious self is a fundamental self. A fundamental self can construct conscious selves out of *itself* by providing the fundamental center point of all conscious unities.

Fifth, a theory of a fundamental self has great explanatory benefit. For if personal substance is primary, then we can shave off impersonal units from the base of our theory of the world. Mindless units are unnecessary posits, on my analysis. If I am right, then just as there is no need to explain thunder by appealing to magical deities, there is no need to explain contents of consciousness by appealing to mindless units of reality. There is a simpler way: all the things we see (through the window of our own consciousness) are explainable in terms of things we know in consciousness. If consciousness is primary, then we can explain everything in terms of one basic kind of reality (conscious, personal substance), from which all other things have their form.

Sixth, the primacy of personal substance also predicts the unification of many things we see in the universe. From the biggest things to the smallest things, there is organization. This organization is explicable in terms of its connection to a unifying, foundational source. This foundational source can unify all the dimensions of reality we experience in consciousness: thoughts, feelings, intentions, value, emotions, and so on. Its personal nature predicts its power to produce a unified reality in accordance with its own conscious unities.

If personal reality is fundamental, we can also explain why consciousness is not randomly thrown together into meaningless noise. By its power to think, it can form the informational "material" states that organize laws. By its power to visualize, it can form spatial structures within a universal field of awareness. By its power to intend, it can organize the world according to lines of purpose and expansion. By these powers, personal reality could form a stage for all reality. On this stage, one might not be surprised if sequences of thoughts, feelings, and emotions would emerge along lines of order, even into epic stories.

Seventh, and finally, we considered how fundamental reality could provide the fundamental center point of all beings. A fundamental self is the right kind of thing to construct conscious beings out of its own substance. Nothing else could.

By my analysis, then, I am led to this vision of reality: the primary nature of reality is not dead, mindless stuff, but is alive and personal.

All these steps lead to a vision of who you are. In this vision, your ultimate nature and origin have deep roots. You are not rooted in the mindless grains of cosmic debris. You are deeper in than the atoms. Beneath the atoms is the quantum field. And beneath the quantum field is the "I" in all beings. This "I" gives the quantum field its structure, information, and organization. This "I" also gives you your life, form, and present sense of self. The picture, then, I present of you includes a picture of a familiar first-person reality in the depths of all things.

THE DESTRUCTION PROBLEM

Writing this book has helped me to realize something else, which I had not understood before. I realized something about what it might take to destroy us. There is a link between the construction problem (of constructing conscious beings) and a *destruction* problem. I will describe this destruction problem here.

To set up the problem, I begin with an observation. I observe that I continue to exist. In this moment, I am aware of myself sitting on a chair. This awareness extends across time: I recognize myself from moment to moment as being me—the same me. While my thoughts come and go, I remain. If I stand up, there I am. My identity—as me—does not change, as far as I can tell. Like a blue sky, I remain in the background of the many things that fly through me.

Of course, this vision of my continued existence is not without obstacles, as we saw in our previous examination of personal identity. There are deep questions about how a person could maintain identity, especially in a sea of changes. For example, how could you be the same you if things that make you (atoms, fields, thoughts) you are constantly changing? These questions have led some to shave off their own first-person self. Then "you" are not a substantive reality at all.

Still, I do not think "you" need to shave off your existence. For, as I have argued, I think the puzzles of identity grow primarily out of a "mindless-dead-stuff-is-first" paradigm. In the mindlessness paradigm, you are made of constantly changing dead stuff (atoms, fields, etc.). Then the core of who you are is a sea of changing things. We can drop this assumption. Instead, as I have proposed, your core identity is not in flux if you are made fundamentally of a single, universal self. Then your identity does not need to be based in changing parts. By pulling out the sea of changing things from our analysis of who you are, we pull out the deepest roots of the problems of personal identity.[1]

Suppose, then, that you do indeed exist and can continue to exist. Then what?

Then we may wonder, how long might a being like you continue to exist? If you have continued up to this point, you might expect to continue to continue. But for how long? Will you only continue for as long as certain atoms hold a certain formation? Which atoms? Why those atoms, and why that formation?

---

[1]For a more detailed examination of these matters, some readers may wish to revisit the steps involved in my analysis of personal identity.

These questions directed my mind to the destruction problem. The destruction problem is the mirror image of the general construction problem we have seen. According to the construction problem, certain materials are the wrong materials for constructing a first-person conscious self (for many reasons). Suppose so. Then there is a parallel problem with using those same materials to remove a self.

To draw out this connection, consider again the prospect of making a first-person self out of sand. According to the construction problem, we cannot turn sand into a conscious self merely by changing its third-person, spatial, or sandy aspects. For example, we cannot turn the sand into someone who feels cold by packing snow on top of the sand. We need another material. But if third-person changes to sand cannot, on their own, make a first-person self *start to exist*, it is unclear how those same changes could make a first-person self *cease to exist*. Could kicking down a sand-castle destroy a first-person self?

I am using sand to illustrate a general destruction constraint. What is true of sand is true of any material that cannot turn into a first-person self. Take any material M. Suppose there is nothing we can do to M to convert M into a first-person self. We can fold M. We can smash M. We can convert M into a computer. Suppose none of these actions make a first-person self, for a self is another kind of being. By symmetrical analysis, these actions also don't remove a first-person self either. For if M is the wrong material to construct a conscious being, then M is the wrong material to destroy a conscious being.[2]

To illustrate further, suppose you were a house constructed out of bricks. Then you could be destroyed by changes to the bricks. The materials that can construct you can also destroy you. If, instead, you are not constructed out of bricks (because you are a first-person conscious self), then those bricks cannot, on their own, destroy you. The materials that cannot construct you cannot, just on their own, destroy you.

---

[2]The principle here is not that whatever can create *anything* can also destroy it. For as Brianna Bode noted to me in conversation, heat can destroy ice, even if heat cannot create ice. Rather, the principle I wish to point to is about the materials for destroying a certain kind of substance. Reason and observation suggest to me at least this: if changing the form of certain materials does not thereby create a certain substance, then changing the form of those same materials does not thereby destroy that same substance. I elaborate on the application of this principle to first-person selves in the main text.

This analysis builds on previous ideas about what a first-person self is. In particular, I am working with the idea that a first-person self has real, substantive existence. According to this idea, you are not a mere arrangement of matter (a hypothesis that leads into the problems we saw with the bodily account of personal identity). Nor are you made of a changing sea of dead stuff. Instead, on my analysis, you are deeper in. Your identity is prior to, and independent from, all these materials.

To appreciate the independence of your existence from the things you see, consider the contents that come into your field of awareness. In this field, things come and go (thoughts, feelings, images, hopes). All the while, *you* do not come and go. You are not those things you see. You are the backdrop, like the sky where the birds fly. As the backdrop, you continue to exist no matter what comes or goes in your field of awareness.

Consider, moreover, you can also continue to exist as things come and go *outside* your awareness. For example, my thoughts outside your awareness come and go, while you continue to exist. In the same way, atoms in a hypothetical brain (outside your awareness) can also come and go. Your specific self does not depend on any of these particular atoms, by my analysis of personal identity. So, while atoms can come and go, you continue to exist. Note carefully: thoughts and atoms alike may take any arrangement in any place, and your identity would be neither made nor destroyed. For your identity is not derived from any of these things.

This picture of your prior existence comes into view by many lights, as we have seen on previous steps. By the lights of reason, direct experience, and science,[3] a first-person self does not depend on a formation of atoms into some arrangement, just as you do not depend on a formation of thoughts into some argument. It is the other way: arrangements of atoms form out of informational states of consciousness (per the informational theory of matter), just as arguments do.

---

[3] As I have sought to show, many observations attest to the power and primacy of your own mental powers to change material states, including brain states. Moreover, while I believe there is evidence of mentality outstripping brain activity (Carhart-Harris et al., "Neural Correlates of the Psychedelic State as Determined by fMRI Studies with Psilocybin," *PNAS* 109, no. 6 [2012]: 2138-21), I do not believe there is comparable evidence of consciousness-related brain activity arising without any prior mentality (or conscious-capable substance).

Our inquiry into conscious unities further supports this analysis. We saw problems with constructing the unity of a conscious field out of disparate parts. For example, we cannot construct a visual experience of a blue sky by piecing the top half of the experience next to the bottom half. Instead, the unity exists as a whole unit. The unity derives from a person's conscious perspective. If that is correct, then a conscious unity does not hinge on the scattering (or moving) of some things—whether images, thoughts, or atoms. Instead, your conscious unity depends on you, a conscious center, that does not consist of an assemblage of things. Then, just as your construction is not explicable in merely terms of gathering things, your destruction is not explicable merely in terms of scattering things.

To recap, destruction is the other side of construction. If certain materials (atoms, thoughts, images, sand, atoms, or bricks) are the wrong materials for constructing you, a first-person being, then those same materials are the wrong materials for destroying you.

We can summarize these considerations into what I call the "destruction argument":

1. Assume changes in third-person bodily states cannot, all on their own, make a conscious self (per the construction problem).

2. Then (by symmetry) third-person bodily states cannot, all on their own, destroy a conscious self. (In other words, third-person bodily changes cannot, on their own, determine *whether or not* a conscious self exists.)

3. You are a conscious self.

4. Therefore, changes in third-person bodily states cannot, all on their own, destroy you.

This result, if correct, has intriguing ramifications for your future. In particular, you have a future. Just has you have *already* continued to persist through a changing sea of thoughts, feelings, and atoms, you will *continue* to continue. You can no more be removed by changing your atoms than by changing your thoughts or visual images. If you are indeed a substantial first-person self, then these things are the wrong kind of things to remove you, just as they are the wrong kind of things to construct you.

So, how long will you continue? That depends on what could destroy you. By my analysis, sticks and stones cannot destroy you, just as they cannot create you. Sticks and stones are the wrong materials to create or destroy a first-person conscious self. Same for molecules: molecules, like mental states, can change you, but they cannot annihilate you.

By these thoughts that have emerged in my mind, I arrive at a fundamental principle of consciousness: conscious selves cannot be created or destroyed by any mere bodily changes. We only change form. If this principle is true, then you will continue. And you will continue to continue, no matter what form your body takes.

SUMMARY

Who are you, really? My answer is this. You are a special kind of reality. You are the kind of reality that can feel, think, intend, hope, dream, and contemplate the ideas of this book. This kind of reality has deep roots. Stardust is not enough to make you who you are. A greater material is required. You are made from the only material that could make you. It is the same material that made me. It is the material that makes all beings and connects everything together. This material is the ground floor of all reality. It is the foundational "stuff" of life. You are made in the image and likeness of the foundation of all reality. Out of this foundation arises *you*—an unshakably valuable, unique, irreplaceable, indispensable, and indestructible expression of the greatest possible kind of reality. This is who you really are.

■ ■ ■

As you exit the cave, you squint your eyes in the bright light. You see some leaves scattering in the wind over some rocks under a blue sky. The leaves and rocks now appear to you strangely unfamiliar. How can there be leaves, rocks, and sky? In this moment, the things "out there" appear infinitely stranger and more mysterious than your own self.

Suddenly, you hear a crash from behind. You turn around. You see rocks falling from the top of the entrance of the cave. To your astonishment, the rocks roll into the shape of a message that spans the length of the cave. The message reads clearly:

You are greater than you can imagine.

BIBLIOGRAPHY

Aristotle. *De Anima.* Translated by Hugh Lawson-Tancred. Harmondsworth, UK: Penguin, 1986.

———. *Metaphysics.* Translated by Joe Sachs. New Mexico: Green Lion, 2002.

Armstrong, D. *A Materialist Theory of the Mind.* London: Routledge, 1993.

Bailey, A. *Monotheism and Human Nature.* Cambridge: Cambridge University Press, 2021.

Bailey, A., and J. Rasmussen. "How Valuable Could a Person Be?" *Philosophy and Phenomenological Research* (2020): https://doi.org/10.1111/phpr.12714.

———. "A New Puppet Puzzle." *Philosophical Explorations* 23, no. 3 (2020): 202-13.

———. "You Needn't Be Simple." *Philosophical Papers* 43, no. 2 (2014): 145-60.

Bailey, A., J. Rasmussen, and L. Van Horn. "No Pairing Problem." *Philosophical Studies* 154, no. 3 (2011): 349-60.

Barnett, D. "You Are Simple." In *The Waning of Materialism,* edited by R. Koons and G. Bealer, 161-74. Oxford: Oxford University Press, 2010.

Baumeister, R. F., E. J. Masicampo, and C. N. Dewall. "Prosocial Benefits of Feeling Free: Disbelief in Free Will Increases Aggression and Reduces Helpfulness." *Personality and Social Psychology Bulletin* 35, no. 2 (2009): 260-68.

Beauregard, M. "Mind Does Really Matter: Evidence from Neuroimaging Studies of Emotional Self-Regulation, Psychotherapy and Placebo Effect." *Progress in Neurobiology* 81, no. 4 (2007): 218-36.

Beauregard, M., and D. O'Leary. *The Spiritual Brain: A Neuroscientist's Case for the Existence of the Soul.* San Francisco: HarperOne, 2008.

Berger, J. "A Dilemma for the Soul Theory of Personal Identity." *International Journal for Philosophy of Religion* 83 (2018): 41-55.

Berkeley, G. *The Works of George Berkeley, Bishop of Cloyne.* Edited by A. A. Luce and T. E. Jessop. 9 vols. London: Thomas Nelson and Sons, 1948–1957.

Bickle, J. "Multiple Realizability." *Stanford Encyclopedia of Philosophy,* 2020. https://plato.stanford.edu/entries/multiple-realizability.

Buddha. *Yamakavagga: Pairs.* Translated by Acharya Buddharakkhita. 1996. www.accesstoinsight.org/tipitaka/kn/dhp/dhp.01.budd.html.

Carhart-Harris, R., et al. "Neural Correlates of the Psychedelic State as Determined by fMRI Studies with Psilocybin." *PNAS* 109, no. 6 (2012): 2138-43.

Carroll, S. "Consciousness and the Laws of Physics." *Journal of Consciousness Studies*, preprint (2021): http://philsci-archive.pitt.edu/19311/.

Chalmers, D. "Facing Up to the Problem of Consciousness." *Journal of Consciousness Studies* 2, no. 3 (1995): 200-219.

———. "What Is It Like to Be a Net?" http://consc.net/notes/lloyd-comments.html.

Churchland, Patricia. *A Neurocomputational Perspective.* Cambridge, MA: MIT Press, 1989.

———. *Neurophilosophy: Toward a Unified Science of the Mind/Brain.* Cambridge, MA: MIT Press, 1986.

Churchland, Paul. *A Neurocomputational Perspective.* Cambridge, MA: MIT Press, 1989.

Cisek, P. "Evolution of Behavioural Control from Chordates to Primates." *Philosophical Transactions of the Royal Society.* December 27, 2021. https://royalsocietypublishing .org/doi/10.1098/rstb.2020.0522.

Crick, F. *The Astonishing Hypothesis: The Science Search for the Soul.* New York: Scribner's, 1994.

Crummett, D. "What if We Contain Multiple Morally Relevant Subjects?" *Utilitas* (2022): 1-18.

Crummett, D., and Cutter, B. "Psychophysical Harmony: A New Argument for Theism." *Oxford Studies in Philosophy of Religion*, forthcoming.

Davidson, D. *Essays on Actions and Events.* Oxford: Clarendon, 1980.

Dennett, D. *Consciousness Explained.* Boston: Little, Brown, 1991.

Descartes, R. *Discourse on Method, Optics, Geometry, and Meteorology.* Translated by Paul J. Olscamp. Indianapolis, IN: Hackett, 2001.

Digdon, N., and Koble, A. "Effects of Constructive Worry, Imagery Distraction, and Gratitude Interventions on Sleep Quality: A Pilot Trial." *Applied Psychology: Health and Well-Being* 3, no. 2 (2011): 193-206.

Diogenes Laertius. *Lives of Eminent Philosophers: An Edited Translation.* Translated by Stephen White. Cambridge: Cambridge University Press, 2021.

Dunlap, K. "The Case Against Introspection." *Psychological Review* 19, no. 5 (1912): 404-13.

Fodor, J. *A Theory of Content and Other Essays.* Cambridge, MA: MIT Press, 1990.

Frankish, K. "Illusionism as a Theory of Consciousness." *Journal of Consciousness Studies* 23 (2016): 11-39.

Fritjof, C., and P. L. Luisi. *The Systems View of Life: A Unifying Vision.* Cambridge: Cambridge University Press, 2014.

Fumerton, R. *Metaphysical and Epistemological Problems of Perception.* Lincoln: University of Nebraska Press, 1985.

Gertler, B. "Self-Knowledge." *Stanford Encyclopedia of Philosophy.* 2015. https://plato .stanford.edu/entries/self-knowledge.

Giustina, A. "Conscious Unity from the Top Down: A Brentanian Approach." *The Monist* 100, no. 1 (2017): 16-37.

Goff, P. *Consciousness and Fundamental Reality.* New York: Oxford University Press, 2017.

———. "Is It a Problem That Physics Is Mathematical?" *Journal of Consciousness Studies* 24 (2017): 50-58.

Graham, G. "Behaviorism." *Stanford Encyclopedia of Philosophy.* 2019. https://plato .stanford.edu/entries/behaviorism.

Harris S. *Free Will.* New York: Free Press, 2012.

Hasker, W. *The Emergent Self.* Ithaca, NY: Cornell University Press, 2001.

Henry, R. "The Mental Universe." *Nature* 436, no. 29 (2005): https://doi.org/10.1038/436029a.

Hiley, B., and P. Pyklkkanen. "Can Mind Affect Matter via Active Information?" *Mind and Matter* 3, no. 2 (2005): 8-27.

Hoffman, D. *The Case Against Reality: How Evolution Hid the Truth from Our Eyes.* New York: W. W. Norton, 2019.

———. "The Scrambling Theorem: A Simple Proof of the Logical Possibility of Spectrum Inversion." *Conscious Cognition* 15, no. 1 (2006): 31-45.

Hoffman, D., and C. Prakash. "Objects of Consciousness." *Frontiers in Psychology* (2004): https://doi.org/10.3389/fpsyg.2014.00577.

Hoffman, J., and G. Rosenkrantz. *Substance: Its Nature and Existence.* London: Routledge, 1996.

Hume, D. *A Treatise of Human Nature.* Edited by L. A. Selby-Bigge. Oxford: Clarendon, 1896.

Huxley, T., and W. Yourmans. *The Elements of Physiology and Hygiene: A Text-book for Educational Institutions.* New York City: D. Appleton, 1868.

Irvine, E. *Consciousness as a Scientific Concept: A Philosophy of Science Perspective.* New York: Springer, 2012.

Jackson, F. *Perception: A Representative Theory.* Cambridge: Cambridge University Press, 1977.

———. "What Mary Didn't Know." *Journal of Philosophy* 83, no. 5 (1986): 291-95.

Jedlicka, P. "Revisiting the Quantum Brain Hypothesis: Toward Quantum (Neuro)-biology?" *Frontiers in Molecular Neuroscience* (2017): https://doi.org/10.3389/fnmol .2017.00366.

John, E. "The Neurophysics of Consciousness." *Brain Research Reviews* 39, no. 1 (2002): 1-28.

Johnston, M. "The Obscure Object of Hallucination." *Philosophical Studies* 120 (2004): 113-83.

Kammerer, F. "The Illusion of Conscious Experience." *Synthese* 198 (2021): 845-66.

Kant, I. *The Metaphysics of Morals.* Edited by Lara Denis. Translated by Mary Gregor. 2nd ed. Cambridge Texts in the History of Philosophy. Cambridge: Cambridge University Press, 2017.

Kastrup, B. *The Idea of the World: A Multi-Disciplinary Argument for the Mental Nature of Reality.* Winchester, UK: John Hunt, 2019.

——. *Why Materialism Is Baloney: How True Skeptics Know There Is No Death and Fathom Answers to Life, the Universe, and Everything.* Winchester, UK: Iff, 2014.

Kim, J. "Events as Property Exemplifications." In *Action Theory*, edited by M. Brand and D. Walton, 159-77. Proceedings of the Winnipeg Conference on Human Action, 1976.

——. *Physicalism or Something Near Enough.* Princeton, NJ: Princeton University Press, 2005.

Kulstad, M. "Leibniz's Philosophy of Mind." *Stanford Encyclopedia of Philosophy.* 2020. https://plato.stanford.edu/entries/leibniz-mind.

Lavazza, A. "Free Will and Neuroscience: From Explaining Freedom Away to New Ways of Operationalizing and Measuring It." *Frontiers in Human Neuroscience* (2016): https://doi.org/10.3389/fnhum.2016.00262.

Leaf, C. *Cleaning Up Your Mental Mess: 5 Simple, Scientifically Proven Steps to Reduce Anxiety, Stress, and Toxic Thinking.* Grand Rapids, MI: Baker Books, 2021.

Leibniz, G. *The Monadology and Other Philosophical Writings.* Translated R. Latta. Oxford: Clarendon, 1898.

Levine, J. "Materialism and Qualia: The Explanatory Gap." *Pacific Philosophical Quarterly* 64 (1983): 354-61.

Libet, B., et al., "Time of Conscious Intention to Act in Relation to Onset of Cerebral Activities (Readiness-Potential): The Unconscious Initiation of a Freely Voluntary Act." *Brain* 106, no. 3 (1983): 623-42.

Locke, J. *An Essay Concerning Human Understanding.* Translated by Peter Nidditch. Oxford: Clarendon, 1975.

Long, J. and Perry, P. *Evidence of the Afterlife: The Science of Near-Death Experiences.* New York: HarperCollins, 2010.

Longenecker, M. "A Theory of Creation Ex Deo." *Sophia* 61 (2022): 267-82.

Ludwig, D. *Pluralist Theory of Mind.* Berlin: Springer, 2015.

Martin, M. "The Limits of Self-Awareness." *Philosophical Studies* 120 (2004): 37-89.

McFadden, J. "Integrating Information in the Brain's EM Field: The Cemi Field Theory of Consciousness." *Neuroscience of Consciousness* 2020, no. 1 (2020): https://doi.org/10.1093/nc/niaa016.

Merricks, T. *Objects and Persons.* Oxford: Oxford University Press, 2001.

Montero, B. "The Body of the Mind-Body Problem." *Annals of the Japan Association for Philosophy of Science* 9, no. 4 (1999): 207-17.

Nelson, R. "Global Consciousness and the Coronavirus—a Snapshot." *The Global Consciousness Project* (2020): https://global-mind.org/papers/pdf/GCP.Corona.edgescience.fin.pdf.

Nisbett, R. E., and T. D. Wilson. "Telling More Than We Can Know: Verbal Reports on Mental Processes." *Psychological Review* 84, no. 3 (1977): 231-59.

Oldofredi, A. "The Bundle Theory Approach to Relational Quantum Mechanics." *Foundations of Physics* 51, no. 1 (2021): https://doi.org/10.1007/s10701-021-00407-2.

Palmer, S. *Vision Science: Photons to Phenomenology.* Cambridge, MA: MIT Press, 1999.

Papineau, D. "The Problem of Consciousness." In *The Oxford Handbook of the Philosophy of Consciousness,* edited by U. Kriegel. Oxford: Oxford University Press, 2020.

———. *Thinking About Consciousness.* Oxford: Oxford University Press, 2002.

Pitt, D. "The Phenomenology of Cognition, or, What Is It Like to Think That P?" *Philosophy and Phenomenological Research* 69, no. 1 (2004): 1-36.

Place., U. T. "Is Consciousness a Brain Process?" *British Journal of Psychology* 47, no. 1 (1956): 44-50.

Plantinga, A. "Content and Natural Selection." *Philosophy and Phenomenological Research* 83, no 2. (2011): 435-58.

Prakash, C., et al. "Fitness Beats Truth in the Evolution of Perception." *Acta Biotheoretica* (2020): https://doi.org/10.1007/s10441-020-09400-0.

Pruss, A., and J. Rasmussen. *Necessary Existence.* New York: Oxford University Press, 2018.

Rasmussen, J. "About Aboutness." *Metaphysica* 15, no. 1 (2014): 117-86.

———. "Against Non-Reductive Physicalism." In *The Blackwell Companion to Substance Dualism,* edited by Jonathan J. Loose, Angus J. L. Menuge, and J. P. Moreland, 328-39. Malden, MA: Wiley-Blackwell, 2018.

———. "Building Thoughts from Dust: A Cantorian Puzzle." *Synthese* 192 (2015): 393-404.

———. *Defending the Correspondence Theory of Truth.* Cambridge: Cambridge University Press, 2014.

———. *How Reason Can Lead to God.* Downers Grove, IL: InterVarsity Press, 2019.

———. "How to Build a Thought." *Thought* 9, no. 2 (2020): 75-83.

Rickabaugh, B. "The Primacy of the Mental: From Russellian Monism to Substance Dualism." *Philosophia Christi* 20, no. 1 (2018): 31-41.

Rolls, E. "A Computational Neuroscience Approach to Consciousness." *Neural Networks* 20, no. 9 (2007): 962-82.

———. "Consciousness Absent and Present: A Neurophysiological Exploration." *Progress in Brain Research* 144 (2004): 95-106.

Rosenberg, A. *The Atheist's Guide to Reality: Enjoying Life Without Illusion.* New York: W. W. Norton, 2011.

———. "Disenchanted Naturalism." *Kritikos* 12 (2015): https://intertheory.org/rosenberg.htm.

Roveli, C. *Reality Is Not What It Seems: The Journey to Quantum Gravity.* New York: Random House, 2014.

———. "Relational Quantum Mechanics." *International Journal of Theoretical Physics* 35, no. 8 (1996): 1637-78.

Russell, B. *The Analysis of Matter*. New York: Harcourt, Brace, 1927.

———. *The Analysis of Mind*. New York: Macmillan, 1921.

———. *The Problems of Philosophy*. New York: H. Holt, 1912.

Schneider, S. "Does the Mathematical Nature of Physics Undermine Physicalism?" *Journal of Consciousness Studies* 24 (2017): 7-39.

Schulte, P., and Neander, K. "Teleological Theories of Mental Content." *Stanford Encyclopedia of Philosophy*, 2022. https://plato.stanford.edu/entries/content-teleological.

Schwartz, J., and S. Begley. *The Mind and the Brain: Neuroplasticity and the Power of Mental Force*. New York: Harper Collins, 2002.

Schwitzgebel, E. "A Phenomenal, Dispositional Account of Belief." *Noûs* 36, no. 2 (2002): 249-75.

Searle, J. "Consciousness." *Annual Review of Neuroscience* 23 (2000): 557-78.

———. *Mind: A Brief Introduction*. Oxford: Oxford University Press, 2004.

———. "Minds, Brains and Programs." *Behavioral and Brain Sciences* 3 (1998): 417-57.

———. *Seeing Things as They Are: A Theory of Perception*. Oxford: Oxford University Press, 2015.

Seth, A., et al. "Theories and Measures of Consciousness: An Extended Framework." *Proceedings of the National Academy of Sciences of the United States of America* 103, no. 28 (2006): https://doi.org/10.1073/pnas.0604347103.

Smart, J. J. C. "Sensations and Brain Processes." *Philosophical Review* 68, no. 2 (1959): 141-56.

Stalnaker, R. "Merely Possible Propositions." In *Modality: Metaphysics, Logic, and Epistemology*, edited by Bob Hale and Aviv Hoffmann. Oxford: Oxford University Press, 2010.

Stitch, S. *Deconstructing the Mind*. New York: Oxford University Press, 1996.

Taliaferro, C. "Masked Man." In *Bad Arguments: 100 of the Most Important Fallacies in Western Philosophy*, edited by Robert Arp, Steven Barbone, and Michael Bruce. New Jersey: John Wiley & Sons, 2018.

Tononi, G. "Consciousness as Integrated Information: A Provisional Manifesto." *The Biological Bulletin* 215, no. 3 (2008): 216-42.

Unger, P. K. *All the Power in the World*. Oxford: Oxford University Press, 2006.

———. "I Do Not Exist." In *Perception and Identity*, edited by G. F. Macdonald. London: Macmillan, 1979.

Van Inwagen, P. "Creatures of Fiction." *American Philosophical Quarterly* 14 (1977): 299-308.

———. *Material Beings*. Ithaca, NY: Cornell University Press, 1990.

Vohs, K., and J. Schooler. "The Value of Believing in Free Will: Encouraging a Belief in Determinism Increases Cheating." *Psychological Science* (2008): https://doi.org/10.1111%2Fj.1467-9280.2008.02045.x.

Wertheimer, M. *Productive Thinking*. New York: Harper, 1945.

GENERAL INDEX

ALSO BY
JOSHUA RASMUSSEN

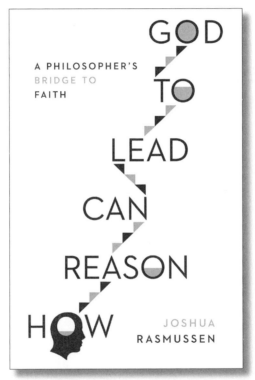

How Reason Can Lead to God
978-0-8308-5252-9